新经典
ENGLISH MAJOR

高等学校英语专业系列教材

U0587396

跨文化沟通

INTERCULTURAL COMMUNICATION

庄恩平
Nan M. Sussman（美）　编著

外语教学与研究出版社
FOREIGN LANGUAGE TEACHING AND RESEARCH PRESS
北京 BEIJING

图书在版编目（CIP）数据

跨文化沟通 ＝ Intercultural communication：英文／庄恩平，（美）萨斯曼 (Sussman, N.M.) 编著． —— 北京：外语教学与研究出版社，2014.3（2024.11 重印）
高等学校英语专业系列教材
ISBN 978-7-5135-4209-8

Ⅰ. ①跨… Ⅱ. ①庄… ②萨… Ⅲ. ①英语－高等学校－教材②文化交流 Ⅳ. ①H31

中国版本图书馆 CIP 数据核字 (2014) 第 044252 号

出 版 人　王　芳
责任编辑　卫　昱
封面设计　孙敬沂
版式设计　涂　俐
出版发行　外语教学与研究出版社
社　　　址　北京市西三环北路 19 号（100089）
网　　　址　https://www.fltrp.com
印　　　刷　三河市北燕印装有限公司
开　　　本　650×980　1/16
印　　　张　17.5
版　　　次　2014 年 4 月第 1 版 2024 年 11 月第 22 次印刷
书　　　号　ISBN 978-7-5135-4209-8
定　　　价　49.90 元

如有图书采购需求，图书内容或印刷装订等问题，侵权、盗版书籍等线索，请拨打以下电话或关注官方服务号：
客服电话：400 898 7008
官方服务号：微信搜索并关注公众号"外研社官方服务号"
外研社购书网址：https://fltrp.tmall.com

物料号：242090101

前　言

　　《高等学校英语专业英语教学大纲》、《高等学校商务英语专业本科教学要求》、《大学英语课程教学要求》，以及2013年上海市教育委员会颁布的《上海市大学英语教学参考框架（试行）》均提出了注重培养学生跨文化交际能力的理念。四部教学大纲对学生听、说、读、写、译等英语交流能力提出了具体的要求，但均未对跨文化交际能力提出具体要求，只有《高等学校英语专业英语教学大纲》对21世纪外语专业学生在工作中的运用能力作了如下概述：外语专业学生在工作中的运用能力主要指能够从事不同文化间交流与合作的能力、交际能力、协作能力、适应工作的能力、独立提出建议和讨论问题的能力、组织能力、知人处事的能力、灵活应变的能力等等。笔者认为，这种能力不仅仅是指跨文化意识或跨文化适应能力，更是一种在实际的工作环境和社会环境中应对并解决由文化差异产生的文化冲突的能力，这就叫跨文化沟通能力。跨文化沟通能力已被美国劳工部认为是21世纪社会人们必备的一种能力；英国工业委员会2011年发布的题为《培养全球能力毕业生——全球能力领导者》的一项报告把与不同文化背景的人合作与共事的能力和沟通能力视为所有能力中最重要的能力；2013年2月欧洲委员会和欧盟委员会在爱尔兰召开的"跨文化城市里程碑盛会"呼吁提高全球公民跨文化能力以应对多元文化的挑战。

　　《跨文化沟通》是一本跨文化案例教材，注重跨文化交际的应用，是中美两位跨文化研究专家长期从事跨文化沟通教学、研究、培训与咨询的实际经历与经验的总结，所有案例、剖析视角、观点都是从跨文化实践中提炼与概括而成。本书共分为三大部分，12个单元。每单元主体部分由四大模块组成：What's Wrong, Reading 1 & Reading 2, Intercultural Lens,

Intercultural Case Study。本书最大的特色在于将跨文化学习视为一个过程，引导学生循序渐进，层层剖析，学以致用。

What's Wrong? 通过典型跨文化交际案例引发学生思考，即以全球化社会所面临的文化差异挑战为导向，提出一个反映时代性、全球性和实时性的跨文化综合案例，旨在培养学生以全球视野观察世界、发现问题的意识与能力。

Reading 1 & Reading 2 通过阅读材料引导学生思考问题背后的原因。该模块提供两篇与单元主题相关的文章，让学生通过阅读积累相关跨文化知识，并通过讨论培养学生的思辨能力。

Intercultural Lens 通过提供与单元相关的多种跨文化视角与观点，拓展学生的跨文化知识、提高学生的跨文化意识、培养学生的跨文化技能，旨在培养学生以跨文化视角思考问题与分析问题的能力。

Intercultural Case Study 通过案例培养学生跨文化敏感性，即在跨文化时代中文化差异或文化冲突无处不在、时刻发生在我们的身边。

在每单元最后，还专门设立了两个学习专栏：Learning Culture Through Proverbs和Online Research—Using Key Words。第一个专栏旨在引导学生通过学习谚语了解其传达的文化价值观，并通过分析其文化价值观，了解人们的行为特征，即学习谚语、了解文化、发现行为，三者融为一体；第二个专栏旨在培养学生通过搜集、整理信息，提高自主学习的意识与能力。

在现实的跨文化交往中，沟而不通的现象比比皆是，这不是因为一方未听懂另一方所说的话，也不是语言表达不妥所致，而是未能理解另一方所表达的背后的含义，这就造成沟而不通或无效沟通的现象。因此，《跨文化沟通》教材更注重职场中的沟通与沟通技能的训练，注重开拓跨文化思维、培养跨文化敏感性，注重培养以国际视野观察当今社会所面临的跨文化挑战的意识与能力、培养国际化教育环境下及跨文化职场环境中的跨文化沟通能力。

《跨文化沟通》一书得到了上海大学重点通识课程建设项目的支持，

该课程面向全校学生授课。

　　本教材编写得到了外语教学与研究出版社的大力支持。在此，我们表示衷心的感谢。

　　　　　　　　　　　　　　　　　　　　　　　　　庄恩平
　　　　　　　　　　　　　　　　　　　　2013年3月于上海大学

Contents

Part One   Basic Concepts of Intercultural Communication

Unit 1 Culture Behind Language   **2**
- Reading 1   Language, Thought, Culture, and Intercultural Communication   6
- Reading 2   Language Mirrors Values   11

Unit 2 Communicating Interculturally   **23**
- Reading 1   The Link Between Culture and Communication   27
- Reading 2   Intercultural Awareness and Communication   33

Unit 3 Barriers in Intercultural Communication   **47**
- Reading 1   Experiencing Intercultural Communication   50
- Reading 2   Cultural Biases and Intercultural Communication   57

Unit 4 Intercultural Adaptation   **72**
- Reading 1   Internationalisation and Intercultural Competences   76
- Reading 2   Studying Abroad and Culture Shock   82

Part Two   Intercultural Skills

Unit 5 Understanding Cultural Differences   **96**
- Reading 1   Dynamics of Intercultural Communication   98
- Reading 2   Understanding Values Behind Businesspeople   105

Unit 6 Time and Culture   **117**
- Reading 1   Time and Culture   121
- Reading 2   Managing Change in a Past-Oriented Culture   126

Unit 7 Communicating Nonverbally   **137**
     Reading 1   Defining Nonverbal Communication   140
     Reading 2   Nonverbal Communication   144

Unit 8 Different Communication Styles   **157**
     Reading 1   Ways of Reasoning   161
     Reading 2   Teaching Culture: Perspectives in Practice   167

Part Three   Applications of Intercultural Communication

Unit 9 Innovation and Education   **180**
     Reading 1   Differences That Make a Difference   185
     Reading 2   The Global Campus: Challenges and Opportunities   189

Unit 10 Intercultural Training   **200**
     Reading 1   What Are Intercultural Services?   204
     Reading 2   Working Abroad and Expatriate Adjustment   209

Unit 11 Intercultural Business Communication   **223**
     Reading 1   The Theoretical Foundation for Intercultural Business
                      Communication: A Conceptual Model (Part 1)   230
     Reading 2   The Theoretical Foundation for Intercultural Business
                      Communication: A Conceptual Model (Part 2)   236

Unit 12 Public Diplomacy and Intercultural Communication   **249**
     Reading 1   China Needs More Public Diplomacy, Zhao Says   252
     Reading 2   Public Diplomacy Gains Ground   256

Acknowledgements   **266**

Part One

Basic Concepts of Intercultural Communication

Unit 1
Culture Behind Language

When you communicate with people from other countries, it is unlikely that they will have the exact same word or meaning in mind. That difference in thought, however tiny, sends shock waves throughout the communication process. All understanding, therefore, is at the same time a misunderstanding and all agreement of feelings and thoughts is at the same time a means for growing apart. Language plays an essential role in culture learning. Language is a reflection of the cultural environment and its values. Developing intercultural awareness usually goes along with learning a new language and being exposed to a new culture, though not always. In intercultural communication, the role of language is especially important.

What You Can Learn from This Unit

1. Understand how important it is to learn culture through a foreign language;
2. Know that culture gives meaning to words;
3. Understand the meaning behind words;
4. Understand that culture might be a hidden barrier in intercultural communication.

Questions for Intercultural Awareness

1. What is the relationship between language and culture?
2. When learning English, are you trying to understand what cultural values some English words or statements indicate? List some English sayings or proverbs and explain the values they transmit.
3. Can you list some barriers in intercultural communication? Share your view in class.

What's Wrong?

How to Understand Invitation

Carmen and Judy are two mothers who live near each other. They often take their children to the park so that their children can play together.

Carmen: Hi, Judy.

(*Judy and Carmen's children are pleased to see each other and then begin playing together in the sand.*)

Judy: Hi, Carmen. How are you?

Carmen: Fine. I'm glad to see that our children like to play together.

Judy: Yeah, me too. I remember just a month ago they weren't sharing their toys.

Carmen: Now it looks like they're enjoying each other's company.

(*The two mothers continue chatting.*)

Judy: This has been fun. Maybe we could get together at one of our houses sometime. I'm sure the kids would enjoy that.

Carmen: Sure. That'd be nice.

Judy: Well, let's do it.

Carmen: OK.

(*Two weeks later in the park.*)

Judy: Hi, Carmen.

Carmen: Hi, Judy. How are you?

Judy: Fine. How about you?

Carmen: Pretty well.

Judy: I've been so busy lately, but I still want to get together soon. I know our kids would enjoy that.

Carmen: Yes. They would.

Judy: Let's do it soon.

Carmen: OK. That sounds like a good idea.

(*Judy and Carmen continue to talk for a few minutes.*)

Judy: I can't stay long. I promise my kids that I would take them to the library across the street.

Carmen: Yeah. I have to go, too.

(*Carmen and her children begin to get ready to leave.*)

Judy: Let's get together soon. I'll give you a call.

Carmen: OK. That sounds good. Bye.

Judy: Bye.

In the situations above, are Judy and Carmen really interested in getting together at each other's houses? Why or why not?

From a linguistic perspective, we can see that Judy invited Carmen to get together by saying "Maybe we could get together at one of our houses sometime. I'm sure the kids would enjoy that." And Carmen also accepted the invitation by saying "That'd be nice." Judy agreed by saying "Well, let's do it." This invitation was sent each time when they met. But they did not make an exact date to meet. Why did that happen? Was Carmen angry or disappointed with Judy for not making an exact time for the play-date?

From an intercultural perspective, the expression "Let's get together" in English does not have the same meaning as an invitation would have in Chinese. Instead, it may be a conversation closer—a way to end a conversation or an interpersonal encounter without using an abrupt departure expression which may hurt the other person's feelings. Examples of this might be "Sorry I have to go now" or "Sorry I have an appointment right now." Each time that Judy was about to leave, she would use the vague expression "Let's get together" to achieve her purpose of indicating that she needed to depart.

Ambiguous Invitations

In English, a number of expressions sound as if they are "invitations," but they are not. The following expressions are not real invitations because they are ambiguous statements to achieve the pragmatic function to leave.

A: Listen, I have a lot to talk to you about. I think we should try to have lunch together sometime soon.

B: OK.

A: I'll call you.

B: Sounds good.

A: Good talking to you. Let's get together sometime.

B: Sounds good.

A: I'll call you one of these days and we'll set up a time that's good for both of us.

B: Great. Talk to you soon.

Real Invitations

A real invitation should be specific; it has the activity, specific time and place. The following are examples of real invitations.

I would like to invite you over for my birthday party at my house at 8:00 this Friday evening. Can you come?

A: Jim, are you and Claudine free on Saturday night? We'd like to have you over for dinner.

B: Yes, I think we're free. That sounds nice.

A: If you can, let's make it for 8:00 after the kids are asleep.

B: Good idea. See you then.

Change Ambiguous Invitations into Real Invitations

Sometimes a friend is serious about the invitation, but he or she is not sure whether the other person would accept it. In this case he or she would not be specific in uttering a real invitation as stated above; instead he or she would send an ambiguous invitation as a hint to see the other person's response. This avoids embarrassment if he or she receives a refusal. If someone sends this kind of invitation to you, you can employ the following communication strategy to confirm your understanding.

A: Let's get together soon.

B: I'd like that.

A: Good. I'll give you a call.

B: I have got my notebook with me now. How about setting a date now?

A: Uh, sure. I'm free any day next week at noon. How about you?

B: Will tomorrow at 12:00 be OK?

Discussion

1. Are there any misunderstandings between the two mothers? If yes, what is the cause for these misunderstandings?
2. When you hear some expressions that sound like "invitations," will you interpret them as real invitations? Why or why not?

Reading 1

Language, Thought, Culture, and Intercultural Communication

Every language has its unique features and ways of allowing those who speak it to identify objects and experiences.[1] These linguistic features, which distinguish each language from all others, affect how the speakers of the language perceive and experience the world. To understand the effects of language on intercultural communication, questions such as the following must be explored:

* How do initial experiences with language shape or influence the way a person thinks?
* Do the categories of a language—its words, grammar, and usage—influence how people think and behave? More specifically, consider the following question: Does a person growing up in Saudi Arabia, who learns to speak and write Arabic, "see" and "experience" the world differently than does a person who grows up speaking and writing Tagalog in

the Philippines?

Although many scholars have advanced ideas and theories about the relationships among language, thought, culture and intercultural communication, the names most often associated with these issues are Benjamin Lee Whorf and Edward Sapir. Their theory is called "linguistic relativity[2]."

The best-known example of vocabulary differences associated with the Sapir-Whorf hypothesis[3] is the large number of words for snow in the Eskimo language. (The language is variously called Inuktitut in Canada, Inuit in Alaska, and Kalaallisut in Greenland.) Depending on whom you ask, there are from seven to fifty different words for snow in the Inuktitut language. For example, there are words that differentiate falling snow (*gana*) and fully fallen snow (*akilukak*). The English language has fewer words for snow and no terms for many of the distinctions made by Eskimos. The issue raised by the Sapir-Whorf hypothesis is whether the person who grows up speaking Inuktitut actually perceives snow differently than does someone who grows up in southern California and may only know snow by secondhand descriptions. More importantly, could the southern Californian who lives with the Inuit in Alaska learn to differentiate all of the variations of snow and to use the specific Eskimo words appropriately? The firmer version of the Sapir-Whorf hypothesis suggests that linguistic differences are accompanied by perceptual differences so that the English speaker looks at snow differently than the Eskimo speaker.

Numerous other examples of languages have highly specialized vocabularies for particular features of the environment. For instance, in the South Sea Islands, there are numerous words for coconut, which not only refer to the object of a coconut but also indicate how the coconut is being used. Similarly, in classical Arabic thousands of words are used to refer to a camel.

Another variation in vocabulary concerns the terms a language uses to identify and divide colors in the spectrum. For example, the Kamayura Indians of Brazil have a single word that refers to the colors that English speakers would call blue and green. The best translation of the word the Kamayuras use is "parakeet colored." The Dani of West New Guinea divide all colors into only two words, which are roughly equivalent in English to "dark" and "light." The important issue, however, is whether speakers of these languages are able to distinguish among the different colors when they see them or can experience only the colors suggested by the words available for them to use. Do the Kamayura Indians actually see blue and green as the same color because they use the same word to identify both? Or does their language simply identify colors differently than does English?

Do you think that you could learn to distinguish all of the variations of the object "snow" that are important to the Eskimos? Could you be taught to see all of the important characteristics of a coconut or the color? Such questions are very important in accepting or rejecting the ideas presented in the firm and soft versions of the Sapir-Whorf hypothesis.

Researchers looking at the vocabulary variations in the color spectrum have generally found that although a language may restrict how a color can be labeled verbally, people can still see and differentiate among particular colors. In other words, the Kamayura Indians can in fact see both blue and green, even though they use the same linguistic referent for both colors. The evidence on color perception and vocabulary, then, does not support the deterministic version of the Sapir-Whorf hypothesis.

What about all those variations for snow, camels, and coconuts? Are they evidence to support the firm version of the Sapir-Whorf hypothesis? A starting point for addressing this issue is to consider how English speakers use other words along with essentially the one word English has for "particles of water vapor that when frozen in the upper air fall to earth as soft, white, crystalline flakes." English speakers are able to describe verbally many variations of snow by adding modifiers to the root word. People who live in areas with a lot of snow are quite familiar with *dry snow*, *heavy snow*, *slush*, and *dirty snow*. Skiers have a rich vocabulary to describe variations in snow on the slopes. It is possible, therefore, for a person who has facility in one language to approximate the categories of another language. The deterministic position of Sapir-Whorf, then, is difficult to support. Even Sapir and Whorf's own work can be used to argue against the deterministic interpretation of their position because in presenting all of the Eskimo words for snow, Whorf provided their approximate English equivalents.

A better explanation for linguistic differences is that variations in the complexity and richness of a language's vocabulary reflect what is important to the people who speak that language.[4] To an Eskimo, differentiating among varieties of snow is much more critical to survival and adaptation than it is to the southern Californians, who may never see snow. Conversely, southern Californians have numerous words to refer to four-wheeled motorized vehicles, which are very important objects in their environment. However, we are certain that differences in the words and concepts of a language do affect the ease with which a person can change from one language to another because there is a dynamic interrelationship among language, thought, and culture.

Vocabulary

crystalline flakes 片状结晶
referent *n.* [语] 语词所指的对象
spectrum *n.* 光谱

Notes

1. Every language has its unique features and ways of allowing those who speak it to identify objects and experiences.

   一种语言之所以区别于另一种语言，就是因为每种语言使用者感知和认识世界的方式不同。例如，东西方都有龙的传说，但却由于文化的不同，龙所代表的形象也有所不同。在中国文化中，龙是瑞兽；而在西方文化中，龙却是怪兽。中国人自称是龙的传人，龙是华夏民族的图腾；而西方文化中的龙一般带有恶毒、凶狠的意味，与东方的瑞兽完全不一样。所以不同语言中相同的词可以代表不同的含义，这种文化差异就造成了沟通的障碍。本句大意为：每种语言都有其特色和表达方式，让它的使用者可以确定语言所指的实物和事件。

2. linguistic relativity

   "语言相对论"有两层含义：第一，一种文化中的内容，只有用该文化中的语言才能得到充分表达；第二，发源于某一文化中的概念，如果用另一种文化中的语言去讲，意思就会有所不同，至少在人们心目中唤起的意象不同。

3. Sapir-Whorf hypothesis

   20 世纪50 年代，美国人类学家、语言学家萨丕尔和他的弟子沃尔夫提出"萨丕尔—沃尔夫假说"。该理论包括两个基本观点：一是语言决定论（linguistic determinism），也就是语言决定着人们的思维、信念、态度等；语言不同的民族，他们的思维方式也不同。二是语言相对论（linguistic relativity），也就是语言反映人们的思维、信念、态度等；思维是相对于语言来说的，思维模式会随着语言的不同而不同，随着语言的变化而变化。

4. A better explanation for linguistic differences is that variations in the complexity and richness of a language's vocabulary reflect what is important to the people who speak that language.

   语言中的词汇也体现文化差异，影响跨文化沟通的效果。例如，爱斯基摩语中有关雪的词汇就有很多，因为他们的生活离不开雪，但这对于生活在热带的人来说就很难理解，因为他们可能从来没有见过雪。本句大意为：对于语言差异，还有更好的解释，那就是，人们可以根据某种语言中词汇的复杂和多样化的程度，判断出什么样的事物对于该语言使用者来说非常重要。

Discussion from Intercultural Perspectives

1. When you communicate with your Chinese friends in Chinese, are there times when you could not understand what they mean by what they say? How do you account for such differences?

2. When people from different cultures are using the same word or discussing the same thing, for example, a cow or a dragon, will there be no misunderstanding? Why or why not?

3. The following statements are reflections of one's cultural values. Can you illustrate each statement from both Chinese and American cultural perspectives? Discuss them in groups.

   I will try my best to come here.

   I'll be here by 9:00 a.m.

Reading 2

Language Mirrors Values

In addition to reflecting its worldview, a language also reveals a culture's basic value structure. For example, the extent to which a culture values the individual, as compared to the group, is often reflected in its language or linguistic style. The value placed on the individual is deeply rooted in the American psyche. Most citizens of the United States start from the cultural assumption that the individual is supreme and not only can, but should, shape his or her own destiny. That individualism is highly valued in the United States can be seen throughout its culture, from the love of the automobile as the preferred mode of transportation to a judicial system which goes as far as any in the world to protect the individual rights of the accused. Even when dealing with children, Americans try to provide them with a bedroom of their own, respect their individual right to privacy, and attempt to instill in them a sense of self-reliance and independence by encouraging them to solve their own problems.[1]

Owing to the close interrelatedness of language and culture, values (such as individualism in the United States) are reflected in standard American English. One such indicator of how our language reflects individualism is the number of words found in any American English dictionary that are compounded with the word "self." To illustrate, one is likely to find in any standard American English dictionary no fewer than 150 such words, including "self-absorbed," "self-appointed," "self-centered," "self-confident," "self-conscious," "self-educated," "self-image," "self-regard," and "self-supporting." This considerable list of English terms related to the individual is significantly larger than one found in a culture that places greater emphasis on corporate or group relationships.

In the U.S., individual happiness is the highest good, while in such group-oriented cultures as Japan, people strive for the good of the larger group such as the family, the community, or the whole society. Rather than stressing individual happiness, the Japanese are more concerned with justice (for group members) and righteousness (by group members). In Japan the "we" always comes before the "I"; the group is always more predominant than the individual. As Condon reminds us, "If Descartes had been Japanese, he would have said, 'We think, therefore we are.'"[2]

An important structural distinction found in Japanese society is between *uchi* (the in-group) and *soto* (the out-group), or the difference between "us" and "them." This basic social distinction is reflected in the Japanese language. For example, whether a person is "one of us" or "one of them" will determine which conversational greeting will be used, either *Ohayo gozaimasu*, which is customarily used with close members of one's in-group, or *Konnichiwa*, which is more routinely used to greet those outside one's inner circle. Mizutani has conducted an interesting experiment outside the Imperial Palace in Tokyo which is a favorite place for jogging. Dressed like a jogger, he greeted everyone he passed, both other joggers like himself and non-joggers, and noted their responses. Interestingly, 95 percent of the joggers greeted him with *Ohayo gazaimasu* (the term reserved for in-group members), while only 42 percent of the non-joggers used such a phrase. He concluded that the joggers, to a much greater degree than the non-joggers, considered him to be an in-group member because he too was a jogger.

Group members in Japan don't want to stand out or assert their individuality because according to the Japanese proverb, "The nail that sticks up gets hammered down."[3] In contrast to the United States, the emphasis in Japan is on "fitting in," harmonizing, and avoiding open disagreement within the group. If one must disagree, it is usually done gently and very indirectly by using such passive expressions as "It is said that..." or "Some people think that..."[4] This type of linguistic construction enables one to express an opinion without having to be responsible for it in the event that others in the group might disagree. In a study of speech patterns among Japanese and American students, Shimonishi found that the Japanese students used passive voice significantly more than did their American counterparts.

How language is used in Japan and the United States both reflects and reinforces the value of group consciousness in Japan and individualism in the United States. The goal of communication in Japan is to achieve consensus and promote harmony, while in the United States it is to demonstrate one's eloquence. Whereas language in Japan tends to be cooperative, polite, and conciliatory, language in the United States is often competitive, adversarial, and confrontational, and aimed at making a point. The Japanese go to considerable length to avoid controversial issues that might be disruptive; Americans seem to thrive on controversy, debate, argumentation, and provocation, as is evidenced by the use of the expression "just for the sake of argument." Moreover, the Japanese play down individual eloquence in favor of being good listeners, a vital skill if group consensus is to be achieved. North Americans, by way of contrast, are not particularly effective listeners because they are too busy mentally preparing their personal responses rather than paying close attention to what is being said. Thus, all of these linguistic contrasts between Japan and the United States express their fundamentally different approaches to the cultural values of "groupness" and individualism.[5]

Vocabulary

adversarial *adj.* 对抗性的

assert *v.* 坚持（自己的权利、个性等）

conciliatory *adj.* 和解的

confrontational *adj.* 故意寻衅的

consensus *n.* 共识

counterpart *n.* 职务相当的人

disruptive *adj.* 引起混乱的

eloquence *n.* 雄辩

instill *v.* 逐渐灌输

judicial *adj.* 法庭的，法官的，裁决的

predominant *adj.* 占优势的，占主导地位的

provocation *n.* 激怒，挑衅

psyche *n.* 精神

reinforce *v.* 加强，强化

righteousness *n.* 正直

Notes

1. Even when dealing with children, Americans try to provide them with a bedroom of their own, respect their individual right to privacy, and attempt to instill in them a sense of self-reliance and independence by encouraging them to solve their own problems.

本句大意为：甚至在处理孩子的问题上都能体现出美国人的文化价值观，他们给孩子提供自己的卧室，尊重孩子的隐私，让孩子解决自己的问题，尽力灌输给孩子们独立自主的意识。作者举这个例子是想说明美国人的所作所为都是美国文化的反映，这种文化同时反映了他们的价值观。

2. As Condon reminds us, "if Descartes had been Japanese, he would have said, 'We think, therefore we are.'"

笛卡尔的哲学思想基于唯理性的前提："我思，故我在。（I think, therefore I am.）"本句大意为：正如康登提醒我们的那样，如果笛卡尔是日本人的话，他说的便是"我们思，故我们在"了。作者在此是以I和we在不同的文化团体中不同的使用倾向来说明individual-oriented cultures和group-oriented cultures的差别。日本人在发表见解时习惯用we来代替I，从中我们就能看到日本人的集体主义观念在语言表达中的反映，因为日本人认为，集体利益高于个人利益，不能突出个人。

3. Group members in Japan don't want to stand out or assert their individuality because according to the Japanese proverb, "The nail that sticks up gets hammered down."

日本人的这句谚语The nail that sticks up gets hammered down意为"钉子竖起来，锤子打下去"，与中国的"枪打出头鸟"是一个意思。这些语言表达有助于我们理解中、日文化的含义。中国人是历来讲究中庸之道的，凡事跟大部分人一样，便很安全，很保险。日本人的做法也是如此，在众人面前不会轻易发表个人的不同见解，这跟美国人的做法刚好相反。所以我们学习一门外语，目的不仅仅在于理解其中文的意思，或能否翻译成中文，更重要的是能否理解该语言所表达的文化含义，以及在这些文化价值观影响下人们的行为表现。

4. ...it is usually done gently and very indirectly by using such passive expressions as "It is said that..." or "Some people think that..."

作者在此要表达的是日本人在发表不同见解时的语言习惯。为了礼貌待人，日本人说话委婉，表达含糊。他们最讨厌的是正面的语言交锋，因为这不仅会伤害双方面子，还会破坏整个集体的和睦。在这种交际心理的制约下，日本语言就形成了一种模糊委婉的特点。

5. Thus, all of these linguistic contrasts between Japan and the United States express their fundamentally different approaches to the cultural values of "groupness" and individualism.

作者在文中提到的日本和美国语言表达上的差异能够反映出两国不同的价值观，日本人是groupness或者说是collectivism，即集体主义价值观，而美国人则是individualism，即个人主义价值观。作者强调的是语言的使用可以反映出价值取向，从而来证明自己的论题——Language Mirrors Values。

Discussion from Intercultural Perspectives

1. How do you interpret the statement "Language is like a mirror which can reflect people's values"? Can you give some examples to account for your arguments?
2. Can you point out the difference between the Americans and the Japanese in terms of their way of speaking ?

Intercultural Lens

Language is part of the culture and also a carrier of the culture. Culture shapes its people's behavior. When you observe people's behavior, you can better understand the culture if you understand the words or expressions they are using.

Below are some slogans and sayings that may be confusing to people of different cultures. They might interpret the meanings differently from each other. Without fully understanding the culture of the country in which these slogans and sayings are used, you may have some misunderstandings in communication. Therefore it is important to learn the culture of the country whose language you are learning now.

Impossible Is Nothing. (Adidas's previous slogan) **Anything Is Possible.** (Li Ning's previous slogan) These two slogans encourage all employees to be innovative and to imagine that everything is possible to accomplish. The values these two slogans transmit are that these companies are not content with what they have achieved, but instead they strive to be more innovative by doing something different.

Just Do It. This slogan is also well known to all. It represents Nike's corporate culture, which can help us see its employees' attitude to work. Meanwhile, it also carries the American value, work or action orientation, which motivates people to do something, not just talk about something without taking any action.

Don't just stand there, do something! Americans take pride in quickly taking action in the face of problems or opportunities. To them, doing something, even if it proves to be a mistake, would be better than doing nothing. At least, errors can be mended, or can be a good lesson, but inaction accomplishes nothing.

Tell it like it is! This saying teaches the value that frank verbal and written communication is important. Those who are too indirect are likely to be viewed with suspicion, as if they have something to hide, or worse, from an American perspective, have nothing to contribute or lack self-confidence. This is a typical American value and therefore American people tend to be direct in communication. No "beating around the bush!"

Blow your own horn. If you want a job done right, do it yourself. Speak for yourself. These sayings reflect a strong sense of individualism, which can be seen in an emphasis on individual accountability and singling out a specific person for recognition and reward in the workplace.

There might be a misunderstanding for American individualism in China if individualism is translated into Chinese 个人主义, because 个人主义 in China means that someone cares about his or her own interest without considering other persons' interest, and in most cases it would hurt other people for one's own benefit. In America, you can be both individualistic and also care about other people. Americans often talk about a "win-win" situation in which people, groups or organizations all benefit from a solution.

The following are common proverbs in English. Each proverb communicates a cultural value that is so important to Americans.

Proverbs	Chinese Equivalents	Values
1. Remember the roots of your family tree, but you are known by your fruit, not by your root.	不可忘本，但是扬名不是靠出身，而是靠成就。	Equality
2. Discontent is the first step in progress.	不知足是前进的第一步。	Change
3. Men live like fish; the great ones devour the small.	人生犹如鱼，大鱼吃小鱼。	Competition
4. God helps those who help themselves.	天助自助者。	Independence
5. Work while you work, play while you play.	工作时工作，玩耍时玩耍。	Concentration
6. Great gain makes work easy.	所获甚丰，辛劳也觉轻松。	Materialism
7. Time lost cannot be won again.	时间一去不复返。	Cherishing time
8. Poverty is not a sufficient cause for disgrace, but poverty without resolution to help oneself, is a disgrace.	贫穷并不可耻，穷而不争气才可耻。	Self-reliance
9. Well done is better than well said.	说得好不如做得好。	Action

The following are proverbs from various countries. Different as they are, these proverbs express the same or similar values.

Proverbs	Chinese Equivalents	Values	Countries
a) He who speaks first loses.	发言最先，失败最早。	Silence	India
b) The mouth is the cause of calamity.	祸从口出。	Silence	Japan
a) Whoever goes softly, goes far.	做事轻柔婉转者成功的几率高。	Indirectness	France
b) To speak well and be agreeable costs little and achieves a lot.	多说好话多多附和只会利多弊少。	Indirectness	Mexico
a) A hollow drum makes the most noise.	空心鼓最响。	Modesty	Japan
b) A barking dog is never a good hunter.	吠犬不擅猎捕。	Modesty	ROK
a) Life is but a candle before the wind.	人生好比风中烛。	Destiny	Japan
b) Man does not attain everything he desires; winds do not always blow as the vessels wish.	人无法事事如愿，风也不能时时都顺。	Destiny	Arabic countries
a) If you don't know the ford, don't cross the stream.	不识浅滩，不过溪流。	Caution	Russia
b) Be careful bending your head—you may break it.	低头要小心——你可能折断它。	Caution	Italy
a) There is nothing to fear but fear itself.	最大的恐惧是恐惧本身。	Courage	The U.S.
b) The path is not hard to follow because of the rivers and the mountains, but because, men are reluctant to face the mountains and rivers.	道路的艰难并不是因为有山脉和河流，而是因为人们不愿意直面山脉与河流。	Courage	Vietnam

Group Work

Remember people act in certain ways because of their values. Work in groups of three or four to complete the table based on the following instructions:

1. Make a study of Chinese and English proverbs. Identify what these proverbs mean to the people speaking the language and what values these proverbs transmit.

2. After each group completes the table, you can exchange your findings with each other, so you can make a complete table for the work done by all the groups.

Proverbs	Chinese Equivalents	Values	Countries
1.			
2.			
3.			
4.			
5.			
6.			
7.			
8.			
9.			
10.			

Intercultural Case Study

"New Journey" Begins with Warm Words

The first China-U.S. Strategic and Economic Dialogue began on a relaxed and friendly note on Monday with leaders from both countries using wisdom from one another's cultures in their opening remarks.

While admitting he did not have the fluent *putonghua* of Utah Governor Jon Huntsman, who is likely to become the U.S. ambassador to China, U.S. President Barack Obama displayed a knowledge of Chinese history when he quoted ancient Chinese philosopher Mencius during his welcoming address in the Ronald Reagan Building in Washington, D.C.

"A trail through the mountains, if used, becomes a path in a short time, but, if unused, becomes blocked by grass in an equally short time," Obama said. "Our task is to forge a path to the future that we seek for our children—to prevent mistrust or the inevitable differences of the moment from allowing that trail to be blocked by grass; to always be mindful of the journey that we are undertaking together."

Obama also quoted Yao Ming, the Chinese basketball player who is a member of the Houston Rockets, to emphasize the importance of dialogue between China and the U.S.

"As a new president and also as a basketball fan, I have learned from the words of Yao Ming, who said, 'No matter whether you are new or an old team member, you need time to adjust to one another,'" Obama said. "Well, through the constructive meetings that we've already had, and through this dialogue, I'm confident that we will meet Yao's standard."

In her opening speech, U.S. Secretary of State Hillary Clinton stressed the importance of China-U.S. cooperation by citing a

Chinese proverb.

"When people are of one mind and heart, they can move Mountain Tai," she said.

U.S. Treasury Secretary Timothy Geithner, who has spent time studying in China, spoke positively of the country's development in the past 30 years and called for China and the U.S. to work together on mitigating the global economic crisis. Geithner also used a Chinese expression, saying the countries would be "taking the same boat through rain and wind."

Geithner's comment was similar to what Clinton said when she spoke at the Asia Society in New York in February before her trip to Asia.

"'When you are in a common boat, you need to cross the river peacefully together.' The wisdom of that aphorism must continue to guide us today," she said at the time.

State Councilor Dai Bingguo asked senior officials "can we make it?" as he spoke about creating a better future for bilateral relations. And he received applause and laughter from across the hall by answering his own question in English with Obama's presidential campaign slogan: "Yes, we can."

Analyzing the Issues in the Case

1. Can you find a feature of the speeches made by the U.S. senior officials?
2. Why do the U.S. senior officials often quote Chinese proverbs or old sayings in their speeches? Is that the American way of making speeches? What message does this feature of their speeches transmit ?
3. Americans would often quote in their speeches the words or sayings by celebrities. What cultural values does this feature display?
4. State Councilor Dai Bingguo made a joke in his remarks. Why did he do that? Was he trying to be interculturally sensitive and make speeches the American way? Why would Americans tell jokes in their serious and important speeches?

Learning Culture Through Proverbs

Work in pairs and exchange views on the meanings of the following proverbs, then try to find out their Chinese equivalents if there is any, and discuss the values transmitted.

Proverb 1: *Every dog has his day.*
Proverb 2: *More is meant than meets the ear.*

Online Research—Using Key Words

For more information and resources, search the Internet with the following key words:

culture and language, cultural differences in proverbs

Unit 2
Communicating Interculturally

Culture is like an iceberg. The tip of the iceberg is easy to see. It includes the visible aspects such as dress, language, food, greeting rituals, and religious practices as well as the accepted practices and taboos of living and working in a culture. The remaining huge chunk of the iceberg hidden below the surface includes the invisible aspects such as the values, traditions, experiences, and behavior that define each culture.

Venturing into different cultures without adequate preparation can be just as dangerous as a ship attempting to navigate in icy waters without charts, hoping to be lucky enough to avoid hitting an iceberg.

By definition, intercultural awareness means not only becoming culturally sensitive in other cultures but having a solid understanding of your own culture. Cultural differences must be understood and acknowledged before they can be managed.

What You Can Learn from This Unit

1. Understand different aspects of culture;
2. Understand the relationship between culture and communication;
3. Recognize how verbal expressions are influenced by culture;
4. Increase intercultural awareness and sensitivity;
5. Communicate interculturally with English speaking people.

Questions for Intercultural Awareness

1. What are the various aspects of culture, that is, the elements that make up a culture?
2. What is the relationship between culture and communication?
3. Is it possible to learn a foreign language well without learning about the culture where it is spoken as a native language? Why or why not?

What's Wrong?

Global Workplace Communication

I work for an American company, one of the world's largest manufacturers of custom software and consulting providers. Our company specializes in product development, digital platform engineering, and digital product design. The company's headquarters is in Newtown, Pennsylvania, and its branches are located in more than 40 countries.

I am an HR manager based in Shanghai, China and report to the Asia Pacific Human Resources Department. Our team members come from different nations and backgrounds. While the company strategy is to build one team and one culture, and we value collaboration and appreciate cultural differences, intercultural issues are still the main barriers in the workplace.

Language or Culture

We have several colleagues from India. When meeting with them through video, we were confused that Indian colleagues always shook heads from side to side while saying "yes, yes." Seeing what appeared to us as contradictory verbal and nonverbal responses, we did not know exactly what to ask or what to do next. Later, a colleague who once worked in India helped us remove the communication barrier when working with Indian co-workers.

Language or Communication

In our company, we have an assessment platform, in which any employee can create a career map and then revise the career path annually. The map is then submitted to a supervisor. Once the request is approved, the employee must attend an assessment session and be evaluated by the international expert committee.

Some Chinese engineers in our company had strong technical backgrounds with rich project experience, but when questioned by assessment experts, they could not answer the questions or explain their points appropriately.

When the HR manager received the expert committee's assessment report, the HR manager and Chinese colleagues could not understand what the experts meant by the comment "communication problem that Chinese colleagues are facing."

Attending Meetings

Meetings are so common in the workplace, but what happens in a meeting varies greatly from one country to another. Meetings can have a variety of purposes: sharing information, giving instructions, discussing issues and problems, suggesting solutions, making decisions, and so on.

Our HR team members have a meeting every Friday. During the meeting, our boss always encourages team members to share their ideas or comments. Team members from Australia, Poland, etc. are always very responsive and willing to express their ideas, while others from Asia are usually silent. The HR manager always encourages them to be active and to express their opinions, but they don't feel comfortable sharing their views in meetings.

Discussion

1. Why were the Chinese colleagues confused when the Indian colleagues shook heads while saying "yes, yes"?
2. What does it mean by "communication problem" when the assessment experts discover the problems the Chinese colleagues face at the assessment session?
3. Some Asian colleagues keep quiet in the meetings. How would the Western boss interpret their behaviors?
4. Based on your understanding and discussion of the intercultural issues above, what do you think you can do to solve the intercultural problems in the global workplace?

Reading 1

The Link Between Culture and Communication

It has been said that without a culture we cannot see, but with a culture we are forever blind. In other words, each of us is born into a culture that teaches us a number of shared meanings and expectations. We usually learn our own culture's ways of doing, speaking, and thinking so well that it becomes difficult to think, feel, and act as people in other cultures do.

As the basic building blocks of communication, words communicate meaning, but as we have seen, the meanings of words are much influenced by culture. Meaning is in the person, not in the word, and each person is the product of a particular culture that passes on shared and appropriate meanings. Thus, if we want to learn to communicate well in a foreign language, we must understand the culture that gives that language meaning. In other words, culture and communication are inseparably linked: You can't have one without the other. Culture gives meaning and provides the context for communication, and the ability to communicate allows us to act out our cultural values and to share our language and our culture.

But our own native language and culture are so much a part of us that we take them for granted. When we travel to another country, it's as if we carry along with our passports, our own culturally designed lenses through which we view the new environment.[1] Using our own culture as the standard by which to judge other cultures is called "ethnocentrism," and although unintentional, our ethnocentric ways of thinking and acting often get in the way of our understanding other languages and cultures. The ability and willingness to change lenses when we look at a different culture is both the cure and prevention for such cultural blindness. Studying a new language provides the opportunity to practice changing lenses when we also learn the context of the culture to which it belongs.

When linguists study a new language they often compare it to their own, and consequently they gain a better understanding of not only the new language, but of their own language as well. Students who study a foreign language will also learn more about their own tongue by comparing and contrasting the two languages as well. You can follow the same comparative method in learning more about culture—your own, as well as others'. Remember that each culture has developed a set of patterns that are right and appropriate for that culture. If people do things differently in another culture, they are not "wrong"—they are just different! Always thinking that "culturally different" means "culturally wrong" will only promote intercultural misunderstanding.

Learning about American culture along with the American language does not necessitate your becoming "Americanized" and acting just like an American, but it does mean making an effort to understand American people and culture. In other words, it helps you to see like an American without your having to be like an American.[2]

You Can Talk, but What Do You Communicate?

How often have you heard someone say, in an attempt to clarify, "Yes, that is what I said, but that's not what I meant[3]"? Just because what we talk does not mean that we actually communicate what we intend. Communication can be defined as any behavior that is given meaning, whether the behavior is verbal or nonverbal, intended or unintended, consciously or unconsciously performed. So, it is impossible not to communicate, even though one does not always communicate in words.

The clothes we wear, the way we decorate our homes, the cars we drive, the way we address people, the jobs we choose, all these things communicate different things to different people, and they may communicate more—or less—than we intend. It depends on how the receiver of the message sees, thinks, and feels as much as on what the sender says, thinks, and feels. Communication is a very complex process, even among people from the same culture who speak the same language. The potential problems and the likelihood of miscommunication multiply when communication takes place between people from different cultures.

Communicating Interculturally

Intercultural communication occurs whenever a person from one culture does something that is given meaning by a person from another culture. Communication across cultures is made difficult by each person's ethnocentric tendencies to perceive objects, events, and behavior through lenses designed in the person's own cultures. But an honest desire to communicate with people from other cultures, coupled with an attempt to understand cultural differences, will go a long way in helping you become a successful intercultural communicator.

Communicating in a new culture means learning what to say (words, phrases, meaning, structure), whom to communicate with (the role and status of the person), who you are (how you perceive yourself), how you communicate the message (emotional components, nonverbal cues, intonation), why you communicate in a given situation (intentions, values, assumptions), when you communicate (time), and where you can or should communicate. This sounds like an impossible task— but remember, you have learned to do all these things in your own native language and culture, mostly without thinking about them. The difference is that now as an adult learning a second language and culture, you must think about the process.

An awareness of the following potential problem area will help you avoid the difficulties that others have experienced when communicating with people from other cultures:

- linguistic differences in grammatical structure and semantic differences in word meaning and usage;
- the nonverbal aspects of communication, such as gestures and other silent cultural clues;
- preconceived ideas that cloud your ability to see and understand a person as he or she wants to be seen and understood;
- value judgments about the behavior of people based on what you think is "right";
- anxiety or discomfort that defeats your intentions and creates discomfort for the person with whom you are trying to communicate.

Notice that only one of these problem areas is directly related to the linguistic aspects of communicating in second language and culture. To be an effective intercultural communicator you must pay attention to the social, psychological, and cultural aspects of communication, not just the grammar. Much evidence shows that communicating interculturally is not easy, but that does not mean it is not worthwhile or is to be avoided. As we approach the twenty-first century, we have no choice, given the world we live in. If we are going to survive on this necessarily international globe, we must learn to communicate interculturally.

But we need not dwell on the dark side. Learning to be a successful intercultural communicator[4] can be an exciting, enjoyable and rewarding experience that will open up new doors to both personal and professional growth and satisfaction.

Developing Cross-Cultural Awareness

Developing cross-cultural awareness usually goes along with learning a new language and being exposed to a new culture; such exposure reveals both cultural similarities and differences. And sometimes it is the similarities between cultures that surprise us as much as the differences. Once a little four-year-old American traveling in China was overheard exclaiming, "Look, Mommy, that little Chinese boy is eating ice cream, too."

Cross-cultural awareness is the ability to understand cultures—your own and others'—by means of objective, non-judgmental comparisons. It is an appreciation for, an understanding of, cultural pluralism—the ability to get rid of our ethnocentric tendencies and to accept another culture on its own terms.

Studying a second language without learning the culture is like learning how to drive a car by studying a driver's manual and never getting behind a steering wheel. We study a foreign language in order to communicate with people who have learned their native language not in a classroom, but in natural, everyday interactions with people and situations in their culture. They have learned the intentions behind words and phrases mostly without consciously thinking about them; it has been part of their culture and they have taken it for granted. We, however, as adults learning a second language, must make a conscious effort to examine the cultural context of the language we want to learn.

It is very difficult to be entirely objective when we observe another culture. Having been brought up within the context of a particular culture, we have been influenced and shaped by its values, even if we cannot articulate them. Although it is very hard to observe another culture with pure objectivity, it should be one's goal to do so. We must remember that in comparing cultures, "different" does not mean "bad" or "inferior"—it just means "different."

It is important to remember that although many moments of discomfort occur when we are interacting with people from other cultures, no one culture is inherently better or worse than any other. Each culture has its own set of values, norms, and ways of doing things that are considered "right" for it. That one culture's way of doing things is right for its people does not necessarily mean it is "right" for everybody, and herein lies the potential conflict in cross-cultural encounters.

Becoming more aware of the influence of cultural values has many positive consequences. It leads to better understanding of ourselves and of others. We become more tolerant and less defensive, and we can enjoy cultural differences as well as the similarities. After all, variety is the spice of life!

Vocabulary

articulate *v.* 清晰地表达

blindness *n.* 盲点

ethnocentrism *n.* 种族（或民族）中心主义

inherently *adv.* 内在地，固有地

spice *n.* 趣味，情趣，风味

Notes

1. …our own culturally designed lenses through which we view the new environment.
   这里culturally designed lenses意为"文化透镜"，以此来说明人们都是通过自己的文化视角来观察新环境，评判是非。在单一文化环境中我们应该学会换位思考，不能以自己的观点作为是非的标准，在多元文化环境中我们更应该学会以跨文化视角分析不同的观点与现象。

2. Learning about American culture along with the American language does not necessitate your becoming "Americanized" and acting just like an American, but it does mean making an effort to understand American people and culture. In other words, it helps you to see like an American without your having to be like an American.
   这段话阐述了两个观点：一是学习一种语言就是在学习所学语言国家的文化，因为语言是文化的传播工具；二是学习美国语言与文化不是让学习者的行为像美国人一样，而是以此帮助学习者更好地了解美国社会与美国人的行为。

3. …that is what I said, but that's not what I meant…
   我们用自己的母语进行交流时，是否也常用此表达回答对方？难道我们就听不懂对方说的话吗？我们当然都能听懂对方的话，但我们不一定都

能理解对方所指的意思，理解这一观点对学习跨文化交流很有帮助。

4. a successful intercultural communicator

这里提出一个概念a successful or effective intercultural communicator而不是an intercultural communicator，因为在跨文化语境中任何人都是an intercultural communicator，但不都是a successful or effective intercultural communicator。

Discussion from Intercultural Perspectives

1. Do you agree that culture gives words their meanings? Can you identify two "culturally-loaded" words or phrases in English and in Chinese? How do you understand the statement "Meaning is in the person, not in the word..."?

2. What does the statement "Always thinking that 'culturally different' means 'culturally wrong' will only promote intercultural misunderstanding" mean?

3. "Each culture has its own set of values, norms, and ways of doing things that are considered 'right' for it. That one culture's way of doing things is right for its people does not necessarily mean it is 'right' for everybody..." According to this statement, what might occur in an intercultural communication situation? Can you give some examples?

Reading 2

Intercultural Awareness and Communication

We live in a time when the need for understanding and mutual respect across cultural boundaries is imperative. Implicit in the achievement of understanding and respect is the successful interchange between two human beings that we call communication. Language is, of course, a key component of communication, and although the accurate use of linguistic forms is necessary for effective communication, in most communicative situations, the communicators do more than simply talk to each other in grammatically well-constructed sentences; there has to be familiarity with the culture of the language being used by the communicators.

Even between two fluent speakers of the same language there has to be some awareness of cultural differences. I still remember the parting words from a Nigerian student of mine who assured me "I will remember you until tomorrow." I understood his sentiment because I was aware that the English word "tomorrow" in a Nigerian context was a much less definite time expression than the day that follows today—or at least I hope so. The point is that language and culture, as we all know, are linked together and that communication, even between two people speaking the same language can be difficult if there is a cultural difference between the two speakers.[1]

For the average person, a complete assimilation of a second culture may be even more impossible than speaking with flawless grammar and accurate pronunciation. What may be more realistic and valuable than striving for total assimilation of the target culture is the development of an awareness of culture and the intercultural skills that one develops on the way to cultural awareness.

Cultural awareness can be seen as the recognition that culture affects perception and that culture influences values, attitudes and behavior.[2] The development of this awareness can be described as having four sequential stages leading ideally toward toleration and appreciation of cultural diversity.

Intercultural adjustment skills are a range of skills that are implicit in the concept of cultural awareness. These skills must be developed if we are to adjust to living in a new culture or even travel comfortably through a new culture.

In fact, one could make the case that the skills must be developed before an awareness will develop. Using the four stages of cultural awareness as a basis, we can describe four general skills that must be developed at each stage in the process.

Stage One, Recognition

At this stage we recognize the existence and pervasive influence of culture. For most of us, this begins with the growing consciousness of our own cultural group, and except for those individuals in extremely isolated cultural groups, we also begin to recognize the existence of other cultures. A pronouncement such as "I am an American" is the starting point, and implicit in this statement is the recognition that Americans do things in a particular way. Simultaneously, the concept of foreigner also begins to have meaning, and at this stage there is the recognition that foreigners do things differently. As we develop, so does our recognition that cultural differences are not only obvious and concrete (food, shelter, clothing), but subtle and abstract (values, attitudes, mores) as well. It is probably safe to say that as our recognition of foreign cultures increases, so too does our conscious recognition of our own cultural heritage.

At the recognition stage, the key skill is "non-judgmental observation[3]." This is the ability to see and describe culture with minimal judgment that what is seen is good or bad or right or wrong. In other words, we should avoid quick and easy labeling of cultural behavior as "funny" or "dumb" or "backward" or "progressive." Ideally, the intercultural traveler takes on the attitude of a scientist who simply reports what he or she sees. The first step toward understanding is seeing clearly.

Stage Two, Acceptance or Rejection

Almost simultaneously with our recognition of culture and cultural differences there is a reaction that is most often either positive or negative. The techniques in this article attempt to encourage a neutral, non-judgmental attitude of acceptance, but in fact what often occurs is rebellion against our own culture or rejection of the foreign culture.

The set of skills we hope to develop during this acceptance or rejection stage can be labeled "coping with ambiguity." When we become aware of the fact that there is more than one way to behave or more than one way to organize society, it becomes necessary to live with a certain amount of ambiguity until we see enough of the total picture to see how the various pieces of the cultural puzzle fit together.

Stage Three, Integration or Ethnocentrism

At this stage we reach either a somewhat more sophisticated point of view where we begin to act and think biculturally or, at the other extreme, we solidify our monocultural point of view into rigid ethnocentrism. For the ethnocentric individual, the road toward cultural awareness has come to an end.

At this third stage, where we have started to come to terms with the culture in an intercultural situation, we are beginning to develop into a bicultural being who is not only becoming more fluent in the language but is also beginning to take on a second identity. To achieve biculturalism, we must develop a set of skills that can be called "the ability to empathize." This involves not only projecting ourselves into the role of a person in the target culture, but it also requires a willingness to let go of our close identity with our native culture. In the face of an impending identity crisis, when questions such as "Who am I, after all?" begin to emerge, our self image as "a 100% American," for example, must be sacrificed in order to embrace a new identity.

Stage Four, Transcendence

When we reach the final stage of cultural awareness, we are able to value and appreciate our own cultural roots, whether they are native or acquired, and also to value and appreciate all other cultures as well.[4] At this level of understanding, however, we are also able to transcend particular cultures and see their individual weaknesses and strengths, to become, in effect, a citizen of the world, searching for universals but also valuing the vitality and variety of earth's cultures.

Finally, after we have reached the point where we can transcend culture and see ourselves as a product of culture, but no longer a prisoner of culture, and when we can see the strengths and weaknesses of the cultures we embrace, we need a set of skills that can be labeled "the ability to respect." This is what understanding is all about. It is important to note, however, that the ability to respect still allows for disagreement and criticism. We can, after all, adopt an attitude of "live and let live" while both showing respect for another way of doing things and questioning whether it is the only or best way.

More importantly, however, we should remind ourselves on a daily basis that theories and frameworks such as the four stages of cultural awareness apply only to an idealized individual, and that individuals not only look different from each other, but also think, feel and grow in ways that never quite match the idealized "we" of the preceding paragraphs. Ultimately, the journey toward cultural awareness is made by individuals who, like the six blind men in Saxe's poem[5], may never know the whole truth or the best answer, but whose handicap should not prevent them from the search.

Vocabulary

assimilation *n.* 吸收

come to terms with 与某事妥协，对某事让步

empathize *v.* 有同感，产生共鸣

impending *adj.* 逼近的，即将发生的

let go of 放手

monocultural *adj.* 单一文化的

rebellion *n.* 反抗，不服从

simultaneously *adv.* 同时发生地，同步地

transcend *v.* 超过，超越

Notes

1. The point is that language and culture, as we all know, are linked together and that communication, even between two people speaking the same language can be difficult if there is a cultural difference between the two speakers.

   本句大意为：问题的要点是，语言和文化是分不开的，即使交流双方讲相同的语言，但如果文化不同，也会出现沟通障碍。此句说明，即使我们能用英语流利表达，也就是说没有语言障碍，文化差异也会造成交流障碍，说明了文化在跨文化交流中的重要性。

2. Cultural awareness can be seen as the recognition that culture affects perception and that culture influences values, attitudes and behavior.

   cultural awareness意为"文化意识"，指对文化多元性的意识和对文化差异的宽容态度。本句大意为：具备文化意识就是承认文化影响人们的感知，承认文化影响人们的价值观、看法和行为。

3. non-judgmental observation

   "客观观察"指在看到及描述一种文化时，将主观情感降到最低限度。也就是说，我们应当避免草率、轻易地给某些文化行为贴上标签，断定其为"有趣"、"无聊"、"落后"或者"先进"。作为跨文化旅人，最好秉持科学家式的观察态度，客观地讲述自己的见闻。

4. …we are able to value and appreciate our own cultural roots, whether they are native or acquired, and also to value and appreciate all other cultures as well.

本句大意为：对待我们自己的文化，无论是本土的，还是借鉴外族的，我们都能以重视、欣赏的眼光去看待。当然，对待其他文化，我们也能持相同的态度。

5. the six blind men in Saxe's poem

在萨克斯的诗《盲人摸象》（"The Blind Men and the Elephant"）中，六个盲人去"看"大象。他们通过触摸，分别认为大象像一堵墙、一支长矛、一条蛇、一棵树、一把扇子、一根绳子。事实上，他们摸到的是大象的不同部位，分别是大象的躯干、象牙、象鼻、象腿、象耳、象尾。

Discussion from Intercultural Perspectives

1. Each culture has its own way of saying and doing things and therefore each person tends to make a judgment based on his or her own culture. What would happen if each person sticks to his or her own judgment?

2. Since cultural differences are unavoidable in intercultural communication, what role can intercultural awareness play then?

3. How would you understand the statement "…also to value and appreciate all other cultures as well"?

Intercultural Lens

1. In pairs or in groups, discuss the questions in the following situations.

These questions will help you become more familiar with typical, polite English responses. Analyze any response that would be different from what would be said in Chinese. Discuss how different responses might lead to misunderstandings.

Situation 1

A foreign visitor expresses his gratitude to your boss by saying "Thank you so much for all you have done for me in the past few days." Your boss replies politely by saying in Chinese 这是我们应尽的职责. If you were the interpreter for the visitor, how would you translate what the boss said into English? And why?

A. "It is our duty to help you."

B. "It is our pleasure."

Situation 2

If someone compliments your scarf, how would you respond to it appropriately?

A. "I'm glad you like it and you can take it if you want to."

B. "Oh, it's cheap."

C. "Thank you. I like it too."

Situation 3

You and someone else are waiting for a lift. When it comes, you would like the other person to enter first. What is the appropriate way to say it if the other person is American?

A. "Go ahead."

B. "Please."

C. "After you."

Situation 4

If two people are walking ahead of you and you want to walk past them, what would you do or say?

A. You just pass the two people without saying anything.

B. "Excuse me."

C. "Sorry. Would you let me pass?"

Situation 5

You are at the dinner table and want to eat something on the other side of the table. What would you do or say?

A. Stand up and stretch out your hand to it yourself.

B. "Excuse me, could you pass me..., please?"

C. "Sorry, could you pass me..., please?"

Situation 6

Your English teacher explains some points from the text in class, but you don't understand them, what would you do or say?

A. Nod your head and smile.

B. Look at the teacher blankly.

C. "I'm sorry. I still don't understand. Could you please give an example?" *or*
    "Could you please repeat the point that is relevant to...?"

Situation 7

Suppose you are discussing a proposal made by a Westerner, but you don't think you would accept it, because it is highly demanding and far beyond your expectation. In order to be polite, you reply to him by saying you would like to think about it without saying "Yes" or "No." How would he interpret your message?

A. This is a positive message and you would likely accept it later after your
    consideration.

B. This is a refusal.

2. Learn how to use "Excuse me," "Thank you," and "Sorry" in the following situations.

"Excuse me," "Thank you," and "Sorry" are the oil that makes the American machinery of social interaction run smoothly. People from other countries are often surprised and confused at the amount of apologies and thanks that Americans express. Yet Americans expect to hear these words frequently, on all sorts of minor social occasions.

With a partner, decide which of these expressions should be used in the following situations. (In some cases, only one of these expressions is correct, and in other cases more than one expression can be used.) Write down the expressions and then act out the situations.

Example:

After dinner, at a friend's house, you burp.

"<u>Excuse me</u>."

Situation 1

On a bus, you touch another passenger's arm accidentally.

"_____."

Situation 2

A friend tells you how nice you look today.

"_____."

Situation 3

In a restaurant, you go up to two waitresses who are having a conversation to find out where the bathroom is.

"_____."

Situation 4

The shop assistant gives you a shopping bag after you pay for it.

"_____."

Situation 5

You are five minutes late for class.

"_____."

Situation 6

In class, you ask your teacher to repeat a homework assignment.

"_____."

Situation 7

Your teacher hands back your homework.

"_____."

Situation 8

During a conversation with a friend, you can't stop sneezing.

"_____."

Situation 9

You ask a stranger in the street where the bus stop is.

"_____."

Situation 10

You dialed the wrong number.

"_____."

3. Practice your communication skills when meeting with Americans by choosing the most appropriate answer in each situation.

1) One of your American friends says, "How are you doing?" He or she expects you to respond with "_____."

   A. I'm having a bad day

   B. I'm fine, thank you

   C. Sorry, but I'm in a rush

   D. I've been sick all day

2) After exchanging business cards, Americans will likely _____.

    A. ask you to explain the meaning of your name

    B. admire the quality of your business card

    C. look at your title to see if you are an important person in your company

    D. ask what you do

3) When talking with Americans, you should _____.

    A. keep a half foot away

    B. keep two arms' length away

    C. keep one arm's length away

    D. avoid making eye contact

4) When meeting with American executives for the first time, you should _____.

    A. hand your business card to them immediately

    B. wait for them to hand their business cards to you

    C. shake hands with them and exchange cards after a few minutes of discussion

    D. wait until the end of the meeting to give them your business card

5) In a business introduction, Americans may ask you to call them by their first name because _____.

    A. they are not interested in business

    B. they like harmony in discussion

    C. their last name may be hard to pronounce

    D. they want to be comfortable during the discussion

4. Analyze the following behavior and sayings. Then work in groups and try to understand the values behind people's behavior. Also, try to predict people's behavior once you know their cultural values.

1) Are you a TGIF (Thank God It Is Friday) or a TGIM (Thank God It Is Monday) person?

    TGIF people are glad to see Friday arrive because they look forward to a weekend without work. TGIM people dread Friday; they see the weekend as an unnecessary interruption in their work schedule. TGIM people are often workaholics. Just as alcoholics are addicted to alcohol, workaholics are addicted to work—but do they suffer from it?

2)　What does it mean by learning?

In the United States learning is usually a process that involves asking questions in order to open the doors to understanding. From kindergarten to graduate seminars, students who ask questions are rewarded.

While in cultures like Asia, Latin America, and South Europe, learning generally does not come from asking questions. Learning means receiving and taking in what is given by teachers and some teachers may speak through written texts.

3)　Work smart, not hard.

The most efficient approach when undertaking any form of work is to minimize your own effort whilst maximizing the potential benefits or impacts that may flow from it. Which is more important? Working hard or working smart? Why?

4)　You are what you do.

In the United States, an individual is often judged by what he or she does for a living. At social and professional gatherings, people are expected to introduce themselves and to strike up a conversation. "How do you do?" is often followed by "What do you do?" Once they know what a person does they have a basis for deciding whether or not they are interested in this person enough to continue the conversation.

Intercultural Case Study

Fuyao American Factory

The world's largest auto glass production plant located in Dayton, Ohio, America, but owned by Fuyao Glass Industry Group Co., Ltd. (Fuyao Group), officially opened on October 7th, 2014.

The Fuyao Auto Glass Production facility occupies a total area of 45 hectares with 170,000 m^2 production plant. The plant has adopted the state-of-the-art equipment, together with the world's leading technologies and a variety of craftsmen in fulfilling the demands of different automobile manufacturers. With over 2,000 local employees and the projected annual production of 4.5 million units of auto glasses, the plant will be supplying 1/4 of the American auto market's demand on auto glass. Therefore, Fuyao Group has attracted wide attention and heated discussion.

When a company moves from the domestic market to the international market, it is not simply an extension and expansion in the region, but a process of merging with different cultures in different countries. However, different countries and regions have their own work cultures. The problems caused by the changes in the external environment have become the difficult problems that multinational enterprises must face and overcome.

Fuyao Management Style in Fuyao American Factory

China and the U.S. are different in their cultures, so it is natural that they have different management styles. For example, there are differences in leadership, talent management, performance assessment, and employee engagement and motivation. Therefore, American workers have an ambivalent attitude toward Fuyao management. Though workers who had been laid off from the U.S. automobile industry are grateful to Fuyao for providing employment, they still find it hard to adapt to Fuyao management style. They also have difficulties adopting the Chinese management practices in Fuyao American Factory. Finally, those differences are problematic at different managerial and worker levels in the factory.

Different Cultures and Different Behaviors

In a training session for Chinese staff who will be working in the U.S., they are told that Americans are over-confident yet they require motivation to complete their jobs. American employees always complain about management in the factory, saying that Chinese managers give orders without providing an explanation for the tasks. In addition, Chinese managers are puzzled that they can't get effective feedback from American workers. In order to ensure productivity in the manufacturing facility, Chinese staff should learn how to manage problems when working with American employees.

Different Attitude toward Work

Projects can suffer when international investors are unfamiliar with the American work culture. This is true for many executives coming from China. Chinese managers consider American workers to be lazy, undisciplined, and inefficient. Many American workers, however, who believe in individualism, consider work-life balance to be paramount, and view time on the job as a way to make money in order to enjoy life. A common adage is "work to live, not live to work." Loyalty to one company has decreased in the past decades, especially today in which the low unemployment rate allows employees to frequently change jobs.

Both Chinese and American workers and managers in Dayton factory need to become aware of the cultural differences in work values and attitudes. The Chinese managers need to be culturally flexible and create cultural integration strategies so that the enterprise can achieve profitability soon. In an interview, Fuyao Group President Cao Dewang said, "I am very proud to say that we are a private company from China and we also stand for China's manufacturing industry. The United States is far away from China. If they need to know more about China's factories and manufacturing, they should come and visit my factory. Now my factory in America is open to local residents once a month." According to Cao, he once talked to the U.S. government officials about how China and the United States should learn from each other's strengths to make up for their deficiencies. It's a good thing for the world.

Analyzing the Issues in the Case

1. What are the intercultural problems that you can discover from Fuyao American Factory?
2. What suggestions would you make to promote the understanding of Fuyao's corporate culture for American workers?
3. Discuss what kind of competence is urgently needed for managers to solve the problems that have occurred in Fuyao American Factory.

Learning Culture Through Proverbs

Work in pairs and exchange views on the meanings of the following proverbs, then try to find out their Chinese equivalents if there is any, and discuss the values transmitted.

Proverb 1: *East is East, and West is West, and never the twain shall meet.*

Proverb 2: *The early bird catches the worm.*

Online Research—Using Key Words

For more information and resources, search the Internet with the following key words:

culture and communication, cultural differences between the East and the West

Unit 3

Barriers in Intercultural Communication

What is intercultural communication? Why do we study intercultural communication? What are the barriers to smooth intercultural communication? These questions may challenge you but after reading the materials in this unit, you will have a clear picture of intercultural communication, its focus and its development history. The main point is that intercultural communication has become more and more essential because companies are expanding their businesses into global markets, governments are negotiating across borders and millions of people are studying and working in countries other than their native ones. Hopefully, you will feel a need to develop intercultural competence, with which you can deal with cultural differences when you face them.

What You Can Learn from This Unit

1. Understand culture, communication and intercultural communication;
2. Know the relationship between globalization and intercultural communication;
3. Gain insight into the nature of mobility and its impact on communication;
4. Become aware of the diverse factors influencing the development of intercultural communication;
5. Understand the barriers to intercultural communication.

Questions for Intercultural Awareness

1. What role does intercultural communication play in the age of globalization, and what effect does globalization have on intercultural communication?
2. What is the value of diversity in doing business?
3. Are cultural gaps becoming wider or narrower along with globalization? How can people bridge the gap effectively between different cultures?

What's Wrong?

A Clash of Cultures in Toyota's Recall Hearing

Akio Toyoda's appearance before U.S. legislators on February 24, 2010 represents not just a fact-finding mission by committee members and a public relations move by Toyota, but a clash of cultures that in many ways created the recall controversy.

They turned a rather ordinary recall into a brand-threatening crisis. Indeed, a key reason why Toyoda is in the hot seat is that the company leadership responded in a very Japanese fashion. The cultural conflicts in Toyota's recall hearing can be classified as follows:

Decision-Making Process and Group-Oriented Culture

Toyota's decision-making process is painfully slow, but the international media and concerned customers don't want to wait so long for answers. Anytime the public hears "brake" and "problem" in the same sentence, they want quick answers.

Toyoda's long silence in the hearing is a hallmark of the Japanese culture's emphasis on consensus building. In Japan the decision-making process is really the planning process, so you don't see a lot of rapid response to a strategic issue.

Individual Responsibility and Group Responsibility

In harmony-loving Japan, company heads are rarely management professionals, and are picked more to be cheerleaders for the rank-and-file.

In a Japanese company, the top man isn't the one calling the shots. He is looked up to as a symbol, a bit like the emperor. That's why Japanese company policies don't ever change even if presidents change.

Given such differences in corporate cultures between Japan and the U.S., it wasn't unusual that Toyoda initially said his U.S. executives were the best people to testify at the House Committee on Oversight and Government Reform on Toyota's recalls, now reaching 8.5 million vehicles globally for sticky gas pedals, braking glitches and faulty floor mats.

In three news conferences, Toyoda has stayed true to form as a Japanese president and left the details of the defects and quality measures to another executive. He has focused on sending the message that he is sincere and ready to correct where the esteemed "Toyota Way" of production has gone astray.

As Japanese companies are group-oriented, don't look to one person to steer a company, unlike the West, where executives are hired for ideas and leadership.

Japanese presidents are team leaders who coordinate everyone's views and care intensely about peer opinion because confrontation must be avoided.

Japan has a special phrase to describe such behind-the-scenes consensus-building, *nemawashi*, which translates as "laying the groundwork." Neglecting *nemawashi* is considered a foolish and sure way to walk into failure.

Nemawashi is bureaucratic and time-consuming, but once a decision is made, everyone is on the same page, and action proceeds quickly without infighting.

There is usually no strong leader, who can push radical change within a Japanese firm.

Japanese managers build their careers by moving up within the company and it is unusual for top executives to be recruited from outside the company. That makes for insular management that may be clueless about what's happening outside their companies.

Cultural Differences in Media Coverage

There is a huge difference in how Japanese media cover companies. They are careful not to upset or annoy business leaders too much, because they don't want their access to information or press conferences blocked because of negative reporting.

In the West, big, successful companies like Microsoft, Google or GM are targets of aggressive media. That's the trade-off for visibility and success.

American Direct and Japanese Indirect Cultures

How the Americans and the Japanese view Toyoda's performance at the congressional hearing may be very different because of cultural differences in body language.

Japanese people, when in an apology mode—especially before an authority like the U.S. Congress—will be very humble. That means Toyoda didn't try to look people in the eye when he was answering questions from congressional leaders. From a Western perspective, that can be mistaken as weakness or perhaps trying to hide something.

Also, Japanese language tends to be indirect. The committee members peppered him with direct questions and "be a bit of political theater." In response to the questions, Toyoda should have stuck to the key message that he will put customers first, do everything it takes and won't allow this to happen again.

Toyoda has got to walk a very fine line of polite respect—which Japanese have in bucket loads—and the confidence of being head of one of the largest, most respected companies in the world.

Discussion

1. Discuss the cultural differences that can shape Americans' and the Japanese's behavior.
2. What would happen if people are ignorant of cultural differences in intercultural communication?

Reading 1

Experiencing Intercultural Communication

Communicating with someone from a different cultural background can be exciting and scary, frustrating and enlightening. It can be confusing and overwhelming, but it can also be a learning experience. And there is no one "right" way to experience intercultural interaction. You live in an increasingly diverse society, which means that you will experience many intercultural interactions. New means of communication, as well as new ways of thinking about culture and communication, make it a truly challenging time to live in.

Why is it important to focus on intercultural communication and to strive to become better at this complex form of interaction? We can suggest six reasons, or imperatives, to study intercultural communication: economics, technology, demographics, peace, self-awareness, and ethics. (This excerpt will focus on the first two imperatives.)

The Economic Imperative

You may want to know more about intercultural communication because you foresee tremendous changes in the workplace in the coming years. This is one important reason to know about other cultures and communication patterns. In addition, knowing about intercultural communication is strategically important for U.S. businesses in the emerging transnational economy. Intercultural scholars Bernardo Ferdman and Sari Brody observe that "increasing globalization and a more diverse domestic workforce are push factors (Organizations that do nothing will lose ground), whereas the benefits to be had from working effectively across differences are pull factors (Organizations that take advantage, it is argued, will do better and be more competitive)."

The Workplace Given the growing cultural diversity in the United States, businesses necessarily must be more attentive to diversity issues. As the workforce becomes more diverse, many businesses are seeking to capitalize on these differences: "Once organizations learn to adopt an inclusive orientation in dealing with their members,[1] this will also have a positive impact on how they look at their customer base, how they develop products and assess business opportunities, and how they relate to their communities." Benefiting from cultural differences in the workplace involves not only working with diverse employees and employers but also seeing new business markets, developing new products for differing cultural contexts, and marketing products in culturally appropriate and effective ways. From this perspective, diversity is a potentially powerful economic tool for business organizations.

The Global Economy Businesses all around the world are continually expanding into overseas markets in the process of globalization. They sometimes make more money from overseas sales than from domestic sales. For example, in 2003, Nike made $5.1 billion in overseas sales compared to $4.6 billion at home. Signing up big-name athletes like Brazilian soccer star Ronaldo to sell its shoes and clothing has resulted in tremendous sales in Europe, Asia, and Latin America. In addition, U.S. and European banks and construction companies are competing for lucrative contracts in the rebuilding of Iraq, where American officials estimate that the country's annual gross national product totaled at least $29 billion before the war.

However, rampant globalization has many critics who point out the downside of businesses finding cheap labor abroad—U.S. manufacturers have lost more than 2.4 million jobs since 2001, or more than 2,600 jobs a day. Many people blame the Chinese, whose exports to the United States have more than doubled in the past five years, totaling more than $110 billion in 2002. While U.S. exports to China are rising, they are less than one-fifth of what China shipped to the United States in 2003. After Canada and Mexico, China is the third-largest supplier of goods to the United States.

Opponents say that while globalization is producing great wealth, it is also the cause of growing poverty and inequality on the planet. At the world level, the top 20 percent now has 82 times as much as wealth as the bottom 20 percent, compared to a 30-to-1 ratio in the immediate postwar period.[2] Half the world's people live on less than $2 a day, and one-fifth live on less than $1 a day. Also, 800 million are chronically hungry, and new evidence shows that the World Bank (responsible for some of these figures) has, if anything, underestimated the numbers of the destitute. These kinds of inequalities can lead to resentment, despair, and ultimately to intercultural conflicts.

In addition, there are other considerations in understanding the global market. Moving operations overseas to take advantage of lower labor costs has far-reaching implications for corporations. To help bridge the cultural gap, many companies employ cross-cultural trainers, who assist people going abroad by giving them information about and strategies for dealing with cultural differences; such trainers report that Japanese and other business personnel often spend years in the United States studying English and learning about the country before they decide to build a factory or invest money here. By contrast, many U.S. companies provide little or no training before sending their workers overseas and expect business deals to be completed very quickly. They seem to have little regard for cultural idiosyncrasies, which can cause ill will and mistrust, increase negative stereotypes, and result in lost business opportunities.

In the future, economic development in Japan and other Asian countries (including Singapore, ROK, and China), as well as in Latin America, will create even more demand for intercultural communication. Economic exchanges will drive intercultural interactions. This development will create not only more jobs but also more consumers to purchase goods from around the world—and to travel in that world.

The Technological Imperative

In the 1960s, media guru Marshall McLuhan coined the term "global village" to describe a world in which communication technology—TV, radio, news services—brings news and information to the most remote parts of the world. Today, people are connected—via answering machines, faxes, e-mail, electronic bulletin boards, and the Internet—to other people whom they have never met face to face.

Technology and Human Communication These monumental changes have affected how we think of ourselves and how we form intercultural relationships. In his book *The Saturated Self*, psychologist Kenneth Gergen describes the changes that occur as technology alters patterns of communication. In past centuries, social relationships typically were circumscribed by how far one could walk, but they evolved with each technological advance—whether it be the railroad, automobile, telephone, radio, TV, or movies. These relationships have now expanded exponentially. We can be "accessed" in many ways, including e-mail, faxes, phone, and express mail, and be involved simultaneously in many different relationships, all without face-to-face contact.

What does this have to do with intercultural communication? Through high-tech communication, we come into contact with people who are very different from ourselves, often in ways we don't understand. The people we talk to on e-mail networks may speak languages different from our own, come

53

from different countries, be of different ethnic backgrounds, and have had many different life experiences.

Mobility and Its Effect on Communication Not only do we come in contact with more people electronically these days, but also we come in contact with more people physically. Our society is more mobile than ever before; U.S. families move, on average, five times. Of course, there are still communities in which people are born, live, and die, but this happens far less often than it once did.

Mobility changes the nature of our society, and it also affects the individuals involved. One of the authors of this paper, Judith, remembers moving every few years while she was growing up. She was always facing a new group of classmates at a new school. One year, just prior to attending a new high school, she wrote in diary:

> I know that the worst will be over soon. Always changing schools should make me more at ease. It does not. I like to meet strangers and make friends. Once I get to know people, it'll be easier. But I always dread the first day, wondering if I'll fit in, wondering if the other kids'll be nice to me.

Many families move because of divorce. As of 1999, only half of the children lived with both birth mother and birth father—down from nearly three-quarters in 1972. Of the other half, some lived with one parent or in stepfamilies or extended families (such as grandparents), or shuttled back and forth between parents' houses. And some children commute between different geographical regions of the United States. For example, they might spend the summer with Dad in Chicago and the rest of the year with Mom and stepfather in Phoenix. These new family configurations increase intercultural contact as generational, regional, and sometimes cultural differences help frame the cultural notion of what constitutes "family." Increasing mobility also increases the probability of encountering cultural differences related to food (smelt in Chicago versus Sonoran cuisine in Phoenix), languages, and regional ways of life (riding the EL in Chicago versus driving to strip malls in Phoenix[3]).

Families also relocate for economic reasons. A U.S. company might expand its operations to Mexico and relocate corporate personnel with the company. The rise of the European Union makes it much easier for Europeans to work in other European countries. For example, Irish citizens can work in Belgium, Belgians can work in France, and the French can work in Ireland. Increasing technology and mobility in a shrinking, interdependent world means that we can no longer afford to be culturally illiterate.[4] Rather, we all need to be more aware of cultural differences and learn to bridge those differences. Even people who never move may increasingly encounter others who are culturally different and so need to learn new strategies to communicate with them.

Vocabulary

circumscribe *v.*　限制，约束

chronically *adv.*　长期地

configuration *n.*　构造，结构

destitute *adj.*　一无所有的，贫困的

downside *n.*　不足之处，负面，缺点

exponentially *adv.*　以指数方式，越来越快地

imperative *n.*　动因

inclusive *adj.*　包容广阔的

lucrative *adj.*　可赚大钱的，利润丰厚的

rampant *adj.*　猖獗的，肆虐的，失控的

shuttle *v.*　穿梭往返（两地）

Notes

1. Once organizations learn to adopt an inclusive orientation in dealing with their members...

   本句大意为：一旦各组织学会包容地和其成员打交道……

2. At the world level, the top 20 percent now has 82 times as much as wealth as the bottom 20 percent, compared to a 30-to-1 ratio in the immediate postwar period.

本句大意为：在当今世界，上层20%的人拥有的财产是底层20%的人的82倍之多，而二战结束初期这一比例是30:1。

3. riding the EL in Chicago versus driving to strip malls in Phoenix

EL 是elevated train的缩写，意为"高架（铁路）列车"；Phoenix是美国亚利桑那州的首府和最大城市，译为"菲尼克斯"或"凤凰城"；strip mall泛指商业购物区。本句大意为：在芝加哥坐高架列车与驾车前往凤凰城的商业购物区相比。

4. Increasing technology and mobility in a shrinking, interdependent world means that we can no longer afford to be culturally illiterate.

culturally illiterate指在文化方面的无知、狭隘。本句大意为：在一个日益收缩和相互依赖的世界里，不断进步的科技及日益频繁的迁移意味着我们不能在文化方面无知，否则要付出代价。

Discussion from Intercultural Perspectives

1. Intercultural scholars Bernardo Ferdman and Sari Brody put forward the concepts of "push factors" and "pull factors." Explain the two factors and their relationships.

2. How do you account for the statement "Economic exchanges will drive intercultural interactions"?

3. According to paragraph eight, is it necessary for some companies to employ cross-cultural trainers? Why or why not?

4. Based on your understanding of the two imperatives for intercultural communication study: the economic imperative and the technological imperative, what cities in China have already shared these features? Has intercultural communication in these cities become a daily activity in all areas? Can you give some examples to support your viewpoint?

5. As a student or a future professional in the 21st century, how important is it to know about the barriers existed in intercultural communication? Why do you think so? What would you do right now?

Reading 2

Cultural Biases and Intercultural Communication

Intercultural communication, by definition, means that people are interacting with at least one culturally different person. Consequently, the sense of security, comfort, and predictability that characterizes communication with culturally similar people is lost. The greater the degree of interculturalness, the greater the loss of predictability and certainty. Assurances about the accuracy of interpretations of verbal and nonverbal messages are lost. Terms that are often used when communicating with culturally different people include "unknown," "unpredictable," "ambiguous," "weird," "mysterious," "unexplained," "exotic," "unusual," "unfamiliar," "curious," "novel," "odd," "outlandish," and "strange." As you read this list, consider how the choice of a particular word might also reflect a particular value. What characteristics, values, and knowledge allow individuals to respond more competently to the threat of dealing with cultural differences? What situations heighten the perception of threat among members of different cultural groups? To answer questions such as these, we need to explore how people make sense of information about others as they categorize or classify others in their social world.

Ethnocentrism

All cultures teach their members the "preferred" ways to respond to the world, often labeled "natural" or "appropriate." Thus people generally perceive their own experiences, which are shaped by their own cultural forces, as natural, human, and universal. The belief that the customs and practices of one's own culture are superior to those of other cultures is called "ethnocentrism."[1]

Cultures also train their members to use the categories of their own cultural experiences when judging the experiences of people from other cultures. Our culture tells us that the way we were taught to behave is "right" or "correct," and that those who do things differently are wrong. William G. Sumner, who first introduced the concept of ethnocentrism, defined it as "the view of things in which one's own group is the center of everything, and all others are scaled and rated with reference to it."

Ethnocentrism tends to highlight and exaggerate cultural differences. As an interesting instance of ethnocentrism, consider beliefs about body odor. Most Americans spend large sums of money each year to rid themselves of natural body odor. They then replace their natural odors with artificial ones, by using deodorants, bath powders, shaving lotions, perfumes, hair sprays, shampoos, mousse, gels, toothpaste, mouthwash, and breath mints. Many Americans probably believe that they do not have an odor—even after they have routinely applied most, if not all, of the artificial ones in the preceding list. Yet the same individuals will react negatively to culturally different others who do not remove natural body odors and who refuse to apply artificial ones.

Another example of ethnocentrism concerns the way in which cultures teach people to discharge mucus from the nose. Most Americans purchase boxes of tissues and strategically place them at various locations in their homes, offices, and cars so they will be available for use as needed. In countries where paper products have historically been scarce and very expensive, people blow their noses onto the ground or the street. Pay attention to your reaction as you read this last statement. Most Americans, when learning about this behavior, react with a certain amount of disgust. But think about the U.S. practice of blowing one's nose into a tissue or handkerchief, which is then placed on the desk or into a pocket or purse.[2] Now ask yourself which is really more disgusting—carrying around tissues with dried mucus in them or blowing the mucus onto the street? Described in this way, both practices have a certain element of repugnance, but because one's culture teaches that there is one preferred way, which is familiar and comfortable, the practices of other cultures are seen as wrong or distasteful.

To be a competent intercultural communicator, you must realize that you typically use the categories of your own culture to judge and interpret the behavior of those who are culturally different from you. You must also be aware of your own emotional reactions to the sights, sounds, smells, and variations in message systems that you encounter when communicating with people from other cultures. The competent intercultural communicator does not necessarily suppress negative feelings, but acknowledges their existence and seeks to minimize their effect on his or her communication. If you are reacting strongly to some aspect of another culture, seek out an explanation in the ethnocentric preferences that your culture has taught you.

Stereotyping

Journalist Walter Lippmann introduced the term "stereotyping" in 1922 to refer to a selection process that is used to organize and simplify perceptions of others. Stereotypes are a form of generalization about some group of people.[3] When people stereotype others, they make assertions about the characteristics of all people who belong to a given category. The consequence of stereotyping is that the vast degree of differences that exist among the members of any one group may not be taken into account in the interpretation of messages.

Stereotype inaccuracy can lead to errors in interpretations and expectations about the behavior of others. Interpretation errors occur because stereotypes are used not only to categorize specific individuals and events but also to judge them. That is, one potentially harmful consequence of stereotypes is that they provide inaccurate labels for a group of people that are then used to interpret subsequent ambiguous events and experiences involving members of those groups.

Prejudice

Prejudice refers to negative attitudes toward other people that are based on faulty and inflexible stereotypes.[4] Prejudiced attitudes include irrational feelings of dislike and even hatred for certain groups, biased perceptions and beliefs about the group members that are not based on direct experiences and firsthand knowledge, and a readiness to behave in negative and unjust ways toward members of the group. Gordon Allport, who first focused scholarly attention on prejudice, argued that prejudiced people ignore evidence that is inconsistent with their biased viewpoint, or they distort the evidence to fit their prejudices.

The strong link between prejudice and stereotypes should be obvious. Prejudiced thinking depends on stereotypes and is a fairly normal phenomenon. To be prejudiced toward a group of people sometimes makes it easier to respond to them. We are not condoning prejudice or the hostile and violent actions that may occur as a result. We are suggesting that prejudice is a universal psychological process; all people have a propensity for prejudice toward others who are unlike themselves. For individuals to move beyond prejudicial attitudes and for societies to avoid basing social structures on their prejudices about groups of people, it is critical to recognize the prevalence of prejudicial thinking.

Discrimination

Whereas prejudice refers to people's attitudes or mental representations, the term "discrimination" refers to the behavioral manifestations of that prejudice. Thus discrimination can be thought of as prejudice "in action."[5]

Often, biases and displays of discrimination are motivated not by direct hostility toward some other group but merely by a strong preference for, and loyalty to, our own culture. Thus the formation of our cultural identity can sometimes lead to hostility, hate, and discrimination directed against non-members of that culture.

Vocabulary

breath mint *n.* 薄荷糖

condone *v.* 宽恕，原谅（大多数人认为不道德的行为）

deodorant *n.* （除体臭的）除臭剂，体香剂

discharge mucus 排出体液

exaggerate *v.* 夸大，夸张，言过其实

exotic *adj.* 异国风情的，外国情调的（含褒义）

outlandish *adj.* 古怪的，奇异的

prevalence *n.* 普遍，盛行，流行

propensity *n.* 倾向

repugnance *n.* 厌恶，强烈的反感

weird *adj.* 古怪的，奇异的

Notes

1. The belief that the customs and practices of one's own culture are superior to those of other cultures is called "ethnocentrism."

   本句大意为：认为自己的文化、习俗优于其他文化、习俗的观念被称为"种族（或民族）中心主义"。种族（或民族）中心主义是一种主观主义的态度：偏爱本群体的生活方式，以自己的生活方式为标准，否定或贬低其他群体的生活方式和文化成就。其实，每一种文化都具有其独创性和充分的价值，每一种文化都是一个不可重复的独立的体系。一切文化价值都是相对

的，各种族（或民族）文化在价值上是相等的。种族（或民族）中心主义是跨文化沟通的障碍，是一种应该摒弃的思想观念。

2. But think about the U.S. practice of blowing one's nose into a tissue or handkerchief, which is then placed on the desk or into a pocket or purse.

本句大意为：但是想一想美国人的习惯，他们用纸巾或者手帕擤鼻涕，然后把用过的纸巾或者手帕放在桌子上，或者装进口袋或钱包里。作者在本段例举了不同国家（地区）的人们清洁鼻腔的做法，解释种族（或民族）中心主义的弊端。

3. Stereotypes are a form of generalization about some group of people.

stereotype指刻板印象，是跨文化交际理论中的一个重要概念。本句大意为：刻板印象是指对某类人群的一种（比较固定的）笼统的概括。

4. Prejudice refers to negative attitudes toward other people that are based on faulty and inflexible stereotypes.

prejudice在本文中特指文化偏见。本句大意为：文化偏见是指基于错误、陈旧的刻板印象而形成的对他人的消极态度。

5. Whereas prejudice refers to people's attitudes or mental representations, the term "discrimination" refers to the behavioral manifestations of that prejudice. Thus discrimination can be thought of as prejudice "in action."

本句大意为：偏见指对人们的态度或心理表征，而"歧视"则是这种偏见心理的行为表现。因此，歧视行为可以理解为人们将偏见心理"付诸行动"。

Discussion from Intercultural Perspectives

1. In what way does ethnocentrism become a barrier to communication? Why is it difficult to see our own ethnocentrism? Discuss the impact of ethnocentrism on communication.

2. Can you list the phenomena reflecting stereotypes held by foreigners and yourself when you communicate with them?

3. What are the differences and similarities among ethnocentrism, stereotyping, prejudice and discrimination? Discuss their features with examples.

Intercultural Lens

The pictures and diagrams below feature the relationship between language, communication and culture. Look at each picture and interpret it from an intercultural perspective. Specific requirements and questions are stated under each picture and diagram.

Culture Is like an Iceberg

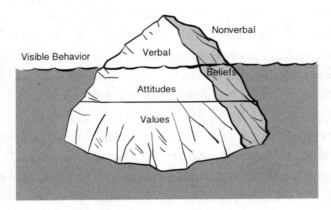

Explain what "Culture is like an iceberg" means to you.

What Goes Wrong with the Ship

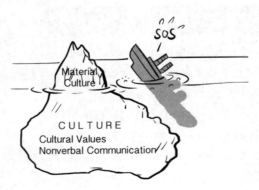

Analyze the barriers in intercultural communication.

Different Perception

What do you see from the picture and what does it mean to you? Can you see this picture from a totally different perspective?

What are they talking about and what does each refer to?

Common Ground for Perception

What does shared knowledge mean in terms of intercultural communication?

Mascot for 2008 Beijing Olympic Games

When the mascot for 2008 Beijing Olympic Games was translated into English (see above), the English version was put on the Beijing Olympic Games Committee website. Right after its appearance people started to argue against its English translation *Friendlies*. One year later, this version was taken off from the Committee website and replaced by a new version *Fuwa* (see below), which ended the argument for the mascot translation.

1) What might be the interpretation of *Friendlies* for 福娃 by English speakers?
2) What's your view of *Fuwa* for 福娃 in its translation?
3) Discuss the differences between the two translation versions and tell what you can learn from it.

Mascot for the Shanghai World Expo

1) What is the English version of 海宝?
2) What do you think of its translation and why do you think so?

A View from a Managerial Perspective

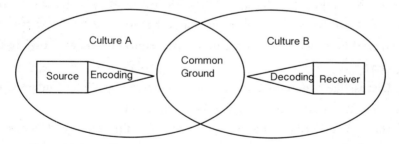

Look at the diagram. Suppose Culture A is Chinese Culture and Culture B is Western Culture. If you view this diagram from a managerial perspective, what is your understanding of the common ground between Culture A and Culture B? Does it mean that this is something two cultures share? In this case, we can conclude that the more common ground two cultures share, the fewer differences they keep. Therefore, to be effective in intercultural communication, we need to develop more common ground.

A View from an Intercultural Perspective

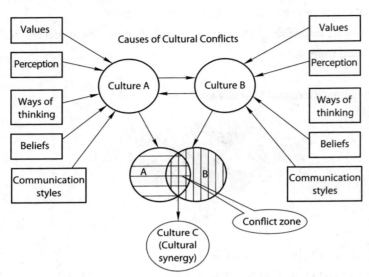

Look at the diagram. When people from two different cultures (Culture A and Culture B) are working together, say in a Sino-U.S. company, are they in the common ground area, which means they share everything when they are working together as stated before (see "A View from an Managerial Perspective")? Or are they in the conflict zone as shown in this diagram?

Discuss the feature of Culture C in this diagram and why Culture C can function well in a cross-cultural company management.

Have you noticed that the two diagrams present different views? Discuss the reasons and try to present one convincing argument to tell the difference.

Intercultural Case Study

A Clash of Cultures in Toyota's Recall Hearing

Akio Toyoda, the grandson of the founder of Toyota, and Yoshimi Inaba, the company's North American president, appeared on February 24, 2010 before the House Oversight Committee to offer an apology and explanation for the defects that have caused their vehicles to sometimes accelerate out of control.

Throughout hours of testimony, Toyoda and Inaba used words such as "shameful" when describing past events, and "modestly" and "humbly" to describe how they will approach their responsibility for safety in the future.

Toyoda reminded the committee that he is in some ways the human embodiment of the car company, and that he, more than anyone, would want to repair the damage.

"All the Toyota vehicles bear my name," Toyoda said in his opening statement. "When the cars are damaged, it is as though I am, as well."

The day didn't start well for the automaker.

"There is striking evidence that the company was at times more concerned with profit than with customer safety," Towns said.

Then Transportation Secretary Ray LaHood excoriated the company for being "safety deaf"—that is, not hearing and reacting to the numerous complaints of customers. The National Highway Traffic Safety Administration has said that as many as 39 deaths may be linked to unintended acceleration in Toyota vehicles.

But through demeanor and apology, Toyoda and Inaba seemed to defuse at least some of the anger.

"I am deeply sorry for any accidents Toyota drivers have experienced," Toyoda said.

Again: "I sincerely regret accidents."

And when pressed later on the problems, he offered, "Truly speaking, truly, I feel very sorry for the members of the Saylor family who ended their life with Toyota vehicles. I extend the condolences from the deepest part of my heart."

So how did the famed automaker lose its way? Toyoda even seemed to line up with what has been a popular theory among business analysts in recent weeks.

"Toyota has, for the past few years, been expanding its business rapidly," he said. "Quite frankly, I fear the pace at which we have grown may have been too quick."

LaHood and some lawmakers suggested that one of the company's key problems may have been arrogance, or at least a refusal to hear in Japan what drivers in the United States were saying.

Toyota North America has "some great people there, very professional, good people. We work with them. They make recommendations to Japan," LaHood said. "The decisions are made in Japan."

Some lawmakers referred to the cultural divide between the two nations and the way their governments and corporations operate.

Delegate Eleanor Holmes Norton asked LaHood about the "notorious" culture of secrecy in Japan and wondered if he and the NHTSA had trouble "penetrating that culture" when investigating Toyota's troubles.

"Yes, we've had some issues." LaHood said. "That's why I picked up the phone and talked personally to Mr. Toyoda."

"I said, 'Look, this is serious,'" LaHood recalled. "'Lives are being lost.' Right after that, they started taking action."

And LaHood said that as U.S. officials recognized a problem last year, Transportation Department Acting Administrator Ron Medford had to travel to Toyota to speak to top company officials "because he didn't think his message was getting to Japan."

LaHood said he upbraided Toyota officials.

"My point is this: Their business model is this—there are a lot of good people in North America, but the decisions are made in Japan," LaHood said.

Others blamed a lack of ethnic diversity in the automaker's management.

"It is my understanding that there are no Americans in the top leadership in Japan," said Representative John "Jimmy" Duncan, Jr. "It might be a good idea to put a couple Americans in the top leadership in Japan."

On the other hand, Representative Geoff Davis, who has a Toyota plant in his home district, complained that the Toyota investigation felt like a witch hunt. He lauded Toyota executives for the "cultural transformation" that his district has undergone, thanks to the company's presence.

Still, the Toyota executives seemed to elude the thunderous condemnations that congressional hearings sometimes evoke. In part, this may have been because of Toyoda's translator—it added a delay and sometimes confusion. Some members thanked Toyoda for having traveled so far. And at least two members of the panel offered *Konnichiwa*.

But Toyota boosters thought Congress had been rude. Paul Atkinson, who represents a Toyota council of dealers, apologized to Toyoda and Inaba for how some congressional leaders asked questions.

"We apologize for the embarrassing way some members of Congress treated you these last few days," he said. "If Bill Gates had been treated the way you were in your country, imagine what would happen. We sincerely apologize."

Aside from the apology, Toyoda offered that the company will add a step to its recall process that will take account of customer safety and that it will form a "quality advisory group" that he will lead, and he said he will establish a new position of "product safety executive." Moreover, he said that he will ensure that members of the management team "actually drive the cars." But more than anything, he seemed to say, there would be a change in attitude.

"We will listen to customer complaints humbly," he said.

Analyzing the Issues in the Case

1. Work in groups of three or four and discuss this story from intercultural perspectives to discover cultural differences behind the testimony.
2. By analyzing the way Toyoda responded to questions and the way Americans asked questions, what cultural differences can you find out?
3. After analyzing this case from the media, you must have increased your intercultural sensitivity, can you find more examples in your real life?

Learning Culture Through Proverbs

Work in pairs and exchange views on the meanings of the following proverbs, then try to find out their Chinese equivalents if there is any, and discuss the values transmitted.

Proverb 1: *Don't go near the water until you learn how to swim.*
Proverb 2: *He who would climb the ladder must begin at the bottom.*

Online Research—Using Key Words

For more information and resources, search the Internet with the following key words:

barriers in intercultural communication, ethnocentrism, stereotype

Unit 4
Intercultural Adaptation

How does one adjust to living and working in another culture? Are there steps or stages to the adjustment process or does it happen all at once? What does the term "culture shock" mean and how does one recover? Many students will be studying and living in another country and worry about whether they will adjust to the new culture. In this unit, concepts relevant to cultural adaptation will be introduced, so as to prepare you for the problems you would encounter in a new cultural environment.

What You Can Learn from This Unit

1. Know what culture shock is and how it occurs;
2. Understand the symptoms of culture shock;
3. How to adapt to a new cultural environment.

Questions for Intercultural Awareness

1. If you study abroad, what might be the first barrier you will encounter?
2. What are the symptoms of culture shock?
3. How do you usually handle cultural barriers when you encounter them?

What's Wrong?

Cultural Barriers in Overseas Study

Ms. Kong was an outstanding college student in her junior year. She was eager to study abroad to experience life in another country. In 2008, she went to a university in the U.K. for one year as an exchange student. She arrived there two weeks before the new term began. For the first few weeks in the U.K., she was busy attending an orientation program and various activities on campus, going to different places like shopping malls, and meeting new friends and classmates. Though she had a tight schedule, she had enjoyed everything she experienced after her arrival.

After about one month, when the initial excitement subsided and her life and study became more normal, she was not as busy. At that point, she was alone most of the time as few people invited her to go out in the evening or on the weekend although she would have enjoyed socializing. Sometimes when she asked her new friends for help, they seemed not as warm and enthusiastic as before. All of a sudden she was aware that her life changed overnight, but she had no idea what would become of her later. Since then she had been overwhelmed with stress, anxiety and depression. She began to feel uncomfortable, worried and impatient all day long so she made phone calls to her family in China every week to share her feelings with her mom. What was worse, she couldn't sleep well most nights and she would feel dizzy all day long.

In order to overcome her depression, her mother came to her university to keep her company and stayed with her for a month. Though her suffering was alleviated a bit, the symptoms reappeared when her mother went back to China. She tried everything she could think about to feel less depressed and lonely, but nothing worked. Finally she decided to return to China after finishing one semester in the U.K.

When she returned home, all the symptoms she had developed while studying overseas disappeared almost immediately. However, from then on, when speaking of her overseas life and study, she became fearful. She concluded that she was not cut out to live in another country.

Though this example highlights only one student's experience, it is not unusual. Many students studying overseas experience similar symptoms of loneliness and some depression although few actually return home prior to the conclusion of their program.

Actually Ms. Kong suffered from a psychological syndrome called "culture shock." This is defined as a transitional period experienced by sojourners (people living temporarily in another country) and the accompanying feelings of stress and anxiety that occur during the early period upon entering a new culture. For those who plan to study or live in a new cultural environment, they should be prepared for culture shock. Knowing what to expect and how to cope with culture shock assists them in coping with these feelings. There is no right or wrong for experiencing culture shock—it happens to almost everyone, although it occurs to varying degrees.

According to researchers of cultural adaptation, a newcomer to a foreign culture often experiences three stages of adaptation:

Stage One: The Honeymoon Stage

In this case, Ms. Kong had a sense of excitement, pleasure, and self-satisfaction about moving to the U.K. for one year as an exchange student. The sense of euphoria is so great that some people call this stage the honeymoon stage. The length of this stage varies significantly from a few days to a few weeks. This is the time when most students take photographs and act like tourists.

Stage Two: The Reality Stage

After a month in the U.K., Ms. Kong began to be aware of the reality of being a college student—going to class, reading the textbooks, taking examinations, and making friends in a new country. She began to feel anxious, restless, impatient, and disappointed. It seemed she had difficulty being with her new friends. People seemed not as friendly as they had been initially. She interpreted their behavior as being unfriendly, not trying to understand her, not listening to her, and not caring about her welfare. She didn't understand why her professors did not simply lecture but expected her and the other students to participate in class discussions. She didn't want to learn from other students; she wanted to learn from the professors.

During this stage, she developed nervousness, depression, excessive homesickness, loneliness, disorientation, and general withdrawal. Some sojourners may stay at this stage for a month or more, and some may get over it soon. Other symptoms include troubled sleep, eating and drinking too much, and speaking negatively about the local residents.

Stage Three: Adjustment and Adaptation

After some months in the new culture, students generally begin to become accustomed to the new environment. They begin to understand the education process and the expectations of the local professors. And they begin to learn how to make friends in the new culture. Students begin to accept the foreign behavior and ways of thinking or at least be able to interpret the actions of their friends using the local perspective.

In the case of Ms. Kong, she did not make the adjustments necessary to move through the second stage, so she was stuck at that stage. Yet almost all people eventually adjust and adapt to the new culture.

There are two cultural lessons we can learn from Ms. Kong's experience. One is that she was not well-suited for an overseas experience. There are some people whose personality and characteristics make it difficult for them to adjust to new situations and deal with the ambiguity of cultural transitions. The other lesson is that she was not aware of the cultural transition process and she was not prepared to adapt herself to a new environment. She had no idea what's wrong with her. The underlying problem behind this case is that our education has not given enough attention to cultural transitions and adaptation. Students are not well prepared for the culture shock they often encounter and they do not know how to overcome it.

Therefore, anyone who plans to go abroad for whatever reasons should receive intercultural training before his or her departure. Learning intercultural adaptation skills is an essential part of intercultural training, which prepares people for culture shock and helps them adapt to the new cultural environment.

1. Would culture shock happen to you if you study abroad? Why or why not?
2. What are the barriers in overseas study and what would you do to cope with them?

Reading 1

Internationalisation and Intercultural Competences

People are more prone today to move from one place to another, to commute to work or visit other countries. Surfing the Internet, watching satellite television, travelling or studying abroad enable frequent intercultural interactions between people. It seems inevitable that future generations, in order to function in a global world, will see the value of intercultural competences and be more prone to seek knowledge and experiences outside their home country. The profound role of higher education and policies on ethnic diversity and internationalisation (student exchange in particular) seems indisputable.

International Student Exchange as an Academic Journey

The primary goals of international student exchange are academic. Thinking that students involved in exchange programmes should study courses similar to those at home and obtain the same competences, some educators are reluctant to encourage studying abroad. With obvious limitations, tolerance is essential when it comes to accepting course equivalencies. Yes, students go abroad to study and learn, but not necessarily the same things they would at home. Also, a great deal of learning takes place outside the classroom setting.

Many students have told me that studying abroad has forced them to structure their studies differently and to develop other skills. Coping with varying teaching styles, mutual expectations (when it comes to the students' independence and responsibility for their education), assessment methods, etc. requires effort. Consequently, this has focused attention on, and broadened, students' academic as well as personal frame of reference.

For this reason, students should take advantage of the academic peculiarities and unique competences that are associated with the host institution. An instrumental view of knowledge—"by taking these particular courses you acquire a certain competence"—should, as far as possible, be avoided. Instead, dynamic competences should be emphasised. The educational benefit lies in detecting differences between "here and there" and then taking advantage of them, as well as the unique competences and expertise of the host institution. Educators need to overcome their reluctance or fear of other methods, perspectives and educational contents. By the same token, they need to overcome their academic ethnocentrism that "our educational system, degrees, programmes, etc. are better than the rest of the world's"—a belief so deeply embedded in their frame of thinking that it is not visible to them.

Some educators claim that their particular subject lacks intercultural or cross-cultural dimensions. For the most part this is not accurate. Engineering, social sciences, medicine, and the arts, to mention only a few fields, invite intercultural or cross-cultural perspectives and themes.[1]

Skilled teachers take advantage of the potential for learning in an international student group. By using their divergent cultural perspectives, the class serves as a "pedagogical melting pot[2]," where students are exposed to varying views, opinions and ideologies. By paying attention to such differences, they learn about the view of others, and become aware of their own frame of reference. Others serve as a mirror through which students obtain an image of their home culture. Against this background, it seems inevitable that the study of other cultures, countries or religions, also encompasses the study of the home culture.

To ensure optimal learning and cultural exchange, "international student ghettos[3]" should be avoided. Instead, one should pursue an approach that embraces the concept of integrated classes, which implies including students from the host culture as well as international students. For obvious reasons, it seems unproductive to send students abroad if they are to be isolated from the host culture. Also connected to this is the importance of having students interact with host nationals who are not students. Students need to be encouraged to explore the host culture in a broader sense. It seems fair to believe that it is when they explore the world "outside the campus" that they get a sense of people's way of life—the dominant culture as well as other ethnic cultures.

International Student Exchange as a Cultural Journey

Being an international student means being a stranger or foreigner in the eyes of the host culture. In this respect, studying abroad resembles the situation that migrants, refugees, diplomats, or people working abroad experience. But there are significant differences. For an international student, the length of the stay abroad tends to be determined in advance—from start to end. The time available to learn the host culture is both limited and shorter. Moreover, international students typically interact with people who are prepared for and, for the most part, appreciate non-native students. The response by the host community is often positive—people are curious, interested and keen to interact with international students. This does not, however, apply to everyone; some are perhaps reluctant because of insufficient confidence in their intercultural communication skills.

As an international student, you are seen as a person with a varying cultural, ethnic and religious background, expressed as differences in religions, values, norms, time conceptions, communication patterns, habits, world views, traditions, gender roles, views of sexuality, etc. Of particular importance are language competences, i.e., skills in the host culture's language. Students do not, by any means, need to be "perfectly fluent," since language skills tend to improve over time. But a sufficient degree of language proficiency is essential for academic results.

International Student Exchange as an Intellectual Journey

"Going international" is an intellectual endeavour. How "successful" or beneficial it turns out to be for the individual depends on his or her attitudes, self-confidence and degree of emotional and cultural coping. For some students, it is the first time their own taken-for-granted culture becomes visible to them, or they realise that other people hold stereotypes and prejudices against them. For other students, the international experience is a troublesome intellectual challenge. They do not understand the new culture, do not reflect on who they are and where they come from, or become too preoccupied with ruminations.

International Student Exchange as an Emotional Journey

"Going international" also needs to be understood as an emotional journey. Leaving home is quite often accompanied by ambivalence. On the one hand, it may feel a relief, exciting and as a "starting all over again" process, with new friends and no personal history. On the other hand, it may bring about feelings of loss, insecurity, uncertainty and anxiety. Sometimes, prior expectations generate uneasiness and anxiety among students. Arriving in a new culture may produce frustration, strain, confusion, disorientation or culture shock. An unfamiliar setting with a flood of new impressions and perceptions is literally exhausting.

Yet the new setting is often perceived as exciting, intriguing and fresh—there are things to discover and people to meet. Every day is a learning experience. This, in addition to the joy of mastering new things, brings about an almost euphoric feeling for some students. Being abroad is like "putting life on hold." It is a period "disconnected" from "real" life, whereas returning home is seen as "going back to reality."

Concluding Remarks and Additional Comments

First, the "success" of internationalisation policies depends on the effectiveness of higher education in taking advantage of inherent human resources—e.g., intercultural competences, professional skills—stemming from "domestic" ethnic diversity. Secondly, establishing and upholding close links to internationalisation issues may increase the status, enhance, enrich and, thus, contribute to the "success" of policies pertaining to "ethnic diversity."

We must help students to become more self-reflexive and self-critical, encourage debates on cultural differences and similarities, promote international experiences and encourage openness and curiosity. We must demand tolerance and respect for other cultures and also take advantage of the ethnic diversity in our student groups.

Vocabulary

ambivalence *n.* 矛盾情绪，矛盾心理

by the same token 同样地，由于同样的原因

encompass *v.* 包含，包括

expertise *n.* 专门知识或技能

divergent *adj.* 多种多样的

intriguing *adj.* （由于奇特或神秘而）非常有趣的，有迷惑力的

peculiarity *n.* 特点，独特性

preoccupied *adj.* 心事重重的

rumination *n.* 沉思

taken-for-granted *adj.* （因为熟悉而）认为……是理所当然的

uphold *v.* 支持，维护

Notes

1. Some educators claim that their particular subject lacks intercultural or cross-cultural dimensions. For the most part this is not accurate. Engineering, social sciences, medicine, and the arts, to mention only a few fields, invite intercultural or cross-cultural perspectives and themes.

   cross-culture和interculture的中文翻译都是"跨文化"，然而两者的研究重点并不相同。前者是对比和分析不同文化交际中的差异，而后者是从交互（interactive）的角度出发，研究跨文化交际动态多变的过程。本句大意为：一些学者声称，他们的研究课题不涉及跨文化层面。在大多数情况下，这种说法是不正确的。仅以几个学科为例，如工程学、社会科学、医药、艺术，这些学科都涉及跨文化视角及主题。

2. melting pot

"大熔炉"指的是当某一族人群进入主流文化后就会被同化，就如进入"大熔炉"一样被融化，这一族人群就会改变其文化特征。该词最早指的是美国的大都市纽约。现在研究发现，许多外国人移民美国之后，虽然能说流利的英语，但他们仍然保留着本国文化的特征。这一现象对美国"大熔炉"社会提出了挑战，于是人们现在比较认同的说法是"沙拉拼盘"（salad bowl），或"马赛克"（mosaic），即多种文化的组合成的文化——多元文化。

3. international student ghettos

留学海外的学生们在面对新环境时，出于对心理、文化、语言等因素的考虑，通常和自己国家的留学生们选择群居在某一地带，形成了"国际学生聚居区"。学生聚居区的租金低，住房条件较差。非学生租房者因为噪音、消防安全等原因，不愿在这一区域居住。"国际生聚居区"的存在不利于城市跨文化发展，政府应该帮助少数族裔学生群体融入主流群体，同时促进主流群体接纳少数族裔学生。

Discussion from Intercultural Perspectives

1. Why does the author claim at the very beginning of this article that it would be essential for young people to develop intercultural competences in order to function in a global world?

2. What do you learn from the statement that "...it seems unproductive to send students abroad if they are to be isolated from the host culture"?

3. How do you evaluate the "success" of internationalisation education according to the statement that "...the 'success' of internationalisation policies depends on the effectiveness of higher education in taking advantage of inherent human resources—e.g., intercultural competences, professional skills—stemming from 'domestic' ethnic diversity"?

Reading 2

Studying Abroad and Culture Shock

Are you planning to study in the U.K.? Are you looking forward to an exciting time, with high expectations of life in Britain?

If you have been to the U.K. already, then you will roughly know what to expect. If it is your first time in the country—and perhaps your first time abroad—you may find that settling in is not an automatic process. It requires a bit of effort. You may be surprised, and at some stage you will probably use the term "culture shock" to explain your reactions. But what exactly is culture shock? What does it feel like? Can you prevent it? Probably not, but you can minimise its effect. Read on and find out how. You may settle in more easily if you know in advance how you are likely to feel after your arrival.

Research into Culture Shock

For over thirty years, culture shock has been a bona fide field of research for European and American anthropologists and psychologists. They have studied the reactions and experiences during the first few months in a new country of travellers and diplomats, businesspeople and international students.

Some researchers describe five stages; others believe it is a six or even seven stage process. Not everyone experiences the exact stages but most travellers will go through the highs and lows, the positive as well as the negative aspects of living in a new culture. The different stages roughly are as follows:

At first you are excited by the new environment and a few frustrations do not spoil your enthusiasm. When experiencing some difficulties with simple things like making telephone calls or using public transport, you tend to down-play negative emotions.

Then follows a period in which cultural differences in behaviour and values become more obvious. What previously seemed exciting, new and challenging is now merely frustrating. You may feel isolated and become withdrawn from life around you. You seek security in the familiar. Food from home, possibly even what you never particularly enjoyed, becomes a focus, maybe an obsession.

In the next stage you may reject what is around you, perhaps becoming opinionated and negative. You may feel that everyone is against you and that nobody understands you. Limpet-like you cling to other students from your home country, hoping to have your negative stereotypes of the British and life in Britain reinforced. However, you are beginning to re-assert yourself.

Based on your successes in negotiating a variety of social situations and, maybe, increased language skills, your self-esteem grows. You can accept the negative differences and tolerate them. Knowing that you cannot change your surroundings you now enjoy certain aspects of British culture and feel relieved and strengthened from having overcome the difficulties. You may even feel a sense of belonging.

The Symptoms[1]

Just as everyone's experience of culture shock is unique, the symptoms associated with it vary, too. They can range from the physical—headaches, lethargy, sleep problems, loss of appetite, and digestive irregularities—to the psychological—irritability and anger over minor frustrations, confusion about morals and values. Suffering from culture shock often leaves people feeling moody, isolated, and insecure.

Researchers believe that the beginning of the negative phases happen most often within two to six months of living in a new culture, but many travellers experience the full gambit of emotions associated with culture shock in a much narrower time span.

Not Everyone Experiences Culture Shock

Research has shown that the more well-travelled and practised at absorbing, accepting and adapting you are, the more easily you overcome culture shock.

If you are confident of speaking the language and possess a thorough knowledge of your new home, you can feel settled after a relatively short period.

If you have adjusted well to your new environment, you would perform competently the roles that each social context requires and thus avoid the frustrations resulting from inappropriate behaviour.

Preparing for Culture Shock[2]

What strategies can you use to minimise, and cope with, culture shock? Research has shown that our expectations affect how we react to a new country. Therefore, thorough pre-departure preparations are necessary:

- Read the very useful booklet "How to live in Britain" (from the British Council).
- Perhaps you know someone who has lived in the U.K., or—better still—studied at the university or college you are going to. Talk to them but beware, they may indulge in some nostalgia when looking back on their student days. Ask them what problems and disappointments they have experienced. Contact former students and find out whether the institution you are going to supports an alumni group in your country.

Do not rely on TV or cinema films to provide you with cultural pointers. British soap operas and films only give you a stereotypical and often idolised view.

How to Overcome Culture Shock

After arriving at your new university or college, the following suggestions may assist you in reducing the strain of culture shock:

- Be aware of the signs, including the physical symptoms.
- Soon after arriving, explore your immediate environment. Having taken advice on personal safety, walk around and get to know your neighbourhood. Create a mental map of your surroundings.
- Be courageous and introduce yourself to your neighbours. If you live in university accommodation, there are likely to be other students who feel just the way you do.
- Locate useful places such as the post office, the doctor's surgery and the university welfare office so that you know where they are when you need them.
- Read a local newspaper and find out what the topical issues are. If you are well informed, you can hold conversations with British people without always feeling as the outsider.

- If you are unsure of your English, boost your confidence by remembering that most British people do not speak a foreign language. Make an effort at improving your language skills by watching TV and listening to the radio. Your institution may run free courses for international students.

- Take a break from studying and take part in social activities. Enquire about things like etiquette and dress code if you are at all unsure.

- Ask questions about social customs from people with whom you feel comfortable. You will always find someone who will assist you in finding out about life in Britain. This can be a two-way exchange, with you telling people about life in your home country.

- Keep in touch with your own culture. The university's International Welfare Officer should know, for instance, where the nearest temples and mosques are and where you can buy the cookery ingredients that you are used to from home.

- Avoid mixing only with compatriots or other international students. Contact with British people allows you to adapt more quickly. By asking questions you have a point of contact when trying to make friends.

- A good way of meeting British people is to take part in a hosting scheme where British families invite international students into their homes for a meal, or a weekend stay. Ask the International Welfare Officer about this.

- Ask yourself which situations irritate or confuse you the most. Are you sure that you have always understood people's reactions to you, or could it be that you misinterpret their behaviour?

- Avoid comparing them with us, good with bad. Establishing why people behave the way they do and then placing their behaviour in a social or economic context is more helpful.

- Help to reduce stress on your body by keeping fit physically.

- If you are feeling very low, talk to someone about it. This could be your fellow students, your landlord, or university staff such as the International Welfare Officer or Student Counsellor.

- Write down things you like and do not like. Can you change them? If not, perhaps you can find a way of living with them.

- And finally, remember that other students probably go through the same experiences as you do. Even British students have to adjust to living away from home.

Adapting to a different climate, different social conventions and different cultural values can be a complex and sometimes painful process, but coming out at the other end is rewarding and definitely worth the effort!

Vocabulary

bona fide *adj.* 真正的，真实的
gambit *n.* 开局
lethargy *n.* 无精打采
nostalgia *n.* 怀旧之情
obsession *n.* 痴迷，着魔

Notes

1. The Symptoms
   文化休克不是病，但它的表象像是一种病症，如身体不适、没胃口、头疼、咳嗽、萎靡不振等，起初你会误以为自己生病了，但服药之后也未见效果。其实这是文化休克的典型特征，所以你要做好跨文化适应的准备。

2. Preparing for Culture Shock
   除了学习本单元介绍的一些内容之外，我们还建议你尽早为出国计划做准备。你可以从学校所开设的课程中选择一些与异国社会与文化相关的课程，如跨文化沟通课程，了解跨文化交流中可能会出现的文化障碍，以及如何克服文化障碍。如有可能，你还应该参加临前文化培训，这种跨文化培训有益于留学生适应异国生活和学习环境。同时你必须认真参加开学前的orientation program，这个课程能帮助学生做好在该校生活与学习的准备，减少文化休克。

Discussion from Intercultural Perspectives

1. What suggestions would you make to those who plan to study abroad? Why?
2. According to this article, what should students do in order to reduce culture shock?
3. What is your attitude toward culture shock? Why do you think so?
4. Should intercultural training be required of those who intend to undertake overseas internship or to study abroad? What do you expect to learn from it?

Intercultural Lens

Improving Adaptation

Reading 2 provided you with some ideas about how to minimize the negative effects of cultural adaptation. Let's review them in more detail. Here are 10 tips for a successful cultural transition.

- Recognize that overseas adaptation is a process composed of many large and small adjustments, and that almost everyone experiences some negative emotions when they move to another country. This awareness is an important step. If you do not expect these changes, you may experience more severe symptoms.
- Before you travel to another country, learn as much as you can about the geography, history, politics, and education system of that country. You would be surprised at how many people travel to another country and know very little about it. The Internet will help with the research as will reading newspapers from that country.
- Think about what makes you happy and bring some of these objects with you. Perhaps certain music—put it on your iPod. Perhaps pictures of your family—take a few of them to put in your dormitory. Perhaps a special

article of clothing—pack that sweater.

- No doubt in the last few days before you leave home you will be busy packing, visiting family and friends and will not get too much sleep. Try to get as much sleep on the airplane as possible. Adjusting to a new culture is tiring for your body, so you need to have enough sleep and eat nutritious meals.

- Don't forget that there would be physical and physiological changes during the first week or two. Jet lag will disrupt your sleep patterns. You will be tired during the day but unable to sleep at night. It takes about one week for your body to adjust to the new time schedule. Differences in climate, food and water would combine to cause some problems for your digestive system. In the beginning, you may want to find the nearest Chinese restaurants—and they are everywhere in the world—until you become more adventurous and seek out local food. But be aware that American or British Chinese food will taste different from what you are accustomed to. Chefs have adjusted their cooking styles and ingredients to suit the palates of the locals!

- If an orientation program is available for you, attend it. You will learn lots of details about the university, the place in which you will live, and transportation system. Plus, you will meet other international students and the staff of the International Office. You might also encounter local students who are interested in meeting international students. These students may become "cultural interpreters" for you. It is important to ask local residents to help in answering the question: "Why do Americans or the British act this way?"

- You will observe many local behavior, language usage (slang), and ways of thinking that will seem odd to you. At this point, it is important that you remind yourself that each culture has an internal logic to it that, while different from the Chinese, makes sense according to its history. Stop yourself from making negative comments about the new culture. The behavior and ways of thinking of your hosts are different, not bad.

- Recognize when you are starting to feel lonely or homesick. E-mail family and text friends back home. But also try to find activities in the local city that could make you feel better (e.g., join the university table tennis club or some other student club). Take advantage of all the inexpensive activities at the university including music concerts, plays, clubs, and sports. Visit the university counseling center to speak with a student counselor. They are available to assist students who are having any type of problem.

- Sometimes culture shock manifests itself as a physical illness—headaches, colds, stomach aches. If you are feeling ill, visit the university doctors. But also realize that you may be experiencing physical symptoms of culture shock.
- Realize that it may take you a while to figure out the customs and ways of thinking of this new culture. You need to be patient and observant. Notice how local students handle different situations. And most importantly, you need to keep a good sense of humor.

Most international students adjust within the first year. Believe it or not, you will make many small changes that you don't even realize until you return home.

Then you will see that indeed you have changed some behavior and ways of thinking to fit into the new culture. At that point, it will feel strange being back in China!

Adaptation Exercises

1. Interview Chinese students who have lived overseas. Ask them what aspects of the overseas culture were puzzling and how they coped with their culture shock.
2. Interview international students on your campus. Ask them what aspects of Chinese culture were puzzling and difficult to adapt to.
3. Make a list of how you now cope with anxieties and worries. Become aware of the coping skills you currently have.
4. Watch two movies (Chinese or Western) or read two books that have to do with cultural adaptations. How do the characters adjust and cope? Are they successful? What about the coping styles they use? Are they positive coping styles (trying new things, meeting new friends) or negative coping styles (sleeping too much, taking alcohol or drugs, withdrawing from classes)?

Sharing Author Zhuang's Experience

China is now undertaking reform in the education system, curriculum design and teaching methodology. As part of the reform process, many universities choose to offer international programs and curricula. Though this reform has just taken its initial step, we have made tremendous advances in this initiative. More and more students have studied in various parts of the world. Many have participated in overseas internships, primarily in the United States.

With so many Chinese students abroad and very few of them culturally prepared, there are a growing number of serious cultural and legal problems.

For example, some students on overseas internship programs violated local laws and thus were repatriated home within 72 hours. These emergencies had stirred up anxiety and worry among students and teachers alike. Some universities were at a loss when facing this issue. When the first repatriation case happened at my university, an emergency meeting was called to discuss how to deal with this challenge and what to do with these students. The atmosphere at the meeting was so serious that each faculty member and administrator expressed concern and regret for those students. However, the first author of this book, Zhuang, pointed out possible intercultural factors related to this issue. He made the following statements at the meeting for resolution of the problem:

- Those repatriated students are suffering due to their ill-preparation for overseas study. The students were not aware that some ethical, legal, or acceptable behavior in China may be considered illegal or grossly inappropriate in another country. Therefore, our education system, rather than the students themselves, should be responsible for the innocent behavior of those students who were studying abroad.
- Students and universities should learn a bitter lesson from these experiences and should take some measures to help students fully prepared for their

study abroad or overseas internship.

- Intercultural training or an intercultural communication course should be an essential part of the teaching curriculum if the education reform policy of internationalization is to be implemented successfully.

This frank discussion helped free students from any punishment in the university, changed some school administrators' stereotypes of management and education, and also called attention to the critical need for intercultural awareness and adaptation education in the age of internationalization.

Since then, some interculturally related courses have been included in the teaching curriculum, and pre-departure intercultural training is now a requirement for exchange students and overseas internship programs.

Intercultural Case Study

Customary or Illegal

A couple from Denmark traveled to New York City, bringing their 14-month baby with them. One evening, they were strolling along the city streets with their child in a carriage. The baby had fallen asleep and the parents decided to have dinner at a small restaurant. They parked the carriage outside next to the large window of the restaurant and went inside.

Passersby were alarmed when the saw the child alone. They went inside the restaurant looking for the parents. However, the parents refused to bring the child inside the restaurant, stating that this was a custom in Denmark and that they could see the child through the front window. One of the passersby then called the police. The police arrived, took the baby and placed it in temporary foster care. The mother explained that they were from Denmark and this was customary in Copenhagen. When the parents objected about the baby being taken away, they were arrested, strip-searched and jailed for two days for endangering the life of the baby and disorderly conduct. Later a judge returned the child to them after four days in foster care. City officials scolded them for ignoring American customs. The legal charges were later dismissed.

Analyzing the Issues in the Case

1. Work in groups of three or four and discuss this story from an intercultural perspective to discover cultural differences between the Danes and Americans.
2. What American values are reflected in this situation? What Danish values?
3. How might you avoid an intercultural problem when you travel or live abroad?

Learning Culture Through Proverbs

Work in pairs and exchange views on the meanings of the following proverbs, then try to find out their Chinese equivalents if there is any, and discuss the values transmitted.

Proverb 1: *There's more than one way to bake a cake.*
Proverb 2: *All work and no play makes Jack a dull boy.*

Online Research—Using Key Words

For more information and resources, search the Internet with the following key words:

culture shock, reverse culture shock, cultural adaptation

Part Two

Intercultural Skills

Unit 5
Understanding Cultural Differences

People act on the basis of their values, those priorities in life that are important. Much behavior observed at home and abroad reflect some core values. For example, the American value of directness can be seen in the blunt way people speak to one another or in the way the education system rewards expressing personal opinions in class. By contrast, in much of Asia, indirectness is valued so people are found to be more reserved in social interactions or academic settings. Being able to identify and understand the values guiding people is crucial to understanding and learning how to adapt oneself to a new cultural context. In order to understand the significance of messages from people of different cultures, you need to understand the ways they look at the world and the cultural values that influence them.

What You Can Learn from This Unit

1. Understand cultural differences through the framework of four cultural dimensions;
2. Understand the values that form the foundation of people's thinking and behavior and therefore, cultural differences;
3. Understand the differences in behavior and thinking between individualistic and collectivistic people;
4. Understand the hidden causes for misunderstandings in intercultural communication;

Questions for Intercultural Awareness

1. Which aspects of culture can shape people's behavior? For example, history, politics, geography, economy, values, beliefs, and ways of thinking.
2. Which aspects of culture can become barriers in an intercultural workplace?

What's Wrong?

Intercultural Competence or Managerial Competence?

Laura Fischer is the CEO of Global One, a multinational mobile communications company. She was recently appointed the CEO both for her technical aptitude and for her multicultural management skills. Her first challenge was to chair the executive director's meeting, composed of the American director of marketing, John Miller, the German operations manager, Hans Schmidt, the Japanese construction manager, Nato Suzuki, the Arab financial director, Mohammed Salleh, and the Chinese director of research and development, Li Chen. What a challenge!

After a brief introduction by each director to present the status of his division's objectives and activities, Fischer opened the floor to the directors' feedback. Schmidt immediately questioned the data Suzuki presented and its sources. Suzuki responded briefly, but sensed an argument developing. Not wanting to break up the harmony with Schmidt, Suzuki suggested that the two of them meet later. In the meantime, Miller tried to defend Suzuki's position, at which point Miller and Schmidt got into a heated debate. Salleh tried to intervene, pointing out that everyone should listen to what each director had to say.

In order to proceed with the meeting, Fischer now had to utilize her multicultural expertise and draw on the other members of the team who had been listening more than participating. She again invited Suzuki to present his rationale, experiences, and final opinions on the data presented. Believing in teamwork, Suzuki took the opportunity to ask the other board members to clarify some of the points discussed, before finally giving his opinion. Fischer then requested that Chen elaborate on the data presented, realizing that he had been waiting for an invitation. Like Suzuki, Chen responded without drawing any conclusion and left the decision to the chair, valuing the senior person's authority. He then turned to Salleh and requested more money for research. Salleh categorically refused, stating that he was solely in charge of finances and that the entire budget had already been allocated. Chen bowed to his authority. Fischer now decided to wrap up the debate and come to a conclusion on the disputed issue. Miller immediately recommended a democratic vote: "Let's do it and fix it later if any problems arise," while Schmidt insisted on delaying any vote before all the data was in.

Suzuki smiled nervously and pointed out that the debate had to be continued until a decision was made and all were in agreement. He suggested that more time be taken in order to help everyone settle down, perhaps during lunch and even with a round of golf. For his part, Salleh supported Miller's suggestion for a vote.

Discussion

1. What are the problems the top managers are facing now at the multinational companies?
2. What competence does the CEO, Laura Fischer, display in chairing the board meeting?
3. What competence would be basic and essential for global managers? Why?

Reading 1

Dynamics of Intercultural Communication

During the 1980s, a great deal of research uncovered factors related to cultural themes. One of the major works during this decade was by Hofstede in which he analyzed questionnaire data from multinational corporate employees in over forty countries. He asked extensive survey questions and applied these to a statistical process resulting in four central factors. These four factors were called "Hofstede's Cultural Dimensions[1]," including individualism-collectivism[2], masculine-feminine cultures[3], power-distance[4], and uncertainty avoidance[5].

Individualism-Collectivism

The concepts of individualism and collectivism have encouraged a significant amount of research. For example, Harry Triandis surveyed anthropologists and psychologists from many parts of the world and concluded individualism-collectivism is one of the most powerful relationship indictors.

Individualism concerns personal achievement. In contrast, collectivist cultures are those that emphasize community, groupness, harmony, and maintaining face. We would expect the accompanying communicator style to be correlated with each of these cultural dimensions. For instance, one could expect a great deal more assertive behavior, self-disclosure[6], and other personal-advancement issues to arise in an individualistic culture. On the other hand, we could expect far more strategies of people pleasing, solidarity, relational issues, and face saving to occur in a collective culture.

Empirical research by Kim, Sharkey, and Singelis confirms the interactive or communication qualities associated with each facet of this cultural dimension in their study of Koreans (collectivists) and Americans (individualists). They indicate significant communication expectations across a number of studies, which have been adapted and summarized here.

Individualists emphasize:
- concern for clarity, directness;
- truth telling, straight talk;
- meeting personal needs and goals rather than group needs and goals;
- self-referent messages, more "I" than "we";
- more independent;
- linear pattern of conversation.

Collectivists emphasize:
- indirect communication;
- concern for others' feelings, avoiding hurting others, saving face (not causing embarrassing situations);

- avoiding negative evaluation from a listener;
- less goal direction;
- more interdependent, group concerned;
- fewer linear patterns of conversation.

Hofstede statistically identified the cultures that fit into these categories. Among the top individualistic cultures are the United States, Australia, Great Britain, Canada, the Netherlands, New Zealand, Italy, Belgium, and Denmark. The top collectivist cultures are Colombia, Indonesia, China, ROK, Thailand, Singapore, Mexico, and Japan. Notice that the collectivist cultures tend to be Asian and Latin-American, while the individualistic cultures tend to be North American and European.

Although Hofstede is frequently credited for this factor, individualism-collectivism, Harry Triandis also has numerous pioneering works applied to this area. He observed that people can act collective-like (He calls them allocentric) or individual-like (He calls them idiocentric) across any culture. Also, Sudweeks underscores the importance of the individualism-collectivism dimension in developing more effective intercultural communication and sensitivity. For instance, she reminds us to be familiar with in-group norms, be aware of the collectivist's discomfort with competitive situations, and generally avoid saying "No" or criticizing in environments such as U.S. classrooms.

Masculine-Feminine Cultures

Hofstede's work borrowed a gender metaphor to describe differentiation in cultures. By suggesting characteristics traditionally associated with masculinity or femininity, Hofstede's masculine cultures are those that exhibit work as more central to their lives, strength, material success, assertiveness, and competitiveness. Masculine cultures also differentiate gender roles more than feminine cultures. Feminine cultures are those that tend to accept fluid gender roles, embrace traits of affection, compassion, nurturing, and interpersonal relationships.

There are also communication style differences that seem to emanate from these cultures. The masculine cultures tend to use more aggressive styles of communication. Their problem-solving methods and conflict-management techniques would center around bottom-line issues, strict coping and debriefing information techniques. In contrast, the feminine cultures are probably much more capable of reading nonverbal messages and are better prepared to deal with ambiguity. Perhaps not so surprising is that masculine cultures display higher levels of stress and also have lower percentages of women in technical and professional jobs when compared to feminine cultures.

The highest masculinity index scores come from Japan, Austria, Venezuela, Italy, Switzerland, Mexico, Ireland, Great Britain, and Germany. The countries with the highest feminine scores are Sweden, Norway, the Netherlands, Denmark, Finland, Chile, Portugal, and Thailand. Hofstede observed that machismo is present in the Caribbean, but not particularly evident in the remainder of South America. This point could be debated at some length, based on evidence from other sources. Also as stated by Lusting and Koester, we would agree with their alternative label "achievement-nurturance" as preferred terminology for this factor.

Power-Distance

Still another dimension of Hofstede's research involved what he called the power-distance index. Cultures with a high power index are said to accept inequality as the cultural norm. In other words, these cultures are vertical— that is, they are hierarchical cultures. People expect hierarchy, and authoritarian style communication is more common in these case. We could expect much more oppressive behavior in high power-distance cultures, as well as more formalized rituals signaling respect, attentiveness, and agreement. Countries highest in the power-distance dimension are the Philippines, Mexico, Venezuela, India, Singapore, Brazil, France, and Columbia. In general, many of the African countries exhibit a high power-distance index as well.

Those countries that are low in power-distance are more horizontal.[7] That is, they are not fundamentally organized around hierarchical relationships. The countries with the lowest power-distance scores are Austria, Israel, Denmark, New Zealand, Ireland, Sweden, Norway, Finland, and Switzerland—mostly European-style countries.

Several theorists are grappling with the reasons to explain the power-distance phenomenon, including ecological, technological, and climate issues. Such arguments have merit along with other potential causes such as migration patterns, tribal and ethnic origins, and religion. Data are incomplete at this time but the cultural roots of power would be fascinating in any discussion in future research.

Uncertainty Avoidance

Obviously, some cultures have a high need for information and certainty. For them, avoiding uncertainty would be very difficult without increasing the number of rules of behavior to compensate for the uncertainty. These cultures include Greece, Portugal, Belgium, Japan, Peru, France, Chile, Spain, and Argentina. Other cultures, however, seem more comfortable dealing with diversity and ambiguity.[8] These include Singapore, Denmark, Sweden, China, Ireland, Great Britain, India, the Philippines, and the United States.

Hofstede's work concerning this factor reminds us that cultures which value avoiding uncertainty will probably exhibit more direct styles of communication. Such a person may seem insistent or even overly aggressive in pursuit of certainty. Identifying with a cultural communicator in a way that allows him or her to feel the most comfort and commonality with the communication interactant is a positive strategy. Anxiety is reduced to the extent that a match is created between communicators and another person.

Vocabulary

anthropologist *n.* 人类学家

commonality *n.* 共性

debrief *v.* 汇报

emanate *v.* 来自

facet *n.* （性格、情况等的）一个方面

grapple *v.* 尽力解决（某困难问题）

linear *adj.* 线性的

machismo *n.* 大男子气概，大男人行为

nurturance *n.* 培养

underscore *v.* 强调

Notes

1. Hofstede's Cultural Dimensions

   "文化维度"是荷兰国际文化合作研究所所长吉尔特·霍夫斯塔德及其同事在对文化因素进行定量研究时采用的概念。霍夫斯塔德认为，影响管理活动或管理决策模式的文化层面主要有四个方面：个人主义和集体主义；价值观的刚柔性；权利差距；不确定性规避。

2. individualism-collectivism

   "个人主义与集体主义"表示个人与群体间的关联程度。个人主义文化注重个体目标，集体主义文化则更强调集体目标。个人主义文化中，人们应当自己照顾自己和直系家庭，而在集体主义文化中，人们期望他们的内群体或集体来照顾他们，作为这种照顾的交换条件，他们对内群体拥有绝对的忠诚。美国、澳大利亚和加拿大属于典型的个人主义的社会，强调个性自由及个人的成就。印度、中国和日本都是崇尚集体主义的社会，强调个人和社会之间的和谐状态。

3. masculine-feminine cultures

   "刚柔性"表示人们对男性和女性社会角色如何分配的认识。阳刚型社会性别角色有明确的划分，阴柔型社会性别角色有所重叠。阳刚型社会的文化成员赞扬成就、雄心、物质、权力和决断性，而阴柔型社会的文化成员则强调生活的质量、服务、关心他人和养育后代。日本、奥地利和委内瑞拉等国属于男性气质比较显著的国家，在这些国家里，男女的社会差异十分明显。而斯堪的纳维亚国家富有女性化气质，男性和女性社会地位平等。

4. power-distance

   "权力距离"表示组织或机构内权力较少的成员对权力分配不平等这一事实的接受程度。权力距离大的文化成员视权力为社会的基本因素，强调强制力和指示性权力，而权力距离小的文化成员则认为权力的运用应当合法，重视专家或合法性的权力。奥地利、丹麦和新西兰等国文化的权力距离指数较低，而马来西亚、巴拿马和菲律宾等国文化的权力距离指数较高。

5. uncertainty avoidance

    "不确定性规避"表示人们对未来不确定性所持的态度。对不确定性规
    避程度较强的文化往往有明确的社会规范和原则来指导几乎所有情况下
    发生的行为，而对不确定性规避程度较弱的文化的社会规范和原则就不
    那么明确和严格。新加坡、丹麦和瑞典等国属于不确定性规避指数较低
    的国家，社会成员会比较容易接受生活中的不确定性；希腊、葡萄牙和
    危地马拉等国属于不确定性规避指数较高的国家，社会成员难以容忍模
    棱两可的现象。

6. self-disclosure

    该表达指将信息"自我表露"，即明确传递信息，不含糊，体现个人主义文
    化群体的沟通方式。

7. Those countries that are low in power-distance are more horizontal.

    作者用vertical和horizontal分别形容高权力距离文化和低权力距离文化。
    前者就像一座金字塔，越往上代表权力越大、地位越高。在组织结构
    中，下属必须层层往上级上报，不得越级；上级下达指示时也是层层往
    下级传递，这种垂直式的组织结构体现组织结构中的等级关系。后者则
    与此相反，文化成员相互平等，不享受特权。这是一种平行式的组织结
    构，虽然有领导与被领导的关系，这种关系仅仅是工作性质不同，但人
    们还是享有平等关系。

8. Obviously, some cultures have a high need for information and certainty. ...
    Other cultures, however, seem more comfortable dealing with diversity and
    ambiguity.

    这里阐述的是"不确定性规避"这一文化纬度，即人们对未来不确定性
    所持的不同态度。一些国家对未来有明确的预期，需要充分的信息，不
    然他们就无所适从，于是他们会采取积极主动的行为，比如提问等方
    式，使不明确的信息变得明确。这种行为方式会被适应不明确信息国家
    的人们认为咄咄逼人；而另一些国家更容易接受未来的不明确性，因为
    他们自己就在这种文化中成长，比如当一方给予另一方含糊的信息时，
    另一方就能理解这种含糊表达的真实含义，因为他也是以这种方式表达
    其真实的含义，所以他能适应这种方式。

Discussion from Intercultural Perspectives

1. Can you list some examples indicating your understanding of the four cultural dimensions?
2. How can you apply the four cultural dimensions to the study of intercultural communication?

Reading 2

Understanding Values Behind Businesspeople

Hard Work

They may appear informal and relaxed, but Americans generally work hard. They will devote long hours—as many as 16 or 18 a day—to their jobs. They may consider their work more important to them than family matters and social relations. Americans use the term "workaholic" to describe a person addicted to work, one who spends as much time as possible on the job and seems to think of little else. Workaholics are by no means rare in the American business world.

American executives often embarrass their foreign counterparts by doing manual work or by doing tasks that elsewhere would be done by lower-status people—tasks such as serving coffee, rearranging the furniture in a meeting room, or taking out a calculator to figure out a problem that came up during a meeting.

Punctuality

Promptness and schedules are important. Meetings and appointments ideally begin and end on schedule. The topic that is supposed to be treated during the meeting or appointment is generally expected to be covered by the scheduled ending time. Delays cause frustration. Getting behind schedule is likely to be considered an example of bad management.

In keeping with their notions about the importance of using time wisely and getting the job done, American executives generally want to get right down to business.[1] They do not want to waste time with formalities or with long, preliminary discussions. In fact, they are usually quite uncomfortable with purely social interactions while they are working.

Impersonal Dealings

Americans generally have no particular interest in getting personally acquainted with the clients or customers with whom they deal. As long as they believe the other party is trustworthy in business dealing and has the ability to deliver whatever product or service is being discussed, the Americans will proceed in an impersonal manner. They value decisiveness and efficiency. Concerns about human relations are lower down in their scale of priorities. Western Europeans are likely to carry on in about the same way, but people from most other parts of the world are likely to find the American approach cold or otherwise uncomfortable.

Even when they seem to be socializing, as at a dinner or reception with business colleagues, their main purpose is more likely to be discussing business than becoming personally acquainted with other people.

Quantitative Reasoning

American businesspeople, probably even more noticeably than American in general, prefer to think and analyze in quantitative terms. They want hard data and facts and figures when they are analyzing a business situation and trying to make a decision. The assumption is that wise decisions are made on the basis of "objective" information uncontaminated by considerations of personal feelings, social relations, or political advantage.

American executives frequently use the term "bottom line," which refers to the final entry in an accounting statement. They want the statement to show a profit. Little else is as important. The purpose of a business is to make a profit, and executives are evaluated by stockholders with reference to their contribution to the company's financial standing.

Writing It Down

The written word is supremely important to American businesspeople. They make notes about conversations, keep files on their various projects, and record the minutes of meetings. A contract or agreement must be written down in order to be taken seriously, and every written word in it is important. It must be the correct word, the one that makes clearest what each party's rights and obligations are.

To Americans in business, then, it seems perfectly natural to consult lawyers about contracts and agreements. Lawyers are trained to select the proper words for important documents and to correctly interpret them. Americans have difficulty understanding that people from elsewhere might consider oral agreements adequate. Businesspeople from abroad might feel insulted by the Americans' insistence on having written agreements, viewing the Americans' attitude as an indication of distrust.

Behavior in Meetings

Meetings are a common phenomenon in the business world, but what actually happens in meetings varies greatly, not just from country to country but from organization to organization. Meeting can have a variety of purposes—sharing information, giving instructions, heightening enthusiasm and dedication, discussing issues and problems, suggesting solutions, making decisions, and no doubt others. Americans like to know explicitly what the purpose of any given meeting is. "What's the point of this meeting?" they may ask.

The leader's role in meeting varies. The leader might be the one who opens the meeting, does all the talking, and then dismisses those who have attended. Or the leader may play the role of a moderator, opening the meeting and then allowing others to discuss matters and make decisions. The role of those attending the meeting differs too. They may be expected to sit quietly and listen, to offer suggestion or comments, or even to challenge ideas others put forth.

In the ideal American meeting, the leader encourages active participation from all those who might have ideas to contribute. The people at the meeting offer ideas and information intended to help illuminate the subject under discussion. They may openly and bluntly disagree with each other. Witnessing such meetings can shock foreigners who are accustomed to more formal, hierarchical arrangements, where the leader firmly controls what takes place and participates either remain silent or mask any disagreement they might have with what others say.

In American meetings, issues are often resolved by means of a vote. "The majority rules," Americans often say—not just in this context but in others, too. The practice of voting in meetings might disconcert foreigners who are accustomed to a system in which decisions must be unanimous or one in which the people in authority are the ones who make the decisions.

Equality

Americans' notions about equality strongly influence what happens throughout business organizations.[2] Although people at various levels are quite aware of the status differences among them, they may not display superiority or inferiority in open ways. Rank-conscious foreigners may feel uneasy by the relatively relaxed and informal interactions they will see between lower status employees and those with higher status.

Another manifestation of the equality assumption is the prevalence of written rules and procedures. If people are considered equal, then they must be treated fairly or impartially, that is, without reference to their own particular personalities. Fairness is best assured, in the typical American view, if there are written rules and procedures that apply to everyone equally. So there are written procedures for hiring, training, evaluating, rewarding, disciplining, and terminating employees. There are written procedures for handling employee complaints. There are job descriptions, safety rules, and rules for taking "breaks" (rest periods) from work. Great stress is placed on carrying out the written procedures completely and correctly.

Foreign visitors are likely to think the constraints Americans impose on themselves by means of their rules are excessive, especially if labor-union rules are added to those of a company.

Turnover

Foreign visitors may see more employee turnover than they are accustomed to. America is still a more mobile society than most (The rate of mobility may have slowed recently), so people change jobs relatively readily. It is unusual to find a strong sense of company loyalty at the lower ranks of a business. People have their jobs to earn a living, and in many ways it does not matter to them just where that living comes from. They do what they are supposed to do (according to a written job description, usually), collect their pay, and go home. Supervisors are often seeking ways to enhance employee allegiance to the company, in the belief that employees who are more loyal will be more productive.

Vocabulary

acquainted *adj.* 认识的
allegiance *n.* 忠诚，效忠
bluntly *adv.* （说话）直言不讳地
discipline *v.* 惩处
disconcert *v.* 使困惑，使尴尬，使不安
illuminate *v.* 阐明，解释
manifestation *n.* 明显迹象，表现
minutes *n.* 会议记录
moderator *n.* 仲裁人，调解人
prevalence *n.* 流行，普遍
turnover *n.* 人事变动（率），人员流动（率）
unanimous *adj.* （决定、表决等）一致通过的

Notes

1. In keeping with their notions about the importance of using time wisely and getting the job done, American executives generally want to get right down to business.
   美国主管对他人的个人生活不感兴趣，习惯开门见山，直接谈生意。他们不喜欢花时间在隐私打听、社交寒暄上，注重工作的效率。这种"脾

性"常常让不同文化背景的人觉得冷漠、难相处。

2. Americans' notions about equality strongly influence what happens throughout business organizations.

美国是一个权力距离指数较低的国家,其社会成员行为独立,彼此平等相待。因此,即便是上级和下级之间,关系也依旧平等自在,并不紧张。相反,在权力距离指数较高的国家,上级和下级之间的等级观念根深蒂固。

Discussion from Intercultural Perspectives

1. What American values do you value most? Why?

2. American executives often do manual work or tasks that elsewhere would be done by lower-status people. How do you interpret this behavior? What value does their behavior transmit? What would Singaporean executives do in similar situations? And what cultural value does their behavior reflect?

3. In an American meeting, people are encouraged to voice their personal opinions. What value does this reflect? Would you offer your opinion in a meeting with Singaporean co-workers? If Americans and Singaporeans are at the same meeting, what would you predict about their behavior at the meeting? And how will Americans and Singaporeans interpret each other's behavior (For example, how will Americans interpret the quietness or indirectness of Singaporeans)?

4. Americans are known for their job-hopping while Chinese have traditionally attached much importance to lifetime employment. Have you noticed that many Chinese have changed their attitudes toward their lifetime employment? What is happening in China in terms of cultural values?

Intercultural Lens

Understanding Cultural Differences and People's Behavior

As we have discussed, Hofstede has suggested four cultural dimensions, each of which includes different value orientations. Every country can be rated on these dimensions. If you know a country's rating on all four dimensions, you can understand and predict much of its people's social and organizational behavior.

In the following descriptions, each dimension has its characteristics of people's behavior to help you further understand cultural differences. The descriptions below is the extreme of each dimension. However, some cultures fall in the middle of the continuum.

Individualism

- People are supposed to take care of themselves, and perhaps their immediate families.
- The autonomy of the individual is paramount.
- Decisions are based on what is good for the individual, not for the group, because the person is the primary source of motivation.
- Key words used to invoke this cultural pattern include "independence," "privacy," "self," and the all-important "I."
- A judgment about what is right or wrong can be made only from the point of view of the individual.

Collectivism

- The group is expected to look out for and take care of its individual members.
- People are required to have an absolute loyalty to the group.
- Decisions are based on what is the best for the group.
- In these cultures, there is a strong belief in obligations to the group,

dependence of the individual on organizations and institutions, a "we" consciousness, and an emphasis on belonging.

Masculinity
- People believe that men should be assertive and women should be nurturing.
- Sex roles are clearly differentiated, and sexual inequality is regarded as beneficial.
- People believe in achievement and ambition, in judging others on the basis of their performance, and in the right to display the material good acquired.
- Teachers praise their best students because academic performance is rewarded highly.
- Male students strive to be competitive, visible, and successful.

Femininity
- People are likely to prefer equality between sexes, less prescriptive role behavior associated with each gender, and an acceptance of nurturing roles for both women and men.
- Friendliness is much more important than brilliance.
- Teachers rarely praise individual achievements and academic performance because social accommodation is more highly regarded.
- Male students try to cooperate with one another and develop a sense of solidarity; they try to behave modestly and properly.

High Power Distance
- People believe that each person has a rightful and protected place in the social order.
- The actions of authorities should not be challenged or questioned.
- Hierarchy and inequality are appropriate and beneficial.
- Those with social status have a right to use their power for whatever purposes and in whatever ways they deem desirable.
- The language systems emphasize distinctions based on a social hierarchy.
- Children are expected to obey their parents without challenging or questioning them.

- The curriculum is likely to involve a great deal of rote learning, and students are discouraged from asking questions because questions might pose a threat to the teacher's authorities.
- Managers are likely to prefer an autocratic or directive decision-making style, whereas subordinates expect and want to be closely supervised.

Low Power Distance
- People believe in the importance of minimizing social or class inequalities, questioning or challenging authority figures, reducing hierarchical organizational structures.
- People use power only for legitimate purpose.
- Children put less value on obedience and are taught to seek reasons or justifications for their parents' actions.
- The education system itself reinforces this value by teaching students to ask questions, to solve problems creatively and uniquely, and to challenge the evidence leading to conclusion.
- Managers prefer a consultative or participative decision-making style, and their subordinates expect a great deal of autonomy and independence as they do their work.

High Uncertainty Avoidance
- People avoid uncertainty; this is one of the cultural values.
- They develop many rules to control social behavior.
- People tend to be worried about the future, and they have high levels of anxiety and are highly resistant to change.
- They demand consensus about societal goals.
- They try to ensure certainty and security through an extensive set of rules and regulations.

Low Uncertainty Avoidance
- People have a high tolerance for uncertainty and ambiguity.
- They believe in tolerating people who behave in ways that are considered socially deviant, and in taking risks and trying new things.

- People tend to live day by day, and they are more willing to accept change and take risks.
- Conflict and competition are natural, dissent is acceptable, deviance is not threatening, and individual achievement is regarded as beneficial.
- They believe in minimizing the number of rules and rituals that govern social conduct and human behavior.

Intercultural Case Study

Studying Abroad

Susanna is a Japanese student studying in an American university. This is her second year in the United States. Though she is proficient in English, she has had hard time in the classroom because Susanna is too shy to speak up in class. When she saw American classmates discussing the issues presented by the professor or other classmates, she expected her professor to ask her for her views, as she is not quick enough to offer her opinion or make a comment. Finally she had the courage to ask her psychology professor a question during a lecture. The professor was very pleased to have Susanna join the class discussion. He replied "Now that's an unusual query," and then answered her question. However, Susanna was unhappy and felt insulted, as she believed that her professor was implying that her question was foolish. So she wondered if the professor was not happy with her attitude in class or her question was strange or too simple. One day when she had a talk with another professor who taught speech communication, she told the story to her in tears. Her speech communication professor was sure that the psychology professor hadn't intended to belittle Susanna and encouraged her to ask him what he had really meant. The psychology professor was upset that Susanna had misinterpreted his comment.

Analyzing the Issues in the Case

1. Why did shy Susanna push herself to pose a question in class?
2. How do American professors usually interpret the behavior of students who don't ask questions or participate in class discussions?
3. What does the word "unusual" in her psychology professor's response really mean to Susanna?
4. Did the psychology professor intend to insult Susanna, or to give her a compliment? Explain.
5. How would you feel if your teacher praised a question you asked, a comment you made, or an answer you gave in class? Why?

Learning Culture Through Proverbs

Work in pairs and exchange views on the meanings of the following proverbs, then try to find out their Chinese equivalents if there is any, and discuss the values transmitted.

Proverb 1: *Those who'll play with cats must expect to be scratched.*
Proverb 2: *He who knows, does not speak. He who speaks, does not know.*

Online Research—Using Key Words

For more information and resources, search the Internet with the following key words:

individualism, collectivism, masculinity, femininity, power distance, uncertainty avoidance

Unit 6
Time and Culture

In intercultural communication, time may influence communication behavior, but not everyone in the world views the concept of time in the same way.

The two most important time systems are called "monochronic time" and "polychronic time." Monochronic time means paying attention to one thing at a time while polychromic time means being involved with many things at once. A thorough understanding of the difference between the two is beneficial for dealing with people from different cultures in an effective manner.

This difference in time orientation is reflected in doing international business. For example, when people with different time systems make business appointments, they might find it so hard to get through a meeting agenda. This is because in some countries meetings begin with an extended socializing time in which time is spent establishing social rapport.

What You Can Learn from This Unit

1. Understand differences in attitudes toward time held by people from different cultures;
2. Understand different words and actions manifested by different time systems;
3. Identify problems and misunderstandings caused by different time systems and apply this knowledge to real global working environment;
4. Define various criteria of punctuality across different cultures.

Questions for Intercultural Awareness

1. Can you identify some examples related to the concept and use of time in your life?
2. How do you personally view and handle time?
3. Do you agree that there is always an appropriate time for a certain thing? (For instance, going out on a date, making a phone call, etc.) Why or why not?
4. How is communication influenced by different attitudes toward time? Explain.

What's Wrong?

Experiencing Different Cultures at Shanghai World Expo

Ecuador Time

Ecuador, a country in northwestern South America, participated in the 2010 Shanghai World Expo. As a member of the participating nations, August 14 was its National Pavilion Day. On this occasion, different kinds of events would be held. There were plans to present its carnival-style entertainment featuring Ecuadorian artists dressed in traditional clothing performing folk songs and dances. Ecuador also planned to exhibit its abundant natural resources and its potential in economy, tourism and trade. Additionally, some seminars would be held to introduce or promote its special programs to the world. Shanghai World Expo officials and other guests from various circles were invited to attend these events.

On August 14, author Zhuang was invited as a guest to attend a banquet at a five-star hotel in Shanghai at 6:30 p.m. The author arrived there at 6:30 p.m., but was much surprised to note that there were no other people in the Banquet Hall except for a few waitresses. Then he went down to the lounge where he saw some people waiting. One was an Expo official who seemed to have lost his patience. He said he had never seen a country without any time conscience and show so little respect for other people. Then he suggested to the author that Ecuadorians should attend intercultural training before participating in international events. At about 7:30 p.m., the Ecuadorian Consul General arrived and at a leisurely pace, entered the Banquet Hall with a group of diplomats from the Consulate and some compatriots who were working at the Pavilion. Having seen people waiting in the lounge, Consul General just waved to them as a greeting without apologizing for the delay or showing any sense of remorse for arriving one hour after the appointed time. The guests followed them and soon the banquet began.

The following day the author was invited to attend the Promotion Seminar given by its Ministers of Travel, and Commerce and Trade. The seminar was scheduled to start at 5:00 p.m., but by then only a few people had arrived. Half an hour later, there was no sign of Ecuadorian presenters or the start of the seminar. Those who arrived at 5:00 p.m. began to ask each other if they had the correct time for the seminar. At about 6:30 p.m., Ecuadorian speakers appeared on the stage and the seminar finally started. More groups of Ecuadorians arrived at about 7:00 p.m. after the seminar started.

Italy Time

In November 2009, the author was invited to attend a forum in Italy and to make some presentations about the Shanghai World Expo and its Intercultural Training Program. The Italians were very interested in this topic as the next World Expo will be held in Milan, Italy in 2015. The invited participants to the forum included government and business representatives. The presentation was scheduled to begin at 9:00 a.m., but it did not start as planned. The host explained to the author that Italians view time differently from Chinese people, but he was sure that there would be more people arriving later. In fact, the host was actually not prepared to start the forum as scheduled but later in the morning. He knew that his colleagues would arrive an hour or more after the appointed start time. Eventually, the group assembled and resulted in a successful forum from an Italian perspective. The success was not due to the forum being well organized but rather to the heated discussions among the speaker, chairperson and the audience. Italians are motivated to have emotional and animated conversations. They enjoy sharing their opinions, arguing with speakers, and trying to persuade their colleagues.

Intercultural Perspectives

We can use the terms "polychronic time orientation" and "monochronic time orienation" to understand how time affects attitudes, behavior and communication. The anthropologist Edward Hall used the term "polychronic" to describe the cultural preference for doing several things at once. Polychronic cultures tend to prioritize relationships over tasks and do not consider time commitments to be binding. Polychrons prefer to work as they see fit without a strict schedule, following their own mental processes. Conversely, monochrons prefer to do one thing at a time, working on a task until it is finished, then, and only then, moving on to the next task. People in monochronic cultures such as the U.S. or Germany prefer promptness, careful planning and rigid commitment to plans.

In the two cases above, punctuality in Ecuador and Italy means that meetings start an hour or more after the scheduled time. Cultural norms, including the use and meaning of time, are agreed-upon by members of a culture. Everyone knows what it means to be punctual. In some cultures it means meeting at the exact scheduled time (as in Germany or Switzerland), or an hour after the scheduled time (as in Ecuador or Italy). As a sojourner to another culture, you will not be able to change this, except in a fixed-hours factory or office environment. You must therefore adapt. If you are not prepared to fit in with their concept of time in their life, or you are not patient enough to accept their concept of time and can't tolerate it, you will be very frustrated. You need to learn to understand their cultural value in doing business because everyday global business activities such as scheduling meetings, participating in conference calls, or planning a project can be affected by attitudes to time. A comprehensive understanding of the different conceptions of time is beneficial for dealing with people from different parts of the world in an effective manner.

Discussion

1. What would happen when people with monochronic and polychronic time orientations make appointments?
2. What would you suggest to those monochronic and polychronic people when they do business with each other?

Reading 1

Time and Culture

Attitudes toward time vary from culture to culture. Philosophers have written about the concepts of time and mankind's focus on its passage for as long as there has been writing. Ancient thinkers, from Plutarch to Heraclitus, and moderns from Proust to Einstein, have written of the value of time to a society and the ways in which its members think about it, use it, and are ultimately overtaken by it. While every discipline from biochemistry to theoretical physics has examined the effects of time on mankind, only cultural anthropology has systematically sought to examine how societies define themselves according to their views of time.

Beginning in the 1930s with Edward T. Hall, anthropologists have been examining and classifying social behavior, with time as a variable. Until his work among the Navajo Nation of the American West, the perception was that cultures thought, wrote, and spoke about time in a fairly straightforward way. Subsequent research from a variety of sources indicated that some cultures with a past orientation view the traditions of what came before as being more important in many ways than the present.[1] Japan, India, China, and numerous cultures of Eastern Europe have always placed a significant value on past achievement and on honoring the lives and spirits of ancestors. Many cultures throughout Asia and the Latin world have a strong sense of the past and the role that traditional values must play in present-day decisions. Cultures with a present orientation are focused on the moment, neither invoking the past nor wondering about the future. Societies with simple patterns of organization, fewer rules and norms, and very little outside influence often exhibit such views. The Bedouin tribes of northern Africa, numerous Pacific Islanders, and the Maoris of New Zealand see time as a seamless continuum that passes over us—a phenomenon we are neither able to understand nor influence. The developed nations of the modern, global economy exhibit still another view of time: They tend to have a strong future orientation, focusing on what's ahead, planning for contingencies that may never come about and anticipating the divisions and demarcations in time that linear, forward-thinkers value.

The concepts of polychronic and monochronic time come from Edward T. Hall. Monochronic (one dimensional) societies are those that are punctual, efficient, and attach importance to being on time. These are mostly linear thinkers who see time as scarce, valuable, something to be saved (or lost), and having a monetary equivalent: "Time is money."[2] Monochronic people feel more comfortable if they are able to stick to the original plans, meet established deadlines, and use their time wisely. In return, they expect others to be prompt, to respect their own use of time, and to adapt quickly to make the most of the time they have been given. They also prefer to focus on one task at a time.[3] For example, global business specialist Richard Gesteland shares this advice: In Germany, Switzerland, or Sweden, you can expect to start off with a few minutes of small talk and then proceed in a linear fashion from item number one to the last item on the agenda with no major digressions.[4] A Swiss friend was once asked whether people in his hometown were all so punctual because they had such good watches. "NO," he replied, "We have such good watches because we are on time." In most monochronic societies, you could gather up all the clocks and watches, and people would still show up on time for work, school, dinner, or the theater. That is simply how they have been enculturated. Nations with a monochronic view of time are usually among the more individualistic cultures, such as the U.S., Canada, and northern Europe, but other collectivistic cultures, such as Japanese (largely because of global economic development), also fall into this category. Keeping to schedule and completing tasks in a timely fashion demonstrate respect for the larger group. (Table 1 shows the varying degrees of time orientation across a range of countries and regions.)

Table 1 Varying Degrees of Dimensions in Business Cultures

Very Monochronic Business Cultures	Moderate Monochronic Business Cultures	Polychronic Business Cultures
Nordic and Germanic Europe	Australia and New Zealand	Arab countries
North America	Russia and most of East-Central Europe	Africa
Japan	Southern Europe	India
	Singapore	Latin America
	China	South and Southeast Asia
	ROK	

In polychronic (multidimensional) societies, people are more relaxed about time because relationships are more important than schedules. Relationships are crucial to developing trust, which evolves through these relationships and ultimately makes for good business. Hurrying any proposition is considered superficial and deadlines are never missed (They are simply adjusted),[5] but that is part of the process. Usually the more collectivistic cultures see time this way, such as cultures from Asia, Latin America, and the Middle East. Other European cultures, such as French, Spanish, and Irish, also fall into this category. They don't want to rush through life—they would much rather spend time over a meal or having a drink with friends. The Arabic saying *Insha'Allah*, which translated means "God willing," is a demonstration of how strong religious belief shapes Arabic thinking in relation to time. People simply do not carry the pretense of knowing what will happen in the future. In Indonesian, the saying *jam karet* literally means "rubber time," and refers to a relaxed attitude toward time. Only a true emergency, such as a death or serious illness, makes people rush. In traditional Mexican culture, *manana*, translated as "tomorrow," means that nothing is so urgent that it cannot be done the next day. In many developing nations, traditional notions of time have come into conflict with more modern, monochronic concepts. Still, nations such as India, Brazil, Mexico, and Vietnam are learning to live with both of these concepts:[6] one time for business (usually with foreigners), and another time for the things in life that really matter.

Vocabulary

anthropology *n.* 人类学

Bedouin *n.* 贝都因人（在阿拉伯半岛、叙利亚和北非沙漠中游牧的阿拉伯人）

contingency *n.* （可能发生的）意外事件，不测事件

continuum *n.* 统一体，连续体

demarcation *n.* 划分，划定，界定

digression *n.* 偏离主题

enculturate *v.* 使适应所处社会的文化方式

Heraclitus *n.* 赫拉克利特（古希腊唯物主义哲学家）

invoke *v.* （在脑海中）唤起，引起，产生

monochronic *adj.* 单元时间制的

Navajo *n.* 纳瓦霍人（散居于美国新墨西哥州亚、利桑那州及犹他州的北
美印第安人）

passage *n.* （时间的）流逝

Plutarch *n.* 普卢塔克（古希腊传记作家、散文家）

polychronic *adj.* 多元时间制的

seamless *adj.* 浑然一体的，无缝的

variable *n.* （数学中的）变量，变元

Notes

1. Subsequent research from a variety of sources indicated that some cultures with a past orientation view the traditions of what came before as being more important in many ways than the present.

   past orientation意为"过去时间取向"，即注重传统、过去，其文化特点是比较保守，比较缺乏创新意识。大部分亚洲国家以过去时间取向文化为主。本句大意为：后来的种种研究表明，在一些以过去时间取向文化为主的人们眼里，传统文化比起当今文化，在许多方面都更为重要。

2. These are mostly linear thinkers who see time as scarce, valuable, something to be saved (or lost), and having a monetary equivalent: "Time is money."

本句大意为：这些大部分都是线性思维的人，他们认为时间是稀少的、宝贵的，是需要节约（或会被浪费）的，而且可以与金钱对等，即"时间就是金钱"。具有这种时间观念的人不会浪费时间，比较守时。

3. They also prefer to focus on one task at a time.

本句大意为：他们更偏向于在一段时间内把注意力集中在一件事情上（即在每一时间段中做一件事，不会在同一时间段中安排两件或三件事）。

4. …you can expect to start off with a few minutes of small talk and then proceed in linear fashion from item number one to the last item on the agenda with no major digressions.

本句大意为：你会发现人们通常在开始时寒暄几分钟，然后进入议程，将日程上的问题逐个进行讨论，其间不再有过多的题外话。持这种时间观念的人不会花过多时间闲聊，见面寒暄之后就会直接进入主题，这是典型的西方人的沟通方式。

5. Hurrying any proposition is considered superficial and deadlines are never missed (They are simply adjusted)...

本句大意为：匆忙达成一项提议被认为是肤浅的，人们从不会超过截止日期（因为人们会一直调整日期）。这说明多元时间制的人们对已作出的时间安排会不断地改变与调整，不像单元时间制的人们那样按计划、按时间安排处事，不轻易改变计划与时间安排。

6. Still, nations such as India, Brazil, Mexico, and Vietnam are learning to live with both of these concepts…

本句大意为：印度、巴西、墨西哥、越南等国家正在试着接受这两个概念，允许它们并存。当单元时间制与多元时间制的人们在谈判时，由于他们对时间概念理解不同，在谈判中必然会产生误解，所以只有双方相互理解，相互调整，交流才会顺利进行，才能取得预期的效果。

1. Is there any unanimous perception of time among culturally different people? Is the concept of time universal or culturally specific? Explain.
2. What do you think of being punctual? How do the Westerners define punctuality with measures of time?
3. "Many cultures throughout Asia and the Latin world have a strong sense of the past and the role that traditional values must play in present-day decisions." Does this notion imply that Asian people are proud of what they have achieved in the past? If yes, is it possible to perceive their cultural values by analyzing what they do? Give some examples to support your response.
4. With your understanding of different time orientations, can you list the different behavior of polychronic and monochronic people? Give some examples to indicate their differences in behavior.

Reading 2

Managing Change in a Past-Oriented Culture

One of the authors of this article (Charles Hampden-Turner) was recently in Ethiopia with a Dutch manager who was terribly frustrated by his unsuccessful efforts to organize a Management of Change Seminar with Ethiopia managers. They all kept harking back to a distant and wealthy era in Ethiopian civilization and would not incorporate any developmental principles that were not based in this past. After a discussion with the Ethiopian colleagues, we decided to study some Ethiopian history books, looking at them from the perspective of modern management. What had Ethiopia done right in that period to make its cities and trade so flourishing? The company also had a rich history within Ethiopia and these records too were studied. The Dutch manager posed the challenge anew.

126

The future was now seen as a way of recreating some of the greatest glories of the past; suddenly, the Management of Change Seminar captured everyone's enthusiastic support.

This is not a remote case applicable only to Ethiopia. All change includes continuity, that is, staying the same in some respects so as to preserve your identity. Many cultures decline to change unless the ways in which they will preserve their identity are made clear to them. Synchronic cultures carry their pasts through the present into the future and will refuse to consider changing unless convinced that their heritage is safe.[1]

A large American telecommunications company introduced a technically superior product on the world market. It planned to focus specifically on increasing sales in Latin America, where it had not been very successful previously. The only serious competitor was a French company which had an inferior product, but whose after-sales support was reputedly superior.

The Americans went to great pains to prepare their first presentation in Mexico. "Judgment day" would begin with a video presentation of the company and its growth potential in the medium-long term. After this, the vice-president of the group would personally give a presentation to the Mexican minister of communications. Also meticulously planned was the two-hour lunch. Knowing Mexican culture, they believed this was where the battle would be fought. The afternoon session was reserved for questions and answers. The company jet would then be ready to leave Mexico City in the last departure "slot." It was tight, efficient and appreciated, right?

Wrong; the Mexican team threw off the schedule right away by arriving one hour late.[2] Then, just as the Americans were introducing the agenda for the day, the minister was called out of the room for an urgent phone call. He returned a while later to find that the meeting had gone on without him.[3] The Mexicans were upset that the presentation had proceeded that the after-sales service contract was separate from the sales contract and that the presentation focused only on the first two years after installation rather than the longer-term future together.[4]

The French, on the other hand, prepared a loosely structured agenda. They determined some of the main goals to be attained by the end of the two-week visit. The timing, the where and the how were dependent on factors beyond their control, so they left them open. A long presentation on the historical background of the French state-owned company was prepared for the minister and his team. It had done business with Mexico's telephone system as early as 1930 and wanted to re-establish a historic partnership.[5] As far as the French were concerned, the after-sales service, which extended indefinitely, was part of the contract. It was the French who receive the order for a product known in the industry to be technologically less sophisticated.

What had gone wrong for the Americans? The main mistake was creating a tight, sequential agenda which was almost inevitably thrown off by Mexican officials who had deliberately built slack into their procedures and pursued agendas which were multiple and (to the Americans) distracting. The belief that the technologically superior product should win the contract is part of the original cultural bias in which each episode within a sequence is separated out. The Mexicans were interested in the product only as part of an on-going relationship, an issue which the synchronic French were also careful to stress.[6] Similarly the Americans separated the after-sales service contract from the rest, presumably because it occurred at a later period. French and Mexican culture sees these time intervals as joined.

The French emphasis on the historical renewal of French-Mexican bonds was also effective with a culture that identifies with Spain and has deep European roots. American sequencing strikes synchronic cultures as aggressive, impatient and seeking to use customers as stepping-stones to personal advantage. If the relationship is genuinely to last, what is the hurry? Because the Mexicans did not agree that technological perfection was the key issue, they did not want to be on the receiving end of a detailed presentation timed to end just before the Americans' departure. They wanted to experience a relationship they could partly control. In synchronic time, the demeanor of the American corporation during the presentation presaged its conduct in the future and the Mexicans did not like it.

However, the biggest advantage the French had was their willingness to spend two weeks dedicated to an agreement and leave it up to their hosts to use those two weeks in a flexible program aimed at synchronizing mutual efforts, rather than trying to agree a schedule in advance. For the French and Mexicans, what was important was that they get to the end, not the particular path or sequence by which that end was reached. Similarly, the details of the equipment were less important to the Mexicans than the responsiveness of the supplier, since they could not know that problems might surface in the future. All they could really ask for, given this concern, was someone willing to alter a schedule to their convenience, and the French showed that they could do that.

Moreover, the Americans had a narrower definition of how the negotiation should end. There should come a deadline when the Mexicans would say "Yes." For the French, and synchronic culture generally, there is no real "end" because the partnership continues. Instead of the efficiency of getting from A to B in the shortest possible time, there is the effectiveness of developing long-term relationships. The Americans also made one more serious mistake. Anticipating that the Mexicans would be late returning from the lunch, as they had been several times, the Americans caucused for half an hour among themselves. This failed to show respect for the buyer. You "give them time" by waiting for them to join you. You do not use that time yourself in a way that makes you unavailable should they enter the room. A "readiness to synchronize" must be shown, as opposed to a mere delay in the sequence.

Vocabulary

caucus *v.* 召开核心会议

demeanor *n.* 举止，风度

episode *n.* 片段

Ethiopia *n.* 埃塞俄比亚

go to great pains 煞费苦心（做某事）

hark back 回想，谈论往事，追忆过去

in the last departure "slot" 在最后一个可以离开的 "契机"

interval *n.* 间隔，间歇

meticulously *adv.* 一丝不苟地

pose the challenge anew 重新提出提议

presage *v.* 预示，预兆（尤指坏事）

reputedly *adv.* 据说

slack *n.* 富余部分，闲置部分

129

Notes

1. Synchronic cultures carry their pasts through the present into the future and will refuse to consider changing unless convinced that their heritage is safe.

   synchronic culture意为"共时性文化",在共时性文化中,人们往往将过去、现在和将来联系在一起,并认为过去和将来都会对现在产生影响。本句大意为:在共时性文化中,人们认为过去贯穿于现在和将来,除非确保他们的文化遗产是安全的,否则不愿意改变。

2. …the Mexican team threw off the schedule right away by arriving one hour late.

   墨西哥团队没有按照美方的要求准时到场参加会议,使美国团队等了一个小时,这是因为二者的时间观念不同。美国属于单元时间制文化(monochronic culture),认为时间是线性的,每个事件之间不会有时间上的重叠,因此人们注重守时,按时完成每一件事;而墨西哥属于多元时间制文化(polychronic culture),认为时间是可循环的,许多事情可以同时发生,并不强调守时。

3. He returned a while later to find that the meeting had gone on without him.

   墨西哥部长因有急事离开会议,回到会议室后发现会议在按原计划继续进行,因此感到吃惊与失望。这是因为美国属于单元时间制文化,活动与会议需要按计划进行,不会因某人(即使是领导)延迟。在墨西哥的多元时间制文化中,时间并不会被严格地规划和管理,时间的安排往往很灵活,而且又会因人(尤其是领导)而随时改变。在本案例中部长以为人们会等他回来再继续会议。

4. …the presentation focused only on the first two years after installation rather than the longer-term future together.

   美国人在报告中只作了两年的规划,而墨西哥人认为应该作长远规划。这是因为墨西哥文化为长期取向文化(long-term orientation culture),倾向于制定长远目标,而美国文化为短期取向文化(short-term orientation culture),更习惯制定许多短期目标。

5. A long presentation on the historical background of the French state-owned company was prepared for the minister and his team. It had done business with Mexico's telephone system as early as 1930 and wanted to re-establish a

historic partnership.

法国代表在报告中没有为将来制定清晰的目标，而是反复重申过去的历史以及与墨西哥以往的合作，这是因为法国文化属于过去时间取向文化（past-oriented culture）。在这种文化中，人们倾向于在当下的生活中保护和维持过去的历史与传统。本句大意为：法国国有公司为墨西哥部长和他的团队准备了一段很长的报告，来讲述双方合作的历史背景。早在1930年他们就与墨西哥电信系统有过合作，他们希望以此为契机再次合作。

6. The Mexicans were interested in the product only as part of an on-going relationship, an issue which the synchronic French were also careful to stress.

墨西哥和法国文化都属于同步文化（synchronic culture），也可称为多元时间制文化，在这种文化中，目标的达成往往与人与人之间的关系密切相关，因此在与他们合作之前，需要先与他们建立良好的关系；而序列文化（sequential culture），也称为单元时间制文化的人们往往对事不对人，将工作与个人情感分开，因此在工作或谈判中不会涉及太多社交活动。

Discussion from Intercultural Perspectives

1. What is wrong with the American businesspeople who made tight schedules when doing business with Mexicans?
2. What are the cultural factors contributing to the French's success in doing business with Mexicans?
3. What is past-oriented culture? What are the features of people's behavior in a past-oriented culture?

Intercultural Lens

1. Understand the concept of time.

Suppose you are in America and are invited to a friend's house for dinner at 6:00 p.m. What time should you arrive?

A. 5:30 p.m.

B. 6:00 p.m.

C. 7:00 p.m.

In North America, these are the reactions you might get if you arrived at these times:

In North America, time is exact. People make plans and arrange their lives around specific times. For example, you should always arrive exactly on time for dinner, a date, or a business appointment. While it is sometimes acceptable to arrive five minutes early, it is considered extremely impolite to arrive late.

2. A survey for students to do on campus.

The following table is designed to help students understand time conceptions in different cultures. For each activity below, are you always punctual, or early (How early is it), or late (How late is it)? If you know friends from other countries, you may ask them for their time conceptions.

Time\nOccasions	China	The U.S.	Other Countries
Have dinner with your friend in a restaurant			
Have a date			

（待续）

（续表）

Time Occasions	China	The U.S.	Other Countries
Appointment with your classmate			
Appointment with your professor			
Business appointment			
Appointment with someone who asks you for help			
Attend public lectures			
Attend classes			
Attend a meeting			
Attend an inauguration ceremony			
Attend your friend's birthday party			
Attend a new year celebration party			
Watch a movie in a cinema			
Watch a sports event			

3. Understand time and people's behavior.

The following table shows different behavior of people with different time orientations: monochronic time and polychronic time. Below the table are specific examples of the behavior. Discuss with your partner and try to match these examples with the behavior in the table.

Monochronic Time	Polychronic Time
Do one thing at a time	Do many things simultaneously
Concentrate on the job	Are highly distractible and subject to interruption

（待续）

（续表）

Monochronic Time	Polychronic Time
Have no tolerance for ambiguity	Have high tolerance for ambiguity
Are committed to the job	Are committed to relationships
Arrival-meeting-conclusion-action	Arrival-meeting-small talk
Adhere to plans	Change plans often and easily
Are concerned about not disturbing others: follow rules of privacy	Are more concerned with those who are closely related (family, friends, business associates) than with privacy
Seldom borrow and lend	Borrow and lend things often and easily
Are accustomed to short-term relationship	Have strong tendency to build life-time relationships

1) People meet by appointment and do not ask personal questions.

2) A manager answers the phone when he is in a meeting.

3) People make appointments with other people at one time.

4) People make things clear by asking. For example, when someone is indirect in expressing his or her view, the other person would ask for clarity so as to make things clear.

5) People do business together because of their relationship or for their future relationship.

6) Once people know each other, they tend to keep this relationship and become good friends. Businesspeople can also become good friends after a deal.

7) People often change their schedule, appointment or plan, for many reasons.

8) People arrive, and start to discuss, exchange views, and then arrive at conclusion. After that they take action.

9) Borrowing or lending is considered too personal. People would go to the bank or public service department for personal needs.

Intercultural Case Study

Time Concept

John works in a big international corporation in the United States. Recently he was sent to an affiliated company in China to work for a short time. He was very excited at first and couldn't wait to come to China since he had never been to China before. But one week after his arrival, he felt very uncomfortable working here. He couldn't stand his Chinese colleagues' attitude toward time. He was unhappy when two senior clerks were late for the first meeting. Soon after the meeting started, he almost got angry when he noticed some clerks were still busy chatting. For him, small talk should be kept to a minimum, and the meeting should be taken seriously. John got more and more impatient when the presentation delivered by the sales manager lasted twenty minutes longer than scheduled. During the discussion period, he expected to see everyone present air their comments and suggestions, but the atmosphere was extremely "harmonious." When a proposal was put forward, people usually gave roundabout and ambiguous responses. He is now at a loss and does not know how to continue his work here or how to adapt to the new working environment.

Analyzing the Issues in the Case

1. Discuss the problems that John had during his first week working in China.
2. Are these typical problems faced by Westerners who work at international companies in China? Explain.
3. When Chinese people work in foreign companies, would there be similar problems? Why or why not?
4. In today's global context, what principles should be applied if you want to develop effective working relationships with your colleagues from different cultures? Can you suggest some specific skills that can be adopted in dealing with these cross-cultural problems?

Learning Culture Through Proverbs

Work in pairs and exchange views on the meanings of the following proverbs, then try to find out their Chinese equivalents if there is any, and discuss the values transmitted.

Proverb 1: *To save time is to lengthen life.*
Proverb 2: *One of these days is none of these days.*

Online Research—Using Key Words

For more information and resources, search the Internet with the following key words:

monochronic time and polychronic time, time orientation (past oriented, present oriented, and future oriented)

Unit 7
Communicating Nonverbally

Nonverbal communication begins even before you say your first word in an interview. As the interviewer walks toward you to shake hands, an opinion is already being formed. And as you sit waiting to give your answers to questions you've prepared for, you are already being judged by your appearance, posture, etc. In other words, what you communicate through your nonverbal signals affects how others see you. However, many people are unaware of the nonverbal messages they have already communicated. Sometimes your nonverbal signals do not match up with the words you're saying, and then it's most likely that misunderstandings have occurred because you communicate with nonverbal behavior subconsciously. Nonverbal communication is one of the barriers in intercultural communication.

What You Can Learn from This Unit

1. Understand the relationship between verbal and nonverbal communication;
2. Recognize how nonverbal behavior is influenced by culture;
3. Interpret behavior culturally and communicate nonverbally.

Questions for Intercultural Awareness

1. Can you list some nonverbal messages in other countries that are different from those in China?
2. How do you use body language, or nonverbal codes to express your feelings and emotions? Why don't you use verbal expressions?
3. Have you noticed some foreigners' nonverbal behavior that you can't understand? Discuss such nonverbal behavior with your partner.

What's Wrong?

U.S. Presidents Bow to Japan's Emperors

U.S. President Obama Bowed to
Japan's Emperor Akihito in 2009

U.S. President Richard Nixon Bowed to
AKihito's Father, Emperor Hirohito in 1971

On November 14, 2009, U.S. President Barack Obama bowed low as he shook hands with Japanese Emperor Akihito upon Obama's arrival at the Imperial Palace in Tokyo. News photos of President Barack Obama bowing to Japan's emperor have sparked debate that Obama was disgracing Americans by groveling to a foreign leader. Critics said the U.S. leader should stand tall as he represents America overseas.

Going the full 90 degrees, Obama has disappointed many Americans because this is not only unnecessary, but also shows his lack of sensitivity to what is accepted in his own culture and the lack of appreciation for the fact that he is the president of an equally sovereign nation which deserves to be respected and deserves a president who upholds his own national dignity in the face of foreign leaders.

President Barack Obama may think it would play well in Japan, but it was not appropriate for an American president to bow to a foreign leader.

A person from Asia states bowing is much of a norm in Asia, but a light bow suffices when talking about showing respect or upholding proper diplomatic decorum with a head of state.

Obama's 90-degree stance unfortunately looks and means *kowtowing* in the majority of Asian cultures or extending a deep apology to someone.

Were these bows by American presidents culturally appropriate to the Japanese? And to the Americans?

Pro Arguments

- In Japan, very low bows like President Barack Obama's are a sign of great respect and deference to a superior.
- It's a gesture of kindness that intends to show "goodwill" between two nations that respect each other.
- It is a respectful tradition for visitors to bow to the emperor in a formal setting.
- President Obama wants to be mindful of other cultures.
- Republican President Richard Nixon bowed in 1971 to Akihito's father, Emperor Hirohito. True, Nixon's bow wasn't as deep as Obama's but a bow like this was accepted.

Con Arguments

- Heads of state do not bow and show obedience to one another.
- The sign of deference goes against State Department protocol, which decrees that presidents bow to no one.
- Obama humiliates himself and Americans by groveling to Japan's emperor.
- Obama's deference has gone too far.

Discussion

1. Why did President Obama bow to the Japanese emperor at the full 90 degrees? What's your comment on this issue?
2. Discuss the two photos above and find out the similarities and differences in nonverbal messages when Obama greeted Akihito in 2009 and Richard Nixon bowed to Hirohito in 1971. What is your interpretation of both presidents' bows from intercultural perspectives?

Reading 1

Defining Nonverbal Communication

What is not said is sometimes as important as what is said. Nonverbal communication is communication through means other than language—for example, facial expression, personal space, eye contact, use of time, and conversational silence. Nonverbal communication also involves the notion of cultural space. Cultural spaces are the contexts that form our identity—where we grow up and where we live (not necessarily the actual homes and neighborhoods, but the cultural meanings created in these places).

Learning Nonverbal Behavior

Whereas we learn rules and meanings for language behavior in grammar and spelling lessons, we learn nonverbal meanings and behavior more unconsciously. No one explains, "When you talk with someone you like, lean forward, smile, and touch the person frequently, because that will communicate that you really care about him or her." In the United States, such behavior often communicates positive meanings. But if someone does not display such behavior, we are likely to react quite differently.

Sometimes we learn strategies for nonverbal communication. For example, you may have been taught to shake hands firmly when you meet someone, or you may have learned that a limp handshake indicates a person with a weak character.[1] Likewise, many young women learn to cross their legs at the ankles and to keep their legs together when they sit. In this sense, we learn nonverbal behavior as part of being socialized about appropriate behavior.

Nonverbal Codes

Personal Space Personal space is the "bubble" around each of us that marks the territory between ourselves and others. How big your bubble is depends on your cultural background. In some cultures, people stand very close together to talk, while in others, they feel a need to be farther apart when talking. This difference in personal space rules can cause misunderstandings and even some discomfort in intercultural interactions. For example, in one university, there were reports of miscommunication between Arab and American students. The Arab students complained that the American students were distant and rude, while the American students characterized the Arab students as pushy, arrogant, and impolite. The problem was that the two groups were operating with different rules concerning personal space. The Arab students were accustomed to standing closer together when talking, while the American students had been raised to do just the opposite.

In fact, some cultural groups are identified as contact cultures, and others as noncontact cultures. Contact cultures are those in which people stand closer together while talking, making more direct eye contact, touch frequently and speak in louder voices. Societies in South America and southern Europe are identified as contact cultures. By contrast, those in northern Europe, North America, East Asia, and the Far East are noncontact cultures, in which people tend to stand farther apart when conversing, maintain less eye contact, and touch less often. Jolanta, a Polish student, talked about her first experience abroad, as the guest of an Italian family, and being overwhelmed by the close physical contact and intense nonverbal behavior: "Almost every aspect of this family's interactions made me anxious and insecure. This included the extremely close personal distance, touching and speaking loudly, all of which was quite overwhelming."

Eye Contact Eye contact is often considered an element of personal space because it regulates interpersonal distance. Direct eye contact shortens the distance between two people, while a lack of eye contact increases the distance. Eye contact communicates meanings related to respect and status, and it often regulates turn taking in conversations.

Patterns of eye contact vary from culture to culture. In many societies, avoiding eye contact communicates respect and deference, although this may vary from context to context. For many Americans, maintaining eye contact communicates that one is paying attention or showing respect. But a Navajo student told us that the hardest thing for her to learn when she left the Navajo

Nation to study at Arizona State was to remember to look her professors in the eye. Throughout her whole life, she had been taught to show respect by avoiding eye contact.[2]

When they speak with others, most Americans look away from their listeners most of the time. They might look at their listeners every 10 or 15 seconds. And when a speaker is finished taking a turn, he or she will look directly at the listener to signal completion. However, some cultural groups within the United States use even less eye contact while they speak. For example, some Native Americans tend to avert their eyes during conversation.

Silence Cultural groups may vary in the relative emphasis placed on speaking and on silence. In most American contexts, silence is not highly valued. Particularly in developing relationships, silence communicates awkwardness and can make people feel uncomfortable. One of the major reasons for communicating verbally in initial interactions with people is to reduce uncertainty. In American contexts, people employ active uncertainty reduction strategies, such as asking questions.[3]

However, in many other cultural contexts, people reduce uncertainty by more passive strategies, such as remaining silent, observing, and perhaps asking a third party about someone's behavior.[4] And silences can be as meaningful as language. For example, silence in Japan is not simply the absence of sound or a pause in the conversation that must be filled. Silence can convey respect for the person who is speaking, or it can be a way of unifying people. Silence in Japan has been compared to the white space in brush paintings or calligraphy scrolls: "A picture is not richer, more accurate or more complete if such spaces are filled in. To do so would be to confuse and detract from what is presented."

Vocabulary

avert (one's eyes) *v.* 转移目光
deference *n.* 服从
detract *v.* 破坏，损害

Notes

1. ...you may have been taught to shake hands firmly when you meet someone, or you may have learned that a limp handshake indicates a person with a weak character.

   沟通包括语言沟通（verbal communication）和非语言沟通（nonverbal communication）。在沟通中，信息的内容部分往往通过语言来表达，而非语言部分则作为提供解释内容的框架，来表达信息的相关部分，二者同样重要。非语言沟通的形式有：目光接触、面部表情、手势、体态、身体接触、空间距离等。人们在不知不觉中，学习掌握非语言沟通技巧，比如，与人见面握手要有力，无力的握手会显得人性格懦弱。

2. ...she had been taught to show respect by avoiding eye contact.

   本句大意为：她受的教育一直都是避免目光接触，以示尊重。本文解读了几种非语言代码（nonverbal codes）在不同文化中的交际功能，如个人空间（personal space）、眼神交流（eye contact）等。以美国为例，大多数美国人在交谈时会注视对方，表示对说话者的尊重，但是在印第安部落，人们却认为谈话时避开对方目光，才是对说话者的尊重。

3. In American contexts, people employ active uncertainty reduction strategies, such as asking questions.

   保持沉默（silence）也是一种非语言代码。如何看待交谈时出现双方沉默的情况？不同文化背景的人们对此理解不同。比如，美国人交谈时，不喜欢沉默，会采取一些积极的策略（如提问）推动谈话进行。他们认为沉默会让气氛尴尬，产生不确定性，而规避不确定性的方法就是语言交流。

4. However, in many other cultural contexts, people reduce uncertainty by more passive strategies, such as remaining silent, observing, and perhaps asking a third party about someone's behavior.

   与美国不同，有些国家认为，交谈中"有时无声胜有声"，沉默也可以传递很多信息。在日本，人们认为沉默是金，沉默是对说话者的尊敬，他们把沉默比喻为书法字画中的留白，作用重大。本句大意为：但是，在其他许多文化中，人们采取较为消极的方法减少不确定性，比如继续沉默、留心观察，还有可能向第三方询问某人的情况。

Discussion from Intercultural Perspectives

1. How does nonverbal behavior affect your intercultural communication? Can you list some possible misunderstandings?
2. How far do you need to keep when you communicate with American people or people from other cultures?

Reading 2

Nonverbal Communication

Differences in nonverbal communication, or body language, are often subtle and can be the source of intercultural misunderstanding. During my first few days at the College of Micronesia, the division secretary was on sick leave. When she returned I introduced myself and asked, "Are you feeling better?" She answered "Yes" nonverbally by raising and lowering her eyebrows. I interpreted her response to mean "What did you say?" So I repeated the question a little more slowly, and again she raised her brows. I asked the question a third time, receiving the same nonverbal response. Out of frustration, I finally said, "I hope you are feeling better soon." About a week later, when I learned that raised eyebrows mean "Yes," I realized that the secretary must have thought me dense for repeatedly asking the same question.

Micronesians use the same shake of the head as Americans as a way to say "No." A frown accompanied by a wave of the hand at chest level is an emphatic "No!" or "Stop it!" Micronesians throw their heads slightly back and to the side to indicate "over there." Depending on the context of the question, the response could mean a few blocks away or the next island over. The apparent ambiguity of that particular response was sometimes confusing. Similarly, if I, as an outsider, were to summon a Micronesian by repeatedly curling my index finger upward,[1] the gesture would imply that the receiver had the status of an animal. More than a few times, I had to control my impulse to use that common American gesture.

Much more difficult was remembering that the proper nonverbal gesture for summoning someone in Micronesia is to make a downward movement of the hand from the level of the head to the shoulder. The first time a Micronesian beckoned me in this manner, I thought he was telling me to "go away." I stood in utter confusion until he finally asked me to "come here."

Touching as a Nonverbal Code

Cultures differ in the overall amount of touching they prefer. People from high-contact cultures, such as those in the Middle East, Latin America, and southern Europe, touch each other in social conversations much more than do people from noncontact cultures, such as those in Asia and northern Europe. These cultural differences can lead to difficulties in intercultural communication. Germans, Scandinavians, and Japanese, for example, may be perceived as cold and aloof by Brazilians and Italians, who in turn may be regarded as aggressive, pushy, and overly familiar by northern Europeans. Cultures also differ in where people can be touched and in their expectations about who touches whom. Finally, cultures differ in the settings or occasions in which touch is acceptable.

Time

As members of a "doing" culture, European Americans are very concerned with time, compartmentalizing it carefully to avoid wasting it.[2] Micronesia is a "being" culture. Micronesians are more likely to listen to their natural impulses— to eat when they are hungry and sleep when they are tired—than to the hands of a clock. Cooking, fishing, and other tasks are determined by mood, weather, or ocean tides. In the remote villages and outer islands, much time is spent relaxing and socializing. The men meet to discuss community affairs or play games. The women weave or socialize over a card game. I had difficulty relating to people in the village who appeared to spend a great part of the day just sitting around doing nothing. I would have been bored but, interestingly, the word "bored" does not exist in Micronesian languages.

In city centers, where people are expected to abide by work hours and class times, Micronesians find the transition to schedules unnatural and confining. It is not considered unusual or rude for Micronesians to arrive later than their appointed time. It would, however, be unusual to meet a Micronesian who was in a hurry or anxious over a deadline. Because European Americans typically view time as a commodity, the time issue causes many misunderstandings. It took most of the first semester for me to understand that student tardiness was not a sign of disrespect or apathy.

During the fall semester I was asked to present a communication workshop to local radio announcers. I had very little time to design the workshop, so I gave the support staff the course materials to duplicate and assemble. Two days before the workshop was scheduled I discovered the duplicating hadn't been completed. I expressed my concern about having the materials on time but was assured that they would be ready. I heard indirectly that if I was in such a great hurry I should do the job myself. Surprisingly, the materials were delivered one hour before I left for the radio station.

I arrived at the station ten minutes early and found only one person there. The general manager and three announcers trickled in over the next 20 minutes. As I was about to begin, the electricity shut down, leaving us without air conditioning or lights. The general manager suggested we move the workshop to the college campus. By the time we drove to the campus and settled into a classroom, 15 minutes were left of the scheduled time. I had time only for a brief introduction and an icebreaker activity. I was disappointed that we lost virtually an entire session and that my preparation had been in vain, yet none of the participants seemed inconvenienced.

Space or Privacy

While the concept of private property does exist, Micronesians tend to be less attached to their belongings than are European Americans. Acquaintances who were Peace Corps volunteers on Pohnpei said this was a frustrating cultural difference that they found difficult to accept. They explained that if they wanted to keep personal possessions such as hair clips, books, or cassette players for themselves, they would have to put them away in a private place. Their Pohnpeian family's attitude toward such items is one of detachment, which is generally true for most Micronesians. For instance, if something is borrowed and subsequently lost or damaged, the owner will not express anger, because people are much more important than possessions in their culture. In contrast, European Americans tend to react to losing a possession with varying degrees of anger and, depending on the object, may perceive a loss almost as a loss of part of oneself.

The issue of privacy was a challenge for me in Pohnpei.[3] As a typical European American, I highly value my privacy, but the concept of privacy is strange in Micronesian cultures because togetherness is the norm. Although most Micronesians have been exposed to American cultural patterns and accept them, they still do not fully comprehend the need for "quiet time" or privacy. Being alone is generally associated with strong emotions—for instance, avoiding an individual or group to keep from expressing strong anger toward others or hiding because of feelings of sadness or great shame. Micronesians may also think that someone desiring solitude is mad or "physically sick and wants to be alone."

The day I moved into my two-bedroom bungalow, the landlord sent his son over to make some repairs on the house. His three sisters followed him over, walked into my living room, tied up the curtains to let the breeze in, and sat down for a chat among themselves. They were as relaxed and natural as if they were in their own home. I, on the other hand, didn't quite know what to do. Should I offer them something to drink? Make small talk? Try to entertain them in some way? The young women were fully engaged in their conversation in Pohnpeian language, so I retreated uncomfortably to my back room to work until everyone was ready to leave. On other occasions, the children in the neighborhood would pile onto my back porch to watch the video playing on my TV. They seemed as interested in what I was doing as in the plot of the film. After some time, I noticed my boundaries relaxing, but I was never fully comfortable with the territorial differences. The most disturbing violations of my privacy were when the young men in the neighborhood looked into my windows at night. The nocturnal habits of a single *menwai* (outsider) woman were apparently entertaining.

I moved back to California in 1990, when I accepted a teaching position at San Joaquin Delta College in Stockton. The first day on campus I met a visiting professor who had been a Peace Corps volunteer in Micronesia. He encouraged me to teach intercultural communication because, he said, "It's an important course, great fun, and a forum for Micronesian tales."

Vocabulary

abide by 遵从，遵守

apathy *n.* 漠然，冷淡

beckon *v.* （招手）示意，召唤

boundary *n.* 限度，界限

bungalow *n.* 平房

detachment *n.* 冷静，超然

duplicate *v.* 复制

Micronesian *n.* 密克罗尼西亚人

nocturnal *adj.* 夜间活动的

porch *n.* 门廊

summon *v.* 召唤，叫来

tardiness *n.* 缓慢，拖沓

trickle *v.* 缓慢而零星地移动

Notes

1. …curling my index finger upward…

   在美国，这一动作表示召唤某人。但是在许多东南亚国家，以及文中作者提到的密克罗尼西亚，这一手势只用于召唤动物。因此，对人用这一手势，是非常不礼貌的。在印度尼西亚和澳大利亚，这一手势也指召唤性工作者。在欧洲许多国家，用食指指着别人是不礼貌的。

2. …European Americans are very concerned with time, compartmentalizing it carefully to avoid wasting it.

   作者提到美国和密克罗尼西亚对待时间的态度不同。美国是"doing" culture国家，许多美国人对一生时间的短促相当敏感，他们认为如果时间浪费了，那是无法弥补的，他们要让每分钟都有价值；而密克罗尼西亚是"being" culture国家，人们做事随心情而定，没有"浪费时间"一说。compartmentalize意为"分割"，即把时间分割成不同时间段，将所做的事情放入不同时间段中完成。本句大意为：美国人（的生活）与时间紧密相关，他们把时间仔细分割成一段一段的，以免造成浪费。

3. The issue of privacy was a challenge for me in Pohnpei.

   个人主义国家和集体主义国家对于隐私的界定大不相同。美国是典型的

个人主义国家，非常重视个人隐私，不打探他人私事，未经允许不进入他人房间、动用他人物品。密克罗尼西亚是集体主义国家，当地人对于个人隐私的概念没有美国人敏感。由于"隐私"问题，产生的文化冲突非常常见。波纳佩岛（Pohnpei）是密克罗尼西亚联邦领土，位于西太平洋。

Discussion from Intercultural Perspectives

1. It is common that Chinese students of the same gender often touch each other while they are talking. How might Western people interpret this behavior? What is the cultural differences behind?
2. Nonverbal message can also contradict verbal message. What might happen if your nonverbal message contradicts your verbal message?

Intercultural Lens

Gestures

Handshaking

Do you know how to greet someone from a different culture?

In India, the hands are placed in a praying position, about chest high, accompanied by a slight bow. It also means "Thanks you" and "I'm sorry."

In the Middle East, a gentle grip is appropriate. A firm grip suggests aggression.

In the U.S. and Europe, you should have a firm handshake with direct eye contact, indicating warmth and respect. In the U.S., two "pumps" of the arms are customary. If you have a soft handshake, also called "fish handshaking," that means you are cold and unfriendly to the other person. In Northern Europe, you will receive a firm, one-pump handshaking.

In the U.S., handshaking is customary in business settings when initially introduced to someone of the same status. In Europe, colleagues shake hands every morning when they arrive at work.

In Japan and ROK, handshaking should be gentle, and you should avoid direct eye contact. Staring at someone is intimidating and disrespectful.

Middle Finger

Holding the fist, knuckles facing outward, and extending the middle finger upward stiffly is an insulting gesture of contempt which is found in many cultures.

A different gesture of contempt, raising a fist upward with a bent elbow and slapping the bicep of the same arm with the other hand, is common in countries that speak Spanish, Portuguese or French.

Index Finger

In North America this gesture means "come here." But this gesture is not used in restaurants in the U.S. to call a waiter or waitress. It is rude to them.

In parts of Southeast Asia, this gesture is used only for calling animals. Therefore, using it to beckon a human would be terribly impolite.

In Indonesia and Australia, it is also used for beckoning "ladies of the night."

In North Africa, the beckoning motion is done with the full hand, waving the hand downward, palm outward.

Thumb Up

The thumb-up gesture has become an almost universal signal for "OK" or "Fine," or "Well done!" in the U.S., Europe, and Asia. But in the U.S. and parts of Europe, it is also used to signal that one is hitch-hiking by slightly bending the wrist to the right side. In Nigeria, however, it is viewed as a rude gesture. Foreigners traveling in Nigeria have innocently tried hitch-hiking only to be roughed up for appearing to be sending insults to passing motorists.

In Australia, flashing the upright thumb and then making a slight jerk upward is generally used to silently signal "Up yours!"

The thumb-down gesture means "It's bad" or "failure" in the U.S. and parts of Europe.

Pointing at the Head with an Index Finger

In the U.S., rotating the index finger around in front of the ear connotes that someone is crazy or has a "loose screw" in their heads.

In China and other Asian countries, it means "think it over."

V Sign

Holding two fingers upright and palm outward signals "victory" or "peace" in more and more countries.

However, the palm and fingers facing inward means "Up yours!" in some countries in Europe. In Australia, New Zealand, Ireland, and South Africa, this gesture signals obscenity.

OK Sign

In most countries, the OK gesture means "Fine" or "No problem."

In France, it means "zero" or "worthless."

In Japan it is the signal for "money."

In Brazil it is considered very rude.

It is an insult in the following countries or regions: Malta, Sardinia, Greece,

Brazil, Tunisia, Italy, Turkey, Russia, and Paraguay.

In some Mediterranean countries it is an obscene gesture.

In several South American countries, it denotes homosexuality.

Touching

In North America, lingering touching between adults of the same gender, men in particular, is seen as an indication of homosexuality. However, it is accepted for men to touch each other if it is a quick touch (e.g., slap on the back) or hug (e.g., in times of greeting, joy or grief)

For some high-contact cultures, such physical displays signal friendship.

Contact cultures: Middle East countries, Latin countries, Italy, Greece, Spain, Portugal, some Asian countries, Nigeria.

Noncontact cultures: Japan, the U.S., Canada, Britain, Northern European countries, Australia, Estonia.

Middle ground: France, China, Ireland, India.

There are cultural differences in the parts of the body where touching is allowed (e.g., shoulders, back, arms) and where touching is prohibited (e.g., top of the head, hands). Other cultural differences include whether it is accepted for men and women to kiss in public. In 2007, the movie star Richard Gere was harshly criticized in India when he kissed on the cheek of an equally famous Indian woman film star. Until recently, Indian movies seldom showed kissing, even when the couple on the screen was portrayed as married.

Nodding and Shaking Head

Nodding and shaking head means different things to different people.

In most countries, nodding the head signals "Yes" and shaking it means "No."

In Hungary, parts of Greece, Turkey, Iran, and Bengal it is the reverse. Nodding the head means "No" and shaking the head means "Yes."

In the U.S., several quick head nods may simply mean that the listener understands the meaning of the speaker's words; it doesn't necessarily signal agreement.

The Bottom of Foot

Showing the sole of your foot is a rude gesture in many parts of the Middle East and parts of Asia like ROK and Thailand.

In 1988 the 24th Olympic Games was held in Seoul. One day when a sports event between the America and the ROK was televised live, an American sports commentator and a South Korean sports commentator sat before the camera. At one point, the American commentator put his leg across the other leg with the sole of his foot facing the South Korean commentator. The following day this photo was carried on the first page of the South Korean main newspaper with a comment: An American sports commentator was insulting the South Korean sports commentator. With much surprise, American newspapers carried this news with the photo in the U.S. It aroused heated discussion in the U.S. An American professor took this photo into her classroom with an air of disbelief. She asked a student from ROK why South Korean people thought this way. When she got an explanation from the student, she seemed not to accept it by saying "UNBELIEVABLE."

Intercultural Case Study

Touching or Not

One American professor was visiting the Philippines for a business trip. She was working with another female professor from a local university. After two days of meetings, the two of them were walking down the street. Suddenly and casually, the Philippine professor began holding the hand of the American professor. This seemed to be a natural gesture for the Philippine and she maintained their walk. However, for the American, this produced a strong physiological reaction. Her heart began to beat quickly and she found herself so distracted that she couldn't pay attention to the conversation they were having. She stopped walking and pulled her hand away. She was wondering if the Philippine professor was making a sexual advance. The Philippine professor was puzzled at the unfriendly behavior of the American.

Analyzing the Issues in the Case

1. What are the touching rules for American women? And for Philippine women?
2. How should we interpret ambiguous intercultural situations? Why does this happen?

Learning Culture Through Proverbs

Work in pairs and exchange views on the meanings of the following proverbs, then try to find out their Chinese equivalents if there is any, and discuss the values transmitted.

Proverb 1: *Silence is also speech.*
Proverb 2: *The eyes are the window to the soul.*

Online Research—Using Key Words

For more information and resources, search the Internet with the following key words:

cultural differences in nonverbal communication, facial expression, posture, gesture, eye contact, personal space, use of time, conversational silence

Unit 8
Different Communication Styles

Since communication style is both cultural and personal, it varies from culture to culture and from person to person. As a result, different communication styles constitute one of the biggest obstacles to intercultural communication. Intercultural communication scholars have done extensive research and identified various communication styles. To meet the challenges created by different communication styles, you need first to know your own communication style. And then through reading and training, you can understand the common communication styles adopted by people from different cultural backgrounds. With that knowledge, you can adjust your personal communication style to suit different communication contexts.

What You Can Learn from This Unit

1. Understand how cultures influence communication styles;
2. Know different communication styles;
3. Identify cultural values by observing communication styles;
4. Avoid misunderstandings resulting from different communication styles;
5. Adjust your communication style in different contexts.

Questions for Intercultural Awareness

1. What are the differences in your friends' communication styles? Give an example to illustrate the differences.
2. What is the etiquette that people should follow in a conversation? Discuss how we take turns speaking and listening.
3. How would you react when someone speaks to you in a language that you cannot understand or in a manner that is very different from yours?

What's Wrong?

Do You Know How You Communicate?

The following are three dialogues on the same topic. You need to analyze them from intercultural perspectives. Try to tell where the communicators are from in each conversation. What is the outcome of each conversation? The important point to bear in mind in judging the three dialogues is to evaluate communication effectiveness. Do the speaker and the listener understand each other's intended message? An ineffective communication situation is one in which the listener fails to understand what the speaker means rather than what the speaker says. Just ask yourself whether this is often the case in your intercultural communication.

Think about the following questions before you read the conversations below:

Question 1: Is this an effective communication?

Question 2: If yes, how did it achieve its outcome? If not, what's wrong with it?

Conversation 1

A: We're going to Surrey this weekend.

B: What fun! I wish we were going with you. How long are you going to be there? (If she wants a ride to the airport, she will ask.)

A: Three days. By the way, we may need a ride to the airport. Do you think you can take us there?

B: Sure. What time?

Conversation 2

A: We're going to Surrey this weekend.

B: What fun! I wish we were going with you. How long are you going to be there?

A: Three days. (I hope she'll offer me a ride to the airport.)

B: (She may want me to give her a ride.) Do you need a ride to the airport? I'll take you.

A: Are you sure it's not too much trouble?

B: It's no trouble at all.

Conversation 3

A: We're going to Surrey this weekend.

B: What fun! I wish we were going with you. How long are you going to be there?

A: Three days. (I hope she'll offer me a ride to the airport.)

B: (If she wants a ride, she will ask.) Have a great time!

A: (If she had wanted to give me a ride, she would have offered it. I'd better ask somebody else.) Thanks. I'll see you when I get back.

When analyzing the above three conversations, you need to first understand which conversation is an effective communication, and which is not. And then you should find out the reasons for the effective one(s) and ineffective one(s). You would fail to see the differences if you analyze them from linguistic perspectives as all the conversations are conducted with the same well-organized sentence structures. But an intercultural perspective can help you perceive those differences and even figure out the causes for the failure or success.

The first two are examples of effective communication as speaker A has achieved her purpose in conducting the communication. The third one is not effective because the speaker does not achieve her expected outcome. Let's analyze the three scenarios as follows.

Conversation 1 is an effective conversation. The two communicators are probably Westerners from the same or similar cultural background. Each knew the other's intention in the utterances, that is, the listener understood the speaker just by interpreting the speaker's coded messages rather than the context in which the conversation took place. In Western countries if the speaker requests the listener to do something, the speaker would make an explicit request in coded messages; otherwise the listener would interpret it as a statement rather than a request. In Conversation 1, when the speaker asked the listener for a favor, the listener made an appropriate response based on the speaker's direct message. As both are from the same cultural background, they can interpret each other's coded message to achieve communication effectiveness. The key to effective communication in this example is the use of direct requests. Both members of the dialogue were prepared for expected directness. Therefore, neither was upset by the direct request. Western, especially North American, communication is based on the premise that people will ask for what they want and listeners will respond to the request however they want.

Conversation 2 is also an effective conversation. The communicators might both be Chinese. Each knew that the other member of the communication understood the meaning, that is, the listener understood the speaker just by interpreting what the speaker meant in this context, not by what she said literally in her message. In this conversation, when the speaker uttered her statement "We are going to Surrey this weekend," she wanted the listener to understand her implication—I need a ride to the airport. She expected that the listener would then offer her a ride. The listener, on the other hand, would interpret the speaker's message as a request in this context, realizing that she needed a ride. Therefore she offered a ride to confirm her understanding of the speaker's message, which proved her clarification to be a successful conversation strategy. The basis of this effective conversation is indirect communication. The listener tried to figure out the speaker's needs without the speaker having to ask directly. The listener might think, "What would I need if I were going away for the weekend?" So there was an empathetic response from the listener. This indirectness also protected the speaker from rejection. By not directly asking for a ride, she did not risk rejection and did not place the listener in a position of losing face.

Conversation 3 is not an effective conversation. The communicators are from dissimilar cultural backgrounds, interpreting each other's message in their own cultural perspective. In this conversation, the speaker thought the listener would accurately interpret her request when she uttered the message. However, the listener interpreted the speaker's message the other way round, believing that the speaker was simply sharing news about her upcoming trip. She didn't interpret the statement as an indirect request for a ride. Not having been offered a ride from the listener, the speaker concluded that the listener was not willing to help. That's the point leading to misunderstanding. This exchange is not simply an ineffective communication between the two members of the dialogue; the misunderstanding that has occurred between them might hinder the development of their interpersonal relationships or collaboration in their workplace.

The conclusion is that it is essential for intercultural communicators to understand that people from different cultures communicate in different ways. Therefore they should learn to interpret messages from an intercultural perspective in order to achieve effective communication and to avoid misunderstandings.

Discussion

1. What might be the causes leading to intercultural communication failure?
2. When two communicators understand what the other is saying, do you think they can achieve effective intercultural communication in the end? Why or why not?

Reading 1

Ways of Reasoning

To understand how Americans think about things, it is necessary to understand about "the point." Americans mention it often: "Let's get right to the point," they will say. "My point is..." "What's the point of all this?"

The "point" is the idea or piece of information that Americans presume is, or should be, at the center of people's thinking, writings, and spoken comments. Speakers and writers are supposed to "make their points clear," meaning that they are supposed to say or write explicitly the idea or piece of information they wish to convey.

People from many other cultures have different ideas about the point.[1] Africans traditionally recount stories that convey the thoughts they have in mind, rather than stating "the point" explicitly. Japanese traditionally speak indirectly, leaving the listener to figure out what the point is. Thus, while an American might say to a friend, "I don't think that coat goes very well with the rest of your outfit," a Japanese might say, "Maybe this other coat would look even better than the one you have on." Americans value a person who "gets right to the point." Japanese are likely to consider such a person insensitive if not rude.

The Chinese and Japanese languages are characterized by vagueness and ambiguity. The precision, directness, and clarity Americans associate with "the point" cannot be attained, at least not with any grace, in Chinese and Japanese. Speakers of those languages are thus compelled to learn a new way of reasoning and conveying their ideas if they are going to interact satisfactorily with Americans.

As these examples indicate, different cultures teach different ways of thinking about things, of gathering and weighing evidence, of presenting viewpoints and reaching conclusions. These differences are evident in discussions and arguments, public speeches, and written presentations.

It is not enough to make a point, according to the typical American notion. A responsible speaker or writer is also expected to prove that the point is true, accurate, or valid. As they grow up, Americans learn what is and is not acceptable as "proof." The most important element of a proof is "the facts." A student might state an opinion and the teacher will ask, "What are your facts?" Or, "What data do you have to support that?" The teacher is telling the student that without facts to support the opinion, the opinion will not be considered legitimate or valid.

Americans assume there are "facts" of life, of nature, and of the universe that can be discovered by trained people (usually called "scientists") using special techniques, equipment, and ways of thinking. "Scientific facts," as the Americans call them, are assumed to exist independently of any individual person who studies them or talks about them. This important assumption—that there are facts existing independently of the people who observe them—is not shared throughout the world.

The most reliable facts, in the American view, are those in the form of quantities—specific numbers, percentages, rates, rankings, or amounts.[2] Many foreign visitors in the States are struck—if not stunned—by the quantity of numbers and statistics they encounter in the media and in daily conversations. "McDonald's has sold 8.7 billion hamburgers," say signs all over the country. "Nine out of ten doctors recommended this brand of mouthwash," says a radio announcer or a magazine advertisement. (Doctors are viewed as scientists and are held in very high esteem.) "The humidity is at 27 percent," says the television weather reporter. "The barometric pressure is at 29.32 and rising. Yesterday's high temperature in Juneau, Alaska, was 47 degrees."

Americans feel secure in the presence of all the numbers. Foreign visitors often wonder what significance the numbers could possibly have.

Citing quantifiable facts is generally considered the best way to prove a point. Facts based on personal experience are also persuasive. Americans accept information and ideas that arise from their own experience or that of others they know and trust. Television advertisers seek to capitalize on this aspect of American reasoning through commercials that portray presumably average people (a woman in a kitchen, for example, or two men in an auto repair shop) testifying that in their experience the product or service being advertised is a good one. Other credible testifiers are people dressed to look like scientists or doctors and celebrities from the worlds of entertainment and athletics.

Of the various ways of having personal experience, Americans regard the sense of sight as the most reliable. "I saw it with my own eyes" means that it undoubtedly happened. In a court of law, an "eyewitness" is considered the most reliable source of information. If a speaker has failed to make his or her purpose in speaking clear, Americans will say, "I don't see the point."

Along with their trust in facts goes a distrust of emotions. School children are taught (but do not always learn) to disregard the emotional aspects of an argument as they look for "the facts." In their suspicion of emotional statements, Americans differ from many others. Iranians, for example, have a tradition of eloquent, emotion-filled speech. They quote revered poets who have captured the feeling they want to convey. They seek to move their audiences to accept them and their viewpoints not because of the facts they have presented but because of the human feelings they share.

A Brazilian graduate student was having difficulty in his English writing class. "It's not just a matter of verbs and nouns," he said. "My teacher tells me I'm too subjective. Too emotional. I must learn to write my points more clearly."

In evaluating the significance of a point or a proof, Americans are most likely to consider its practical usefulness. Americans are famous for their pragmatism, that is, their interest in whether a fact or idea has practical consequences. A good idea is a practical idea. Other adjectives that convey approval of ideas or information are "realistic," "down-to-earth," "hard-headed," and "sensible."

Americans tend to distrust theory and generalizations, which they might label "impractical," "unrealistic," "too abstract," "a lot of hot air," or "just theoretical." A Latin American graduate student, for example, heard himself being criticized (openly and directly) by the American professor in his international organization class. The student had written a paper concerning a particular international organization and had talked about the principles of national sovereignty, self-determination, and non-interference in the internal affairs of other countries. "That's just pure Latin American bunk," the professor said to him. "That's nothing but words and theory. It has nothing to do with what really happens." The embarrassed student was told to write another paper.

Latin Americans and many Europeans are likely to attach more weight to ideas and theories than Americans are. Rather than compiling facts and statistics on the basis of which to reach conclusions, they are likely to generalize from one theory to another or from a theory to facts, according to certain rules of logic. A European visitor in Detroit in the 1960s asked his hosts where the masses of unemployed workers were. His hosts said there were no masses of unemployed workers. "There must be," the visitor insisted, "According to the theory, the capitalist system produces massive unemployment among the workers. You must be hiding them somewhere."

For this visitor, "truth" came not from facts he observed, but from a theory he believed. Americans believe in some theories, of course, but in general they are suspicious of theory and generalizations and more at ease with specific facts.

In some Chinese traditions, truth and understanding come neither from accumulating facts nor generalizing from theories, but from silent meditation. In Zen, truths cannot even be expressed in language. Zen masters do not tell their students what the point is.

Another element of ways of reasoning, beyond considerations about facts and theory as ways of reaching and supporting conclusions, is the matter of cause-and-effect relationships.[3] Americans tend to suppose that most events have some knowable, physical cause. "Things don't just happen," they often say. "Something makes them happen." Very few events are considered to result from "chance" or "luck" or "fate." Religious Americans will ascribe certain kinds of events (such as the otherwise inexplicable death of a child) to "God's will." But these intangible factors are not usually held responsible for what happens to people. Most Americans have difficulty even comprehending the notion, so prevalent in many other parts of the world, that "fate" determines what happens in people's lives.

When people with differing ways of reasoning are interacting, the typical feeling they both get is that the other person "just doesn't understand" and "isn't making sense." Each then tries harder to be more "logical," not realizing that the problem is their differing conceptions of what is logical. Foreigners in America will need to learn that Americans will consider them "not logical," "too emotional," or "fuzzy-minded" if they do not use specific facts to support or illustrate their ideas and opinions, if they speak mainly in terms of abstractions and generalizations, or if they attribute important events to non-material causes.

Foreign students have a particular need to learn how Americans think about things and how they organize their thoughts in speech and writing. Unless they do, they will have trouble writing papers or giving speeches that American audiences (including teachers) will take seriously.

Vocabulary

barometric *adj.* 气压的

bunk *n.* <非正式>瞎说，废话

capitalize on 利用

legitimate *adj.* 公正的，正当的，合理的

recount *v.* 叙述，描述

revered *adj.* 受人尊敬的

stunned *adj.* （因惊讶、震惊而）目瞪口呆的

Notes

1. People from many other cultures have different ideas about the point.

    由于思维方式不同（比如西方直线型思维和东方螺旋型思维），人们表达观点的方式也不同。比如，中国人的思维逻辑语言表达上表现为：首先叙述事件背景，或罗列客观条件，或摆出事实证据，最后作出结论，说明自己的观点。而西方人习惯先表达中心意思，再由此展开，层层推演。

2. The most reliable facts, in the American view, are those in the form of quantities—specific numbers, percentages, rates, rankings, or amounts.

    不同文化背景的人们，思维方式不同，对事物的推理方式也不同。在美国人看来，那些包含大量的具体数字、百分比、比率、排名或者数量的事实，才是最可靠的依据，没有事实支撑的理论是站不住脚的。相比之下，拉美人和欧洲人更侧重于理论研究，他们习惯于从一个理论归纳出另一个理论。而在中国传统文化中，一些真理是通过静坐冥想得出的，只可意会不可言传，即所谓的"禅"。

3. Another element of ways of reasoning, beyond considerations about facts and theory as ways of reaching and supporting conclusions, is the matter of cause-and-effect relationships.

    本句大意为：除了考虑得出结论和支撑结论所需的事实论据和理论依据之外，美国人推理论证的另一个要素就是因果关系。在许多地区，人们相信"人命天定"，但美国人却不同，他们认为绝大多数事件事出有因。思维方式的差异造成跨文化沟通障碍，人们往往因为感到不被对方理解，而越发想要证明自己有逻辑，却不想适得其反。

Discussion from Intercultural Perspectives

1. Is it possible that misunderstandings may arise even when people have no language barriers in communication? Why or why not?

2. Do you think you are to the point when you make your statements? If not, what might happen in intercultural communication?

3. Can you explain why Chinese do not communicate directly? And what should we do if we want to achieve effective intercultural communication?

4. How does culture influence people's communication styles? Describe some cultural values that might produce different communication styles.

5. How would people working in intercultural workplaces communicate with each other if they don't know the different communication styles? And what might be the outcome?

Reading 2

Teaching Culture: Perspectives in Practice

Context

    E.T. Hall (1977) proposed the notion of low context and high context[1] to differentiate between two ends of a continuum. On one end are low-context messages, where the context or situation plays a minimal role in the communication. Low-context messages are explicit, direct, and conveyed primarily through spoken language. ("It's cold in here. Would you please turn the thermostat up to 74°?") High-context messages are on the opposite end of the continuum. They are implicit, indirect, conveyed primarily through the context or the social situation. (In silence, one person shivers slightly and glances quickly at an underling, who immediately turns up the thermostat to an understood setting.) Hall cites numerous examples that illustrate these two extremes.

Low-context messages include communication between two U.S. trial lawyers in the courtroom or two politicians drafting legislation. High-context messages, in Hall's examples, are the unspoken messages expressed and understood by twins, or by people who have extensive networks with others, where the circumstances of the social situation carry the messages.

Another way of looking at the low-context and high-context distinction is to see messages in degrees of explicitness, from explicit to tacit, direct to indirect. Seen this way, some practices require greater explicitness or visibility in the messages, meanings, or understandings, whereas others call for less. In other words, low-context practices like courtroom exchanges or air-traffic control tower communications require explicitness. High-context practices like folk dancing, buying and selling at a cattle auction, or learning through apprenticeship may call for more tacit messages.

The following diagram illustrates how perspectives, underlying meanings, and messages are more tacit in high-context situations and more explicit in low-context situations.

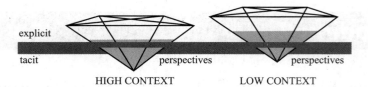

explicit

tacit   perspectives   perspectives

HIGH CONTEXT   LOW CONTEXT

Figure 1 Context in Practices

Looking exclusively at the linguistic dimension in terms of high or low context leads us to degree of directness in language, an important feature of practices. In direct communications, people tend to say what is on their minds and to mean what they say, to "tell it like it is." In indirect communications, people tend to not say what is on their minds and to rely more on suggestion and inference. Craig Storti (1999) offers a useful comparison of interpretations of the same language items by speakers from direct and indirect cultures. When direct communicators say "Yes," for example, they are conveying agreement, approval, acceptance, or understanding. When indirect communicators say "Yes," however, they are expressing politeness and respect and acknowledgment of having heard what the other has said.

A common cultural misunderstanding in language classes involves conflicts between direct and indirect communication style. Tom Kuehn describes a situation where he expected Mexican and South Korean students in his ESL class to ask questions in class when they needed clarifi cation, a classic form of direct communication.

> I was frustrated with a low-English-level South Korean student who never asked questions in class. My goal was to equalize classroom participation, and one aspect of it was to have students ask questions when they didn't understand something during class. I taught techniques of how to ask a question, which the students from Mexico readily adopted, but not the South Korean student. At the end of the course, I interviewed the South Korean student (with a translator) and learned, in her culture, that asking questions in class is an insult to the teacher. Furthermore, she reported, "To learn English one must listen very carefully to the teacher and study hard after class." Through interviewing her, I realized that she was being a good student by not asking the teacher a lot of questions. She could work hard with the homework to grasp a concept she couldn't get in class. Numerous questions would show a disrespect for the teacher. Listening to the teacher is a sign of a good student. There is also the concept of losing face if one is seen as not knowing something the teacher is talking about. It reflects on the student, who must not have studied enough. I realized that I hadn't addressed the underlying values of her culture or mine, and that just teaching techniques wouldn't produce the behavior I was hoping for.[2]

Tom Kuehn's account shows, again, how practices are intimately linked to perspectives. It is not simply about learning how to formulate questions in the new language and observing others perform this practice in class; it's about recognizing that there are cultural perspectives attached to these practices and that these need to be named as well to help students learn to participate appropriately in practices.

Appropriateness

A critical feature of practices is appropriateness, or doing and saying the right thing at the right time in the right way.[3] Knowing what to say and what to do depends on a number of factors, all related to the social situation and the people involved. Not observing the agreed-upon procedures in the proper sequence causes misunderstanding, even conflict. Saying or doing the right thing at the wrong moment, or the wrong thing at the proper moment, also provokes problems. For instance, I have consistently blundered when it comes to *la bise*, kissing the cheek in greetings or leave-takings in France. I know that I need to *faire la bise*, and I know how to do it. However, I'm not always sure how many times to do it—two, three, or four. In fact, one of my exasperated French relatives still announces to me beforehand how many times I should kiss her on the cheek (twice). This does ease some pressure to do the right thing, but at the same time, I'm reminded that I still haven't got it figured out.

Valerie Hansford describes the challenges of teaching the cultural practice of apologizing in a foreign language context: ESOL in Japan.

I teach a required course in ESOL to non-English majors at a university in Japan, and I am required to use the resources selected or approved by the program and department, including texts. I am limited in many ways by the textbook. In this particular textbook, there were a number of communicative aspects (complaining, making requests for personal possessions, etc.), but I chose the function of apologizing to give a specific focus, and also because the manner, style, and timing of an apology varies from culture to culture.

I designed a unit on apologies that spanned four 45-minute lessons and focused on both language and cultural objectives. The primary language objective was the difference between "because" and "so," in the context of apologizing. ("I'm sorry. I'm late because there was a train accident" or "I'm sorry I'm late, so I'll come early tomorrow and help you set up the desks.") Cultural objectives included identifying similarities and differences between Japanese and North American styles of apologizing, including when to apologize. We also explored appropriate nonverbal behavior for each of the styles.

I started to observe both in class and out of class that the "when," or timing, of the apology was also a factor. As the students and I worked through the unit, I learned more about the Japanese cultural aspect of apologizing as well as the styles of a few other Asian countries. (In one of my classes there were six international students.) I also discovered that there are times when my students would use the apologizing form that I had labeled "North American style," but they told me that their parents might not use that form in the same situation.

The most challenging aspect is having students work with "knowing why": to explore the reasons for North American or Japanese apology styles. It is difficult to get students to understand that the objective is for them to make their own guesses and share their ideas rather than to know the "correct" answer. This is especially challenging in this academic setting in Japan where students are hesitant to stand out and generally want to "know" the correct answer before being willing to answer. Two ways I found to address this were: 1) having students work in small groups and then presenting their group's ideas, and 2) having the students write their ideas for homework by giving them specific questions to address. I am still working on ways to address this challenge as I feel that this is an important area for students to develop and broaden their critical thinking skills and because it is an important element in the experiential learning cycle.

The reality is that there are very few opportunities for the students to have experienced the cultural element that I'm focusing on and thus they cannot talk about any previous experiences. Also, once students have learned *about*, *how* and *why*, they have very limited opportunities to use it outside of class. Even so, after completing the unit, the students demonstrated a clear understanding and awareness of the different apology styles. Before class started for the day, in fact, when students came to tell me why they had been absent or that they hadn't completed the homework, they would do so in one of the two styles studied. Other students who were in the room at the time would shout "Ah, Japanese style" or "Ah, North American style." The same occurred after class if a student was late. In effect, the students were making conscious choices in how to apologize.

Vocabulary

apprenticeship *n.* 学徒身份，学徒期

cattle auction 牛畜拍卖

continuum *n.* 统一体，连续体

exasperated *adj.* 恼怒的，烦恼的，愤怒的

leave-taking *n.* 告别，辞别

thermostat *n.* 恒温器

underling *n.* 下属

Notes

1. low context and high context

   语境是使用语言的环境，包括一切主客观因素。美国文化人类学家爱德华·T. 霍尔在1976年出版的《超越文化》一书中，提出文化具有语境性，并将语境分为低语境（low context）和高语境（high context）。在低语境文化中，人们强调的是双方交流的内容，而不是当时所处的语境。低语境文化的特征：外显、明了；明码信息；较多的言语编码；反应外露；圈内外灵活；人际关系不密切。而在高语境文化中，说话者的言语或行为意义来源于或内在化于说话者当时所处的语境，他所表达的东西往往比他所说的东西要多。高语境文化的特征：内隐、含蓄；暗码信息；较多的非言语编码；反应很少外露；圈内外有别；人际关系密切。

2. I realized that I hadn't addressed the underlying values of her culture or mine, and that just teaching techniques wouldn't produce the behavior I was hoping for.

   作者在本段用实例说明高低语境的文化差异。本句中的underlying values of her culture or mine指文化中潜在的高低语境问题，老师与学生的语境文化不同，因此对于学生是否应该向老师提问这一问题，双方处理方式截然相反。本句大意为：我意识到，之前我没有谈及到两国文化价值观的深层差异，仅仅利用教学技巧是不会达到我所预期的效果的。

3. A critical feature of practices is appropriateness, or doing and saying the right thing at the right time in the right way.

   practice作可数名词时，意为"习俗、习惯"。本句大意为：习俗的一个重要特点就是恰当，也就是用最适宜的方式，在最合适的时间，做最恰当的事情，说最妥当的话。

1. Analyze your own communication style according to the descriptions of high-context culture and low-context culture. And discuss with your classmates what would happen to you in intercultural interactions.
2. Have you communicated with someone who has different communication styles? Share with your group.
3. How can you modify your communication style to accommodate your partner's style?
4. Discuss the reasons why Chinese people adopt high-context culture communication style.

Intercultural Lens

Effective communication starts with listening and understanding rather than talking and trying to convince. So, to be effective in communication, it requires both communicators to employ appropriate communication strategies. Communication does not just happen in one way, but in two ways. Therefore, asking and offering feedback are essential in achieving effective communication, but learning to do so requires an intercultural understanding and efforts. The following examples serve as a guide in your intercultural communication activities.

1. Ask questions or offer feedback.

You should learn to ask a specific question rather than a general question if you don't understand what the speaker is saying. The speaker might be confused by your general question because the speaker may have no idea how to answer it or what exactly you meant.

Example 1:

A: Students need to know that organizational communication encompasses not only getting along with colleagues in the workplace, but also various types of business writing.

B: Excuse me, would you please repeat it? *or* Sorry, I don't quite understand you.

→ Improved:

B: Excuse me, what do you mean by "encompass"? *or* Sorry, can you explain the word "encompass"?

Example 2:

A: The only solution to manage cultural conflicts after global mergers is to create cultural synergy.

B: Excuse me, what do you mean by "cultural synergy"? *or* Excuse me, I don't know the word "synergy," could you please explain it to me? *or* Excuse me, I don't understand the meaning of the phrase after the word "create," could you please explain it to me?

2. Offer a specific reply when asked.

Example:

A: The report you wrote is great.

B: Thank you.

A: I gained much information from your report.

B: Thank you.

→ Improved:

A: The report you wrote is great. It has all the information I need.

B: Thank you. I hope you have everything you need for your project. Actually I worked all week gathering the information and writing the report.

3. Clarify or confirm your understanding.

To be effective in communication, you need to clarify or confirm that you have understood the speaker. You may think you understand the speaker, but in most cases, it is otherwise. Therefore misunderstandings occur but you are not aware of it. With clarification or confirmation in communication any possible misunderstanding can be avoided. You may employ paraphrasing to check if your understanding is correct.

Example 1:

A: An increasingly sophisticated set of communication skills will be needed in the 21st century workplace, so it is important that business schools identify (recognize) those components and skill sets that will best serve the future manager, and align (arrange) business communication programs to meet those needs.

B: Do you mean that effective communication skills are needed in the 21st century so that business schools should teach business communication courses to their students? *or* If I understand correctly, you mean that…

Example 2:

A: The word "exciting" has different connotations in British English and in American English. While American executives talk about "exciting challenges" repeatedly, British executives use this word to describe only children's activities (Children do exciting things in Britain, not executives).

B: Does it mean that the same words can have different meanings or connotations in different parts of the world? Is that what you mean?

4. Check the listener's understanding.

Effective communication requires two-way communication, but in most communication activities with Chinese it is one-way communication. The Chinese tends to listen to the speaker without making any feedback so that the speaker may feel uncomfortable as he or she has no idea if the listener understands his or her intended message. Therefore the speaker would check the listener's understanding by asking the following questions. At that time, the listener should be aware that the speaker may have lost his or her patience. The listener should improve his or her communication strategy, otherwise the communication will break down.

Are you with me?

Do you understand what I mean?

Do you follow me?

Are you listening?

5. Showing you understand.

In communication it is important for the listener to show he or she understands as it serves as feedback to the speaker. This is called "nonverbal back channel." However, how people show their understanding of the words and meanings of the speaker varies across cultures. Chinese people show their understanding by nodding their heads accompanied by some vocal messages like "En En" or "Yes Yes." This might be the only feedback given to the speaker throughout the communication. This Chinese communication style might result in some misunderstandings in intercultural communication. Because to the Chinese, nodding or "En En" as a feedback in communication does not always mean they agree with the speaker. But to the Westerners, it might be taken as a sign of agreement. So you should learn to verbalize your feedback in intercultural communication as follows.

Yes, you are right.

I am sorry to hear that.

That's right.

That's too bad.

That's a good idea.

Yes, I will do that soon.

OK, I will talk to him about it tomorrow.

I can't do that tomorrow, for I have another project to do.

I see what you mean but I don't agree with you.

Intercultural Case Study

Listening or Participating

In an office, an American department manager discussed something with his Chinese subordinate. Much to his surprise, he noticed that his Chinese colleague just listened and kept nodding and saying "Yes, OK, En." but never offered any verbal message as feedback. Then the manager wondered if his Chinese colleague understood him or would cooperate with him on their work project. Finally he couldn't refrain from asking "Do you understand me?"

"Yes, I see what you mean," replied his colleague. But the American manager still doubted his Chinese colleague's understanding, and thought that it was so hard to communicate with Chinese.

What Would One Think of the Other? (A for American and C for Chinese)

A: I guess he did not understand me, but why he didn't ask me? How can I work with him any more in the future if he never asks for clarification?

C: He talked too much, and didn't even give me time or a chance to ask him.

A: I gave him plenty of time and opportunities to respond, but he didn't want to share his thoughts or even worse, he might not have any ideas or thoughts on the subject of the project.

An Intercultural Perspective

You will lose many opportunities in your workplace if this is your communication style even though you are competent in your work. The critical lesson is to improve your intercultural communication style, which in turn, can enhance your competitiveness in the workplace or at the university.

Analyzing the Issues in the Case

1. What is the underlying reason for the Chinese communication style?
2. Americans or Westerners expect the Chinese colleagues or students to participate at the meeting or in class. What do they expect the Chinese to do?

Learning Culture Through Proverbs

Work in pairs and exchange views on the meanings of the following proverbs, then try to find out their Chinese equivalents if there is any, and discuss the values transmitted.

Proverb 1: *Do not beat around the bush.*
Proverb 2: *Silence is golden.*

Online Research—Using Key Words

For more information and resources, search the Internet with the following key words:

verbal communication, communication styles, high-context and low-context communication

Part Three

Applications of Intercultural Communication

Unit 9
Innovation and Education

Enculturation of children begins with their parents from birth. Youngsters are being subtly taught how to think and feel and behave in the style of their compatriots. However, by the time when they are five years old or so, in most countries, the second most powerful socialization force asserts itself, namely, the education system. The institution of education, including the length of the school day, the expectations for the roles of teachers and parents in education, the motivation of the students for learning, the methods of teaching, the content of the curriculum, and the interaction among students in the class, works toward shaping the child to embrace the critical values of the culture. For the Chinese, these include respect to authority, interconnectedness with the family, hard work and belief in innovation.

What You Can Learn from This Unit

1. Understand that different cultures have different education systems;
2. Analyze cultural factors that form the foundation of students' behavior in class;
3. Know what teachers and students should do in class in order to cultivate students' innovation;
4. Discover the correlation between innovation and culture in education.

Questions for Intercultural Awareness

1. All people have a grouping of personality traits and characteristics. And some traits are held by many people in a culture. What are the "personality traits" of Chinese university students?
2. Why does the Chinese government call on the nation to increase people's creativity and innovation?

What's Wrong?

Global Debate on Creativity and Education in China and the U.S.

A report in *The New York Times* from 2010, "Top Test Scores from Shanghai Stun Educators" and a *Time* magazine cover story from 2011, "The Truth About Tiger Moms"—have ignited global debates about Eastern and Western education among parents, teachers and children.

In 2010, China participated for the first time in a global standardized test of 15-year-olds, and stunned other nations when Chinese students scored highest in all three subjects—mathematics, science, and reading—vastly outperforming U.S. students, who came in between 14th and 25th out of 65 countries. It's worth noting that China's high-performing Shanghai was the only city in China to participate in the examination that is called the Programme for International Student Assessment (PISA). For Americans, the results are a "wake-up call" to the "brutal truth that we're being out-educated," says U.S. Education Secretary Arne Duncan. What do these results say about China's future, and America's?

Chester Finn, another U.S. government education official commented, "We have to face the fact that China is bent on surpassing us in education, and if America doesn't rise to the occasion, we're going to keep falling behind." "These results reflect something real," says James Fallows in *The Atlantic*, a monthly opinion magazine. "Chinese schools are full of bright and motivated students, and they'll drive China's 'continued development.' But 'don't go nuts.' These tests are fallible. Still, if we're lucky, Americans will be so 'startled' by these results that we'll focus on finally reforming our education system."

President Obama, in a speech to a college audience in North Carolina, recalled how the Soviet Union's 1957 launching of Sputnik provoked the United States to increase investment in mathematics and science education, helping America win the space race. "Fifty years later, our generation's Sputnik moment is back. With billions of people in India and China suddenly plugging into the

181

world economy, nations with the most educated workers will prevail. As it stands right now, America is in danger of falling behind."

In January 2011, Chinese-American mother Amy Chua's book *Battle Hymn of the Tiger Mother* provoked a similarly strong reaction from parents around the country, this time focusing more closely on Chinese parenting. Chua described in detail her parenting methods. Her children focused on two tasks: academic excellence and musical excellence. Each day was filled with hours of homework and musical practice. Participation in afterschool athletics, school plays and clubs, and sleepovers were forbidden. Her daughters were roundly criticized for less than perfect work or performance. Chua believed that mastery in academic subjects and musical instruments would become its own reward and that eventually her children would be pleased to have attained excellence.

Some critics have called Chua an unfair taskmaster, while defenders suggest most American children are coddled. Chua's children are necessarily "superior" to their classmates who are being raised in a more relaxed, Western fashion. However, the superiority may come from Chua's definition of success for her daughters, focusing on music (classical only), academics (specifically math and science) and complete acceptance of parental domination.

Another definition of success is that parenting should help children to develop their talents, gifts and skills that will be highly valued in the society. Therefore Amy Chua's parenting approach isn't the whole picture of Chinese Education. The Chinese government now emphasises more on developing Chinese children's soft skills, such as innovation and creativity. Meanwhile, the United States government is pushing national curriculum standards. So far about 43 states have signed onto the Common Core State Standards Initiative, with the goal of developing one set of standards for every American student to meet.

Chinese feel pride in their students' top-ranked performance in PISA but it should be recalled that there is a close match between the goals and content of the PISA assessments and the examination orientation in China, that is, the skills needed to excel in PISA and the strengths of Chinese students overlap considerably. The same is true of Chinese students' excellent performance each year in the International Mathematical Olympiad.

Faced with China's top score in PISA and parenting practices highlighted in the Tiger Mother's story, we need to ponder why the United States would take these testing differences so seriously. One reason the U.S. media overestimates the dire aspects of the situation is to arouse the nation's awareness of China's strengths and global potential. Further, the attention to the testing discrepancies might serve as a motivation for U.S. educators to fast-track their reform initiatives.

This idea has been supported in an article entitled "The Creativity Crisis" in *Newsweek*. For the first time, research shows that even American creativity is declining. The article notes that creativity scores in this country have slipped as teachers have increasingly been tied to a standards-based curriculum, although it's not clear that the decline is entirely due to a changing education system.

Perhaps it is too early to confirm that U.S. education has its problem or that U.S. creativity is declining. The irony is that, if we look at what China and the United States are doing in their education reforms, China has begun programs aimed at fostering more creativity and innovative thinking and the U.S. schools are now chasing after test scores. China is abandoning pedagogy that focuses on standardized tests and rote memorization and is providing students with more flexibility in course choices and electives. Chinese schools are now encouraging a problem-based learning approach. The United States is moving toward a more rigid program of study for all high schools, and school systems are demanding more homework and more study time for children. Schools are adopting standardized curricula and standardized national testing is made mandatory in the No Child Left Behind law enacted by President George W. Bush's administration.

After comparing the opposing trends in Chinese and American education, you will notice that China is racing toward the American old model, but the U.S. is racing toward the Chinese traditional model.

How can we teach students to be more creative? There are some new findings from psychology that indicates, among Western university students, that one way to foster creative thinking is for students to experience a new cultural perspective. Students who participated in overseas study programs, anywhere in the world, were more creative on psychological tests than students who hadn't studied abroad.

Discussion

1. "...China is racing toward the American old model, but the U.S. is racing toward the Chinese traditional model..." Explain these two models.
2. What might be the barriers in adopting the other country's teaching approach? Why can't they be easily adopted?
3. Is it possible to blend Chinese traditional education model with Western ones? What might characterize such an education model?

Reading 1

Differences That Make a Difference

A newcomer to Japan asked an American consultant who had been in Japan more than a decade if the increasing similarities between Japanese and Western ways were beginning to outweigh the differences. The consultant replied:

"In my experience, the outward similarities just make the subtle differences more difficult to recognize, and therefore even more important. The problem is that the typical American only notices the obvious differences—driving on the left or some guy in a tuxedo taking a leak at the side of the road in the middle of the city.[1] The most important differences are the ones that really make a difference when Japanese and Americans or other foreigners try to work together."

How does one find those differences that make a difference? According to our consultant, there are two rules:

"Rule one: If you notice a difference, realize that difference in itself may not be so important. It is what you do not notice that counts.[2] Rule two: In almost everything in Japan there is some unseen or unstated meaning which is usually not pointed out but which everybody is supposed to know. So my advice is to look for the underlying meanings.

A lot of businessmen coming over here (Japan) these days make the mistake of only focusing on management practices or some other aspects of business, and always comparing them with what Americans would do. My advice is to look for some of the subtle differences in the ways things are done when you don't expect to see any differences. Look at business practices, sure, but also look at what people do at parties, how people talk to each other, and how kids are taught. You'll find some basic differences that make a difference."

A fascinating study conducted a few years ago makes this point precisely. A team of Japanese and American researchers visited several kindergartens in Japan. These included American schools and international schools strongly influenced by Americans (in staffing, language used, and enrollment). Others were *yochien*, Japanese kindergartens. The researchers were interested in children's drawings. They wondered if, given the same instructions, the children from the two cultures would produce significantly different pictures. If Henry drew a picture of the sun, for example, would he color it yellow while Horoshi's sun would be colored red, just like the sun in his country's flag? The answer, as it turned out, was a resounding yes, so much so that almost anybody could sort through the hundred odd drawings and nearly always guess which were done by Japanese children and which were drawn by Americans.

But as culture is more a process than its products, more an event than an object, the truly revealing differences appeared in *how* the children made their pictures. If we take a closer look at what happened when these children were asked to "draw a picture of your family," we can learn a good deal about Japanese and American ways of looking at the world and doing things. We can also anticipate some of the problems that can result when people from both cultures attempt to work together.

To begin with, the seating arrangements in each school were different. In some American classrooms there were individual desks, while in others the children sat on the floor. In all of the Japanese kindergartens, however, the children sat around tables in groups of six or eight. Each group had its own name such as that of a flower or bird and this group served as the basic unit for many of the children's activities.

The roles of the teachers were also different. When the researchers visited a school to ask the children to draw the pictures, the American teachers invited the visitors to "go right ahead and tell the boys and girls what you want them to do." In the Japanese schools, however, all communication was handled by the teacher. She remained authority, the responsible person and "go-between."

How the children began and how they carried out the activity also differed. Usually, as soon as an American child received a sheet of paper he or she would begin to draw. When the picture was finished, the child would hold it up to be collected or would bring it to the teacher's desk. In the Japanese schools the children waited until all of the papers had been distributed. Then, at each table, the children looked at each other and talked a little about what they were supposed to do. Then, table by table, as if by signal, all the children would begin to draw. Throughout the activity, children would turn and look at what the others were doing. Those who finished first waited until the others were done, and when all were finished the drawings were collected.

When children showed difficulty in drawing someone in the family, the responses of the teachers were also different. The Japanese teacher would usually assist the child, not infrequently taking the child's hand and guiding the crayon. (This is truely "hands-on-learning"! It is the same method used to teach Japanese children other skills such as writing and bowing.) In the American schools, the teachers encouraged the children in words: "Just do your best." "It's *your* father and *your* picture and *you* should try to draw the way *you* see him."

Finally, the order in which the family members were drawn was also notably different. For the Japanese youngsters, the order usually began with father, then mother, then older brother or sister. The child would draw himself or herself next, and if there were still younger ones, they would be drawn last. For the American children the order seemed much more random. The only notable tendency was for some children to draw themselves first.

In short, there were cultural differences in the physical arrangements of the rooms, the kind of contact with an outsider that was allowed, the extent of coordination in the beginning and ending of tasks, the role of the person in charge of the activity and the kind of instruction that person offered, and the depiction of social relationships, "the social order." Each of these themes is worth a closer look, for together with other themes, they characterize some of the major features that contrast the two societies and are at the heart of many of the confusions and conflicts that arise when Japanese and Americans work together.

Every person, everywhere, is both an individual, separate from others, and also a member of a group, emotionally tied to others. Cultural background influences whether the independent individual or the interdependent group is given emphasis when we think of ourselves. Japan and the U.S. differ sharply in this regard.

In countless ways, both obvious and subtle, the Japanese are encouraged to think first of being part of the group. "We" always comes before "I." "We" of this family, "we" of this nation, or just "we" who are together in a room talking. One is never fully independent; one must always be conscious of others.

For Americans the individual, not the group, is basic. So many of the values Americans hold dear—equality, democracy, freedom, privacy, and even progress are bound up with the American view of individualism. Cooperation and teamwork are important, to be sure, but these should arise from the choice and desire of the individual.

These are not simply interesting cultural differences. They are very emotional issues. Americans can become upset when a Japanese expresses an opinion beginning with *Wareware nihonjin* ("We Japanese"). "Just give me your own opinion," the American may insist. Likewise Japanese find some expressions of American individualism rude and anti-social. Americans tend to speak in terms that are both personal and also cautious about speaking for others. Nevertheless, the impression given can be one of egotism. A similar problem occurs when an American chimes in to help complete the sentence of a Japanese. Very often the American is simply trying to show that he is listening attentively and understands. The Japanese may find this arrogant and overbearing.

Vocabulary

arrogant *adj.* 傲慢的，目中无人的
chime in *v.* 插话
egotism *n.* 自我主义，自高自大
go-between *n.* 中间人
overbearing *adj.* 专横的，飞扬跋扈的
resounding *adj.* 彻底的，十足的
tuxedo *n.* 男式无尾礼服

Notes

1. ...the typical American only notices the obvious differences—driving on the left or some guy in a tuxedo taking a leak at the side of the road in the middle of the city.

    take a leak 意为"撒尿"（美俚）。本句大意为：典型的美国人只注意到

一些明显的差异——靠路左边开车或某个穿着晚礼服的人在市中心的街边小便。

2. It's what you do not notice that counts.

count 作不及物动词时意为"有价值，重要"。本句大意为：真正重要的是你没有注意到的东西。

Discussion from Intercultural Perspectives

1. The consultant states that "The most important differences are the ones that really make a difference..." What does the consultant mean by "make a difference"?

2. What do you think of the consultant's rules to communicate with Japanese? What are those "you don't notice"? What are the implications of Japanese expressing themselves according to Rule Two?

3. What causes the misunderstandings in the situation in which a Japanese expresses his opinion starting with *Wareware nihonjin* ("We Japanese") and while an American chimes in to help complete the sentence of a Japanese?

4. Discuss the outcome of the drawing lesson taught by American and Japanese teachers from the perspective of developing students' innovation. Which one do you personally prefer?

Reading 2

The Global Campus: Challenges and Opportunities

At the risk of being labeled an alarmist, I propose that it is time to sound the alarm for "internationalized" education[1] at U.S. institutions of higher learning. Confronted with a world that is strikingly different from what it was just a decade ago, the United States faces rapidly shifting economic, political, and national security realities and challenges. To respond to these changes and meet national needs it is essential that our institutions of higher education graduate globally competent students. Without global competence our students will be ill-prepared for global citizenship[2], lacking the skills required to address our national security needs, and unable to compete successfully in the global marketplace. Global competence, as defined in the recently published NASULGC Task Force on International Education's *A Call to Leadership: The Presidential Role in Internationalizing the University*, is the ability "not only to contribute to knowledge, but also to comprehend, analyze, and evaluate its meaning in the context of an increasingly globalized world" (NASULGC, 2004). The skills that form the foundation of global competence include the ability to work effectively in international settings, awareness of and adaptability to diverse cultures, perceptions, and approaches, familiarity with the major currents of global change and the issues they raise, and the capacity for effective communication across cultural and linguistic boundaries.[3]

If the training of globally competent graduates is accepted as one of the chief goals of our system of higher education, our curricula will have to be redesigned to ensure that outcome.[4] Most of our institutions address the need for global competence by adding a diversity or international course(s) requirement—hardly sufficient to instill global competence in our students—or by offering degrees, minors, or certificates in area or international studies. However, there are major shortcomings in the way both area and international studies are generally carried out. Area studies programs tend to be highly descriptive and too often display an apparent abhorrence toward theorizing. The curriculum frequently resembles a cafeteria-style menu: one selection or course from this shelf followed by selections from various other shelves. Somehow, students are expected miraculously to pull together the disparate pieces into some coherent whole. Area studies fail frequently to take advantage of opportunities to generalize from their rich contextual findings to the broader world. International studies programs (particularly when they fall under the rubric of international relations) too frequently manifest a lack of appreciation for the importance of the local and regional cultural contexts. There are few, if any, attempts at applying the theoretical approaches to the empirical context of the regions. Students too often complete these programs without any competence in a foreign language or any knowledge of or any specific grounding in the culture of a society outside of the United States.

Additionally, our area and international studies programs often fail to give appropriate attention to such crucial steps as 1) integrating relevant learning abroad opportunities into the degree, minor, or certificate, 2) incorporating critical thinking skills of knowledge, comprehension, analysis, synthesis, explanation, evaluation, and extrapolation into the learning experience, 3) assessing or evaluating global competence as an outcome, and 4) aligning the area or international studies concentration to a disciplinary major (e.g., biology, anthropology, history, engineering).

This last point deserves further examination and will likely engender controversy among international educators. We must continually ask ourselves if we are doing a disservice to our undergraduate students by encouraging them to spend their undergraduate years pursuing standalone degrees in area or international studies. In my capacity as the University of Pittsburgh's senior international officer, I often meet with heads of multinational corporations, government offices, and NGOs. When I ask these leaders to describe to me what they look for when making hiring decisions, they invariably begin by reminding me that they hire engineers, chemists, economists—in other words graduates with disciplinary expertise. They go on, however, to inform me of the enormous added value they see in graduates who combine a disciplinary expertise with area and international studies knowledge, foreign language(s), and learning abroad experience. It would appear that the assessment of these leaders is consistent with remarks advanced by Thomas L. Friedman in his recent best-selling book, *The World Is Flat*, and with the findings of the 2006 Committee for Economic Development's (CED) "Education for Global Leadership" report. Friedman suggests that companies of the 21st century will seek to hire graduates with disciplinary expertise, especially in engineering, science, and business. But he notes that these same companies in an effort to come to terms with "glocalization[5]," that is, the interface between global economic tendencies and local cultural values, will require that our disciplinary experts possess a familiarity with regional and local cultures, because without knowledge of these cultures our companies are unlikely to be successful in understanding local consumer tastes. Even within the United States, according to the CED report, there is a great demand for globally competent workers who possess the skills to transcend cultural barriers and work together in global teams. The CED report notes that American affiliates of foreign companies employed more than 5.4 million U.S. workers in 2002. Inadequate cross-cultural training of employees in U.S. companies results annually in an estimated \$2 billion in losses.

I proffer an additional criticism of standalone undergraduate degrees in area and international studies. In my view, if we are to achieve global competence, then we are obliged to internationalize the educational experience no matter the discipline. If we require students to select either a standalone major in area or international studies or a traditional disciplinary degree, students most likely will opt for the latter, and we will be left with a situation where only a small number of students will have exposure to an international studies concentration. Global competence cannot be the preserve of only a few students. It is incumbent upon us as international educators to gain deans' and department chairs' buy-in and participation in designing undergraduate programs that will let their students earn area studies certificates or minors truly linked and relevant to their disciplines, or carefully thought-out disciplinary or international and area studies majors in which both disciplinary expertise and area or international studies are fully integrated. The answer is not area studies or disciplines—it is developing a comprehensive and coherent curriculum that will train our students to become globally competent critical thinkers.

In conclusion, there is no single path or recipe for instilling global competence in our students. Many institutions do not have the resources of the large private and public research universities, and will not be able to implement dramatic changes in the short run. Nonetheless, if we are to achieve global competence at our institutions—and there is no excuse for not striving to attain this overall goal—it will require international educators in consultation with administrators, faculty, staff, and students to design and implement a curriculum that is comprehensive, coherent, and accessible to all students, and has as its principal goal the ability to know, comprehend, analyze, and evaluate information in the context of an increasingly globalized world. If we miss this opportunity, we will surely fail to prepare our graduates for the enormous global challenges of the 21st century.

Vocabulary

abhorrence *n.* 痛恨

affiliate *n.* 分公司

align *v.* 使一致

buy-in *n.* 加入

disparate *adj.* 迥然不同的

disservice *n.* 损害，破坏

empirical *adj.* 以科学实验（经验）为依据的

engender *v.* 引起，产生

extrapolation *n.* 推断

incumbent upon 有责任的，有义务的

instill *v.* 逐渐灌输

interface *n.* 相互作用，相互影响

miraculously *adv.* 奇迹般地

opt for 选择

preserve *n.* 专门领域

proffer *v.* 提出

recipe *n.* 秘诀

rubric *n.* 标题

standalone *adj.* 独立的

synthesis *n.* 综合

transcend *v.* 超越，超过，超出

Notes

1. "internationalized" education

   "'国际化'教育"强调加强国际高等教育的交流合作，积极向各国开放国内教育市场，并充分利用国际教育市场。在教育内容、教育方法上

要适应国际交往和发展的需要，要培养有国际意识、国际交往能力、国际竞争能力的人才。教育国际化是应经济全球化而生，是世界经济一体化进程的必然产物。

2. global citizenship

"世界公民身份"并不是一个特殊的身份，而是一个国家公民身份的延伸。我们所住的地方，不论是在哪里，都是世界的一部分，而且在全球化的浪潮下，国与国之间的互动更为紧密，世界上发生的事情最终都会影响到生活在这个世界的每一个人。因此，我们除了要关心自己国家的事，也要关心世界上发生的事；不仅要尽本国公民的责任，也要了解世界公民应负的责任。

3. The skills that form the foundation of global competence include the ability to work effectively in international settings, awareness of and adaptability to diverse cultures, perceptions, and approaches, familiarity with the major currents of global change and the issues they raise, and the capacity for effective communication across cultural and linguistic boundaries.

本句大意为：组成全球能力基础的技能包括：在国际化环境中有效工作的能力；理解和适应多元文化、看法和方法的能力；熟悉全球主要变化和变化引起的问题的能力；有效的跨文化、跨语言沟通的能力。此句涉及一个非常重要的问题，即全球能力是什么？这里所指的全球能力也就是跨文化能力，全球能力或跨文化能力强调工作中的能力，这种工作中的能力必定基于沟通能力、对于多元文化的意识与适应，以及对有关跨文化知识的熟悉。

4. If the training of globally competent graduates is accepted as one of the chief goals of our system of higher education, our curricula will have to be redesigned to ensure that outcome.

globally competent graduates还可以表达为graduates with global competence，英语应尽量避免重复。本句大意为：如果高等教育体系将"培养具有全球能力的大学毕业生"纳入其主要目标，那么为了确保实现这一目标，我们必须重新修订课程大纲（即通过课程大纲以及教学计划的修改培养具有全球能力的大学毕业生以适应社会发展的需求）。

5. glocalization

"全球本土化"是为了强调当全球化的产品或服务与当地文化相结合时更有可能取得成功而产生的一个词。该词最早出现于20世纪80年代晚期，日本经济学家在《哈佛商业评论》发表的文章中提到了这个词，把全球化（globalization）与地方化（localization）结合在一起，描述了本土条件对全球化的反馈作用。全球本土化强调培养global-local 人才，这种人才能够think globally, act locally，即具有全球思维的能力，能根据不同文化需要调整交流方式与处事方式，这种人才才是全球化的社会所需要的。global-local 人才就是interculturally competent 的人才。globally competent people, global-local people, global citizens, interculturally competent people，这些都表达相同的概念。

Discussion from Intercultural Perspectives

1. Can you list some features of global competence from this article and discuss the importance of each feature?
2. "Without global competence our students will be ill-prepared for global citizenship...and unable to compete successfully in the global marketplace." How do you understand this statement and why is it so important in the United States?
3. Faced with global challenges, what should Chinese education do in developing students' global competence?
4. How do you interpret the concept "think global and act local"? And why is it so essential in today's society?

Intercultural Lens

Cultural Values Behind Education

1. Fill in the chart with appropriate information from Reading 1. An example is given in the first row for your reference.

What cultural differences can we find from the study of Japanese and American children's drawings? What values do these differences reflect? After completing the chart, you may understand the cultural differences in Eastern and Western education. This chart is also designed to help you perceive students' behavior behind those cultural differences in education if you take an intercultural perspective.

	Differences	American Values	Japanese Values
Color of the drawing	A Japanese kid colored the sun red like that in the country's flag, while an American kid colored it yellow.	Prefer differences and innovation, encouraging children to do or think as they can.	Prefer imitation, suggesting harmony and stability so that children would follow their teacher's way.
Seating arrangements			
Roles of the teachers			
How the children began and how they carried out the task			
Teachers' responses when children showed difficulty			
The order of family members			

2. Fill in the chart based on your own understanding of China's education.

Speaking of China's education reform, more and more Chinese people cannot help reflecting on the meaning of Qian Xuesen's question about China's education: Why has no university in China managed to develop a way to cultivate innovative talent? (This question was posed in 2005.) As educators or students, we should have to reflect on this critical issue and think what goes wrong with

China's education and what to be done about it. The following chart is designed for you to think about culture-related issues in our education, and to call on the whole nation to create an innovative environment for the whole society.

You may have your own understanding and even different views for each box, but the following chart may map out the general phenomena we are all facing in China.

Behavior in Class	Cultural Values	Consequences for Society
Passive in learning		
Not encouraged to ask questions		
Not encouraged to respond		
Expect to get the answer from teachers		
Learn for examination		
Teachers are authoritarian		
No personal opinion or perspective		
No participation in seminars		

Intercultural Case Study

Improvement of Chinese Students' Entrepreneurship and Innovation

Several years ago there was an educational conference in Beijing and the three keynote speakers were the chancellor of Oxford University, the president of Yale University and the president of Peking University. All three agreed that Western college graduates had less value to their employers upon graduation than Chinese college graduates.

The reason was simple: Western college students are taught concepts and philosophies along with the ability for creative problem solving. They do not memorize the latest data and information in their major area of study. In contrast, Chinese students memorize all the latest data and solutions to current problems, thus equipping them for immediate problem solving competence upon graduation.

In order to adequately equip the Chinese college graduates with creative problem solving abilities, many colleges carried out education reforms focusing on undergraduate student entrepreneurship and innovation. The reforms cover different aspects such as course content, curriculum system and concrete practice, emphasizing project management which was divided into three types, including entrepreneurship, innovation training and practice programs.

With the implementation of the reforms, the Chinese college graduates become more creative and are more competent for jobs in the new global community.

Analyzing the Issues in the Case

1. Look at this issue from a teaching pedagogical perspective and analyze the cultural differences behind teaching pedagogy.
2. Are there any courses or social practice in your university to promote students' entrepreneurship and innovation? If so, list some.

Learning Culture Through Proverbs

Work in pairs and exchange views on the meanings of the following proverbs, then try to find out their Chinese equivalents if there is any, and discuss the values transmitted.

Proverb 1: *The nail that sticks up gets hammered down.*
Proverb 2: *The squeaky wheel gets the grease.*

Online Research—Using Key Words

For more information and resources, search the Internet with the following key words:

culture and education, critical thinking skills, cultural differences in education, culture and creativity

Unit 10
Intercultural Training

As you have learned so far in this textbook, culture is acquired from birth and the enculturation process continues through direct teaching by parents and teachers and through observation of the society by yourself. The enculturation process is so thorough that it is difficult to believe that other ways of thinking and behaving are normal or appropriate. When you will be living in another country or working with co-workers from other countries, it is helpful to undergo intercultural training. You should learn more about the cultural aspects of yourself and the values, modes of thinking and behavior of other cultures. Intercultural training might be offered in a short seminar, a longer workshop, or through online courses, books and instructional CDs. There are both consulting companies and individuals who offer training to you personally or to a group of workers from your company.

What You Can Learn from This Unit

1. Understand why you should undertake intercultural training for overseas assignments;
2. Understand what you should do if you are assigned to work overseas;
3. Understand different types of training programs and different methods of training;
4. Develop your intercultural competence when working with people from different cultures.

Questions for Intercultural Awareness

1. Have you ever heard of the concept of "intercultural training" in China? How much do you know about intercultural training?
2. Who should receive intercultural training and why?
3. What are the purposes and goals of intercultural training?

What's Wrong?

Knowledge or Competence

Three Americans participated in pre-departure training in the U.S. and then began their overseas assignment with a multinational corporation (MNC) in China. As their work developed, they felt that their pre-departure training helped them understand cultural differences when working with Chinese colleagues. They followed through with some of the behavior they were taught, such as exchanging business cards with both hands, and saying *xie xie* or *ni hao*. But they were starting to realize that there were many work customs they didn't understand or they disliked. As time went on, they felt their tolerance of these differences decreasing. They felt that Chinese colleagues didn't contribute a lot to their work or to the company because they never shared their thoughts or ideas at the meeting. Sometimes Chinese colleagues would look at each other and talk with each other in Chinese, but Americans could not understand what they were saying. Their attitude toward their Chinese colleagues grew more negative, which led to more misinterpretations of behavior. When they arrived in China, they thought that Chinese people were hard-working, but now they concluded that their Chinese colleagues were incompetent. They needed to improve their working efficiency because they often couldn't complete their work on time which resulted in frequent overtime. Eventually, the Americans began to publicly comment on the low work efficiency of their Chinese colleagues. As a result, the American general manager established new management regulations and systems to improve their performance. However, there was no improvement in performance.

One day a department managers' meeting was held to discuss each department's work. When a Chinese manager presented his work report, though it was well prepared, the American general manager could not understand what the Chinese manager was saying. He interrupted the Chinese manager's presentation, stating, "Would you please focus on the main points of your work?" This interruption bewildered the Chinese manager, who thought he was focused on the main part of the work, but the American general manager claimed the work report was too general. The general manager's impatience escalated the tension in the office. The communication problem grew into a series of interpersonal and management conflicts, which affected the daily work of the office.

This scenario presents a common intercultural issue that expatriates are likely to encounter during their international assignments. Let's try to determine some of the causes of the office problems. The first cause lies in pre-departure training itself, whose objective was to help the expatriate workers better understand China as a whole, but not the specific cultural features that can determine people's behavior in the workplace. The second cause could be that the intercultural training did not focus on the intercultural problems that the expatriates and the Chinese staff would encounter in the workplace. Accordingly, both the expatriates and the Chinese were not prepared for the problems they faced. Therefore we can conclude that misunderstood cultural differences lead to intercultural conflicts which in turn results in workplace problems.

To achieve success with superiors, subordinates, co-workers, and clients, we strongly recommend that corporate intercultural training programs address the following issues:

Identify the Origin or Source of Potential Conflicts

Articulate the intercultural nature and cause of an identified operational or management problem. Workplace problems with cultural conflicts at managerial levels could be misleading. From managerial perspectives, resolving a problem manifested in one or more cultural differences may require more than examining management or operational procedures. Expatriate or managerial approaches that do not focus on intercultural (or people-related) issues often account for the failures of international assignments and joint ventures, including international mergers and acquisitions.

HR Screening and Trainee Selection

Training can be most effective when employees selected for overseas assignments are those who are motivated to learn about culture and the workplace or are already interculturally sensitive. This characteristic combined with communication skills is required of all international assignees as an essential competence. In the selection of both expatriates and foreign office national hires, candidate screening and trainee selection significantly impact a company's operational and managerial performance and objectives relative to foreign office operations. Managerial and technical expertise cannot always account for cultural differences as reflected in communication.

As evidenced in this case, for example, if both Chinese and American managers are not selected and trained to identify and adapt to each other's work styles, communication would become impaired. As a result, performance levels either deteriorate or fail to improve.

Align Program Training with Requirements

Once an appropriate employee is selected, a training program can be designed. A formal needs assessment process enables the trainers to shape a program that fits the objectives of the specific job (e.g., marketing, finance, and manufacturing) and the goals of the company. Data can be collected that specifies those areas that have the potential for conflicts within the workplace. Lack of preparation for and understanding of cultural differences is cited often within reports of substandard performance during international assignments. Though management may perform intercultural training prior to assignment, such training could fail to address intangible cause and effect aspects of the related international assignment.

Decisions need to be made about the timeline of training as training options mirror the expatriate cycle. Training can be administered prior to departure from home country, on arrival in host country, periodically throughout the work assignment, prior to departing the host country, and on arrival back to home country. In addition to evaluating the training program, management should consider the ability of trainees to understand how their intercultural training supports their international assignments. Intercultural training should focus on culture-specific knowledge, communication styles and ways of thinking, because all these influence employee behavior. Such training can foster intercultural understandings and skills that can promote workplace productivity as well as social assimilation.

Questions

1. What is the objective of intercultural training: intercultural knowledge or intercultural competence? Why?
2. What might be the cause in intercultural training for the failure in dealing with intercultural misunderstandings in the workplace?

Reading 1

What Are Intercultural Services?

Intercultural services involve the delivery to a client of information and skills that enable individuals to quickly adapt and become professionally productive and interpersonally effective when interacting with local people in an unfamiliar culture, or when interacting anywhere with others from one or more unfamiliar cultures. The "client" may be an individual, a couple, a team or working group, a business unit, or an entire organization.

Intercultural services are now viewed as effective and worthwhile by a large and growing percentage of globalizing business as well as by diplomatic corps, international non-profit organizations, educational institutions, military services, missionary societies, and a wide range of other organizations with a global reach and multicultural clientele.

Origins of the Intercultural Field

The intercultural field arose during the 1950s out of two themes, one broad and public, the other focused and professional.

The broad, public theme arose from the terrible memory of World War II and the Holocaust; there was a concern about hate and violence between religions, ethnic, tribal, national, and cultural groups. Intellectually, this theme is best represented by Gordon Allport's widely praised book, *The Nature of Prejudice* (1954). A second feature of this public theme was the reputation for insensitivity, arrogance, and ineffectiveness being earned by some of the Americans who were delivering economic and scientific expertise in non-Western "developing" nations after the war. Their negative impact was revealed by William Lederer and Eugene Burdick's *The Ugly American* (1958) and similar books.

The focused, professional theme was a growing fascination with group-level differences in values and behavior, and a related interest in the adaptation difficulties faced by a person from one group who enters into sustained contact with another group. This was first addressed by anthropologist Edward T. Hall in *The Silent Language* (1959), which described human differences in nonverbal communication, and in *The Hidden Dimension* (1966), in which Hall dealt more broadly with behavioral differences among groups. This nascent research interest soon encountered a specific, real-world challenge.

The Peace Corps[1]

The U.S. Peace Corps was founded in 1961. Before being shipped abroad, the young Americans who signed up received training—data-rich "area studies" courses delivered by lecturers on college campuses. When these enthusiastic, well-intentioned volunteers finally entered villages abroad, most encountered unexpected difficulties. Many were ineffective; some failed completely. The question posed by officials as well as by the humiliated volunteers was, "Could these failures have been prevented?"

Edward T. Hall and other social scientists who examined these failures soon revealed the root of the problems: differences in values among human groups, and the resulting differences in group-level behavioral patterns. For example, they found that valued ideals such as "progress" and "equal opportunity," which motivated the Peace Corps, were not shared by many on the receiving end of its good works. These differences in values led to disagreements about underlying purposes as well as practical projects.

After the conspicuous failures of the early Peace Corps volunteers, the weight of their employer, the U.S. government, was thrown behind the search for understandable and practical solutions.[2] As more was learned about patterned differences among human groups in values and their resulting behavior, new training content and methods were developed. These were put to use for future Peace Corps volunteers, who greatly improved their abilities to work collaboratively with the recipients of their services.

Thus, the intercultural field was able to get off to a secure start during the 1960s. Established academic disciplines contributed to the field's early development.

Antecedent Disciplines

Cultural anthropology is the intercultural field's principal antecedent discipline. Early anthropologists studied one cultural group at a time—the Trobriand Islanders, for example—in great depth and detail. Some current anthropologists continue this work, while others compare and contrast a variety of cultures in order to gain understanding of group-level behavioral differences. The findings of anthropologists add to the store of knowledge that interculturalists use to improve their content, methods and materials.

Interculturalists focus on what happens when members of one cultural group interact with members of another. Both the motivation for, and the outcome of this research are practical: to discover and to apply techniques for enabling individuals to adapt more readily to an unfamiliar set of values, mindsets, perceptual tendencies, and patterns of behavior. The intercultural field may be thought of as a type of applied anthropology.

Psychology is the intercultural field's another main antecedent discipline. Many interculturalists are initially trained as psychologists. Practicing psychologists are drawn to intercultural research because, in their efforts to treat the ills of the human psyche, they come to recognize the extent to which individuals, as they mature, adopt the behavioral patterns enacted by the members of the groups in which they are being raised. When a psychologist is working with a client from an unfamiliar culture, an understanding of the findings of intercultural research often becomes highly applicable.

Sociology, linguistics, social work, and communication are among the other disciplines that have made significant contributions to the intercultural field.

Two Common Misperceptions

Two misperceptions undermine intercultural services deliverers' ability:

The first is the belief by some people that the intercultural field is merely academic and has nothing to contribute to the rough-and-tumble of business dealings and other features of "real life."[3] This is false. The commitment of interculturalists has always been to develop applied solutions. They are dedicated to better enabling all individuals who interact with a wide variety of others—businesspeople, diplomats, educators, refugees, missionaries, soldiers, exchange students, and the family members of all of these—to adapt and more swiftly become successful at cooperating with people from backgrounds that differ from their own. This means that they will gradually become more effective at leveraging differences, combining strengths, developing synergies, building trust, and thereby accomplishing useful work while also deepening their mutual respect and even their interpersonal warmth.

True, some interculturalists are academics. Their research leads to hypotheses that are tested and revised using the established inductive methods of science. People attain doctorates in intercultural communication; well-known, prestigious universities are among those granting these advanced degrees. Cultural guides such as *Encountering the Chinese* as well as learned books, college texts, research reports and monographs, refereed journals, simulation exercises, and other print and non-print training materials are brought to market by mainstream and minor publishers in the U.S. and abroad. These publications now number in the many tens of thousands. The most complete collection of intercultural publications is housed by the library of the Intercultural Communication Institute in Portland, Oregon (visit www. intercultural.org).

The second common misperception is that intercultural work is merely about etiquette and acting agreeably in polite company.[4] "Give and receive business cards with both hands in Japan," for example. It's true that dos-and-don'ts rules of this type usually are mentioned during the delivery of intercultural services. Emphasized far more, however, are differences among the cultures in question in terms of assumptions, values, habits of perception and thought, and patterns of shared behavior.[5] Dos-and-don'ts rules of etiquette represent only a tiny fraction of what the intercultural field is all about.

Vocabulary

antecedent *adj.* 前提的

conspicuous *adj.* 引人注目的，惹人注意的

enact *v.* 展现，表现

humiliated *adj.* 蒙羞的

leverage *v.* 充分利用

nascent *adj.* 新生的

recipient *n.* 接受者

rough-and-tumble *n.* 激烈的竞争

synergy *n.* 协同作用

Notes

1. The Peace Corps
   和平队成立于1961年，通过志愿者从事社会活动、经济项目推动世界和平和友谊。

2. ...the weight of their employer, the U.S. government, was thrown behind the search for understandable and practical solutions.
   由于早期美国和平队志愿者明显的失败，美国政府利用自身影响帮助寻找易于理解并切实可行的解决方案。他们研究不同群体在价值观及行为方面的差异，用新的内容与方法对志愿者们进行培训。

3. The first is the belief by some people that the intercultural field is merely academic and has nothing to contribute to the rough-and-tumble of business dealings and other features of "real life."
   本句大意为：第一个误区是有的人认为跨文化仅仅是一个学术领域的名词，对于复杂混乱的商业行为及"现实生活"毫无贡献。这种观点是错误的，因为跨文化培训能使人与来自不同文化背景的人更好地合作及互

动，这可以惠及很多来自不同行业的人，比如外交官、商业人士、交换生等等。

4. The second common misperception is that intercultural work is merely about etiquette and acting agreeably in polite company.

本句大意为：第二个误区是认为跨文化的工作仅仅与礼仪、礼貌有关系。因为跨文化服务中有很多行为准则。

5. Emphasized far more, however, are differences among the cultures in question in terms of assumptions, values, habits of perception and thought, and patterns of shared behavior.

本句大意为：但是，进一步来讲，跨文化工作更多是有关于假定、价值观、感知与思维习惯，以及共同行为规范的文化差异问题。而且这些行为准则只是跨文化研究的一小部分。

Discussion from Intercultural Perspectives

1. With your understanding of the "origins of the intercultural field," is it necessary to develop intercultural education in China? Why or why not?
2. "Many were ineffective; some failed completely." What are the causes for their failures?
3. How do you interpret the first misperception and can you predict what people or interculturalists will do for intercultural training?
4. How do you interpret the second misperception?

Reading 2

Working Abroad and Expatriate Adjustment

Individuals living and working temporarily outside their native countries are often referred to as sojourners or expatriates. They are characterized by being relocated overseas by an employer, having a clear work assignment, and planning to return to their homelands. They might be missionaries, teachers or students, soldiers, humanitarian or technical assistants, journalists, or corporate employees. This article will focus on the latter group, arguably the largest and among the most researched. Other categories of international workers excluded from consideration in this article are migrants, domestic guests, and illegal workers.

In this article, I will review the concept of enculturation, the model of cultural transitions and why working in a culture other than one's own needs any attention from social scientists.

Enculturation and Cultural Transition Model

Social scientists have long observed that human development of motor, cognitive, emotional, linguistic, and moral processes included enculturation— learning how to think and behave as a member of one's culture. Enculturation spans all human activities. It involves sleeping habits and eating rules, play activities and playmate choices, relations with family members, methods of formal and informal education, careers options and workplace beliefs, health remedies, leisure activities, emotion, motivation, and nonverbal behavior, to name but a few. In short, almost everything humans think and do and feel. During childhood and adolescence, culture settles on people like a comfortable pair of eyeglasses, shaping their view of the world but unobtrusively. Most individuals are unaware of the role that culture has in shaping their values and subsequent behavior and thoughts, all of which are judged by these in-group members as the correct and natural way.

Moving to another culture adds another layer of disorientation and complexity. Basic life assumptions are shaken; skills for the workplace up-ended. Social scientists have identified a cultural transition cycle for sojourners in which the geographic arc is paralleled by a psychological one. Gradual awareness of differences and subsequent adjustments occur throughout the cycle—pre-departure, settling in, adaptation, preparation to depart, and repatriation.

Anecdotal evidence indicates that the adjustment of employees to their overseas assignment is puzzling and difficult and empirical results confirm the observations, indicating that international employees suffer from substance abuse, marital discord, family disintegration, and career disruptions. Estimates are that 16% to 40% do not complete their overseas assignments and return home prematurely. Admittedly, not all researchers agree with these conclusions. Harzing proposes that the return rate has been exaggerated, perhaps by limiting investigations to American expatriates. Upon examining British and European companies, on average only 5% returned home prematurely.

Once employees return home, it is estimated that 50% are dissatisfied with their re-entry positions and 10% to 25% leave their companies, taking their hard-learned cultural knowledge with them, often joining competitors. Consequently, discontent and tension may characterize the whole of the transition cycle, from pre-departure to return, rippling through the employees, their families, and the organizations.

Employees Abroad

The confluence of local and worldwide developments resulted in social science research focus on corporate employees and their adjustment. First, in the 1960s, American business was transforming itself from an inward domestic focus to an international one and with it, a dramatic increase in the number of Americans relocating to other countries. International mergers like Ford-Volvo and British Petroleum with Amoco, acquisitions such as Chrysler by Daimler-Benz and most recently Volvo by Chinese automaker Geely, and newly created joint-venture projects such as Toshiba and Apple Computer's development of multimedia computer products, increased the intercultural contexts in which business was being transacted. While European countries had conducted business across borders for more than a millennium, in the late 20th century, more business was being conducted across the globe, which necessitated locating employees abroad.

Why would employees subject themselves to these painful adjustments? In some industries, such as oil and gas, staff is routinely posted to overseas sites. Those workers who apply for international postings do so for a range of reasons:

intriguing assignment, increased salary and perquisites (e.g., private schooling for children), travel and adventure, and genuine interest in cultural knowledge. While in the past, international rotations might derail career advancement, now it spurs it. The combination of enhanced technical expertise and intercultural learning has made international assignment *de rigueur* for corporate employees seeking advancement.[1] International assignments also can be construed as symbolic capital and current research has been examining the return on the investment of expatriation as well as the variables that affect cultural adjustment.[2]

A second historic factor was the establishment of the U.S. Peace Corps in 1961 and with it, an interest in assisting the cultural adaptation of the hundreds of young adults being sent to developing countries to offer humanitarian and technical assistance. Techniques were designed to educate and train departing volunteers to cope with transition challenges and intercultural work situations.

One final thought: Some have argued that with increased globalization comes cultural homogenization and the fading of cultural differences between countries. The argument continues that as more international business personnel speak English, are educated in the West, and work for international enterprises, business processes, procedures, and structures have become standardized, which in turn further diminishes the influence of culture on workplace beliefs and behavior. It could be concluded that the urgency to prepare employees to live and work abroad has lessened. However, recent studies have indicated that cultural variability in the workplace has been amplified, not weakened with globalization, and that "workways" remain "deeply colored by the palette of historical, ideological, and socio-cultural influences."[3] Further, Berry suggests that globalization has resulted in a range of individual outcomes in addition to the often-assumed assimilation into the host culture and abandonment of home culture. More likely outcomes of globalization include the maintenance of both home and host cultures (integration) or separation from the host culture resulting in a revitalization of the home culture identity.

Vocabulary

adolescence *n.* 青春期

anecdotal *adj.* 轶事的，趣闻的

confluence *n.* 同时发生，会集

construe *v.* 将……理解为

derail *v.* 破坏，干扰

disorientation *n.* 迷惑，头脑混乱

enculturation *n.* 文化适应

homogenization *n.* 同质化

missionary *n.* 传教士

palette *n.* 调色板

perquisite *n.* 额外收入，津贴

prematurely *adv.* 提前

unobtrusively *adv.* 不明显的

Notes

1. The combination of enhanced technical expertise and intercultural learning has made international assignment *de rigueur* for corporate employees seeking advancement.

   把提高专业技能与学习跨文化知识相结合，成为这些跨国企业员工寻求晋升的一种有效方式。因为只掌握先进技术是不够的，只有与跨文化知识相结合，才知道如何将产品向当地宣传。

2. International assignments also can be construed as symbolic capital and current research has been examining the return on the investment of expatriation as well as the variables that affect cultural adjustment.

   本句大意为：外派人员还可以被理解为象征性资本。近期有些研究正在审查移居国外投资的回报率以及影响文化适应的变量。

3. …recent studies have indicated that cultural variability in the workplace has been amplified, not weakened with globalization, and that "workways" remain "deeply colored by the palette of historical, ideological, and socio-cultural influences."

有的人也许认为随着全球化的发展，不同文化间的文化差异会逐渐消失，还有人认为，由于人们都在说英语、接受西方教育的人越来越多，而且在跨国企业中操作越来越规范化，所以文化的影响正在逐渐减少。但是，事实却恰恰相反，随着全球化的发展，文化的多样性逐渐增加而非减少，人们的工作方式仍然受到历史、思想和社会文化因素的深刻影响。

Discussion from Intercultural Perspectives

1. What characterizes an expatriate? How do their experiences differ from those of the immigrants or refugees?

2. Why do we usually become aware of the cultural aspects of who we are when we begin interacting with people from other cultures? Why don't we have cultural awareness before that time?

3. Put yourself in the shoes of a business expatriate. Why would you return home prior to the conclusion of your assignment? Why might you have difficulty re-adjusting to your home city and job?

4. Some people have said that "...as more international business personnel speak English, are educated in the West, and work for international enterprises, business processes, procedures, and structures have become standardized, which in turn further diminishes the influence of culture on workplace beliefs and behavior." Do you believe that the world is becoming homogeneous or cultures are still retaining their unique aspects?

Intercultural Lens

Initiating Intercultural Training

With an increasing contact among people from different cultures, there is a growing demand for both individuals and corporate professionals to engage in intercultural communication for personal and business reasons. More individuals and companies are finding themselves encountering differences in everything from interpersonal communication to perception and values, and have realized that cultural differences are the leading barriers to their understanding of other people and to their successful business dealings.

In order to survive or complete your assignment, you need to acquire intercultural awareness and skills most effectively through intercultural training programs so that you can understand the differences and adapt smoothly to a new cultural environment.

Content of Training

Intercultural training provides people with insight to gain knowledge of a specific culture that contrasts with their own, to increase awareness of different cultures and their influence on people's behavior, and to acquire skills to manage cultural conflicts in intercultural communication. Intercultural training can achieve different objectives, depending on the demands of people and organizations. To be most effective and achieve trainee competence, intercultural training should be designed to teach knowledge of the culture-specific and culture-general and to develop trainees' communication skills and performance competences. However, we notice that a significant portion of training programs focus primarily on the host culture knowledge and cultural awareness. Trainees may discover later that their intercultural training could not help them manage cultural conflicts they are facing in the workplace. Then they begin to doubt the value and effectiveness of such training. An appropriate intercultural training program should cover the following aspects:

Host Culture Training Host culture training focuses on acquiring knowledge of the host country of your work assignment. This is very important for your life and work. This training should include culture-general and culture-specific:

Culture-general introduces trainees to the definitions of culture, how culture is transmitted, and the role of culture in influencing work relationships and work tasks (marketing, human resources management, operations, health care, education, etc.). It summarizes basic facts of the host country such as its politics, history, economics, society, habits, customs and life styles, thus providing the overall framework for thinking about the role of culture in everyday life and work.

Culture-specific teaches about the basic elements of the society such as norms and values, ways of thinking and communication styles and how these elements concretely shape behavior and actions. These contents will help you understand the small details of the host society, thus decreasing intercultural misunderstandings. By learning culture-specific information, trainees can analyze the hidden cultural barriers and take appropriate actions.

Cultural Adaptation Training Cultural adaptation training focuses on the cultural transition cycle which traces the psychological adjustment of sojourners from pre-departure from home country to arrival in the host society to re-entry back home. Such training aims to introduce the vocabulary needed to discuss the transition process and the skills needed to cope with the emotional roller-coaster which is part of the adaptation process. Trainees would learn about the concept of culture shock and its relationship to physiological stress. Following the training, participants should have a smoother adjustment period, having learned to recognize their place in the adjustment cycle and path of adaptation. Adaptation training should include the following:

- stages of the cultural transition cycle;
- emotional reactions at each stage;
- thorough understanding of the psychological and physiological aspects of culture shock;
- review of the symptoms of culture shock;
- introduction to diversity of coping mechanisms to lower culture shock;
- ways to improve interpersonal relations by adapting behavior;

- understanding of the reverse sojourn and similarities and differences with adjusting back to the home country.

Communication Skill Training Communication skill training focuses on actual behavior, both verbal and nonverbal. Differences in thinking and communication are the main obstacles to intercultural communication, especially in the workplaces. These differences are evident in writing, speaking, discussions, and arguments. This training covers the following:

- learn how to write and speak so that the messages sent by the sojourner are received and interpreted the same way by the host country colleagues;
- learn to use and interpret facial expressions, gesture, posture, interpersonal distancing, and eye contact in a culturally-appropriate way;
- learn to express emotion in ways similar to the host country;
- learn to recognize conflicts before they escalate, to avoid them or to approach them in a goal-oriented manner;
- learn how much information to reveal about oneself and what appropriate topics of conversation among co-workers are;
- learn the appropriate use of space within the office or worksite. (How to configure an office, what are low- and high-status space configurations?)

Task-Focused Intercultural Training Following host-culture training, cultural adaptation training, and communication skill training, sojourners begin to face specific job-related tasks. This might include intercultural negotiation, intercultural teamwork building, cultural synergy building, hiring and evaluating staff, marketing products and services, and worker motivation or management. In this case additional half-day or one-day tailored training is required, which should include the following:

- understand different negotiation strategies and different negotiation styles;
- understand the needs and expectations of employees from different countries;
- develop manager's global mindset and global leadership;
- understand cultural differences in intercultural team building;
- develop intercultural competence to approach intercultural issues.

To achieve training effectiveness, there are some important factors that should not be overlooked. First and most critical is that training should be tailored to the requirement of trainees for their specific tasks. This can be accomplished by conducting a formal needs assessment prior to the design and delivery of the training workshop or materials. More often than not trainees make a request for culture training before their departure or after their arrival in their host country, but they would not be specific in proposing content for such training. That is understandable because most sojourners are not aware of the broad effects of culture or cannot articulate their needs. Following training, participants report that while their factual knowledge of the host culture has increased, they are not able to utilize that knowledge when they encounter cultural differences in their workplace. Thus, training should have a practical and skills-based component, enabling trainees to practice their intercultural skills in workplace simulations.

The second important element is the length of training. Intercultural training can range from a half-day to a two-day training or more, depending on the needs of individuals and organizations for their specific assignments. Such training can only begin to prepare trainees for intercultural sensitivity and adjustment to a new cultural environment. However, it will not produce a trainee with well-practiced communication skills and intercultural competence. For those expatriates we would suggest a program of continuous training: two-day training prior to departure from home, post-arrival training, and periodic coaching as trainees face new intercultural situations. For those who study abroad, we suggest, at a minimum, a one-day pre-departure training that combines elements of culture-general, culture-specific, and cultural adaptation. Ideally, the information would be spread over a semester taught as a cultural communication course. This should be required for all departing students. For sojourners engaged in a specific task like business negotiation, though they may not stay for long, they would benefit from a several-day training in which they would learn the cultural concepts and skills behind negotiation and practice their skills by participating in negotiation simulations. With practice and feedback, the trainees will be better prepared for the real business environment.

When to Conduct Intercultural Training

Pre-Departure Training Intercultural training is an essential step to an expatriate assignment, and pre-departure training can increase the chances of your assignment success and better job performance in the workplace, for pre-departure training will assist you to live and work more harmoniously and effectively in your new environment. Pre-departure training can also prepare you to manage cultural conflicts you would encounter in the new environment so that you could take appropriate strategies to approach these issues. For students intending to do an internship or study abroad, pre-departure intercultural training is a must as it can fully prepare you for cultural differences you would encounter when you start your life, study or work over there. If you do or think as you do in your home country, you would be in trouble.

There are still many companies that do not consider the necessity of conducting pre-departure training for expatriates or that make training workshops optional to their employees. Managers often assume that business is conducted the same way everywhere in the world or that their sophisticated and smart employees will learn quickly whatever minor differences exist. However, they would regret the lack of employee preparation once they face cultural conflicts in their business. They would pay a big price for not making a small investment in their employees' knowledge and performance.

Post-Arrival Training Post-arrival training takes place in the first few weeks after arrival. This training is designed to prepare the employees with the readiness to get over the culture shock period followed by more specific understanding of different ways of thinking and communication. Post-arrival training can be designed according to the cultural differences that have been perceived in the workplace, and then solutions to these problems can be worked out. We suggest that intercultural training should be targeted not only to the foreign employees or managers, but also to the local employees and managers who need to work closely with their international co-workers. In the meantime they should attend the training and participate in the discussions to achieve the most effective training.

Remember, intercultural training is suddenly considered when intercultural conflicts occur. Though it is not too late, it takes more time and effort to achieve effectiveness after misunderstandings and tensions have arisen.

Who Needs Intercultural Training

Who needs intercultural training and why intercultural training is imperative? In fact, this is an obvious and easy question to answer if you look at your community, your colleagues in the office and your friends. No matter whether you are a government official, or an employee in a business organization, your workplace is made up of people from many different ethnic and cultural backgrounds. If you are a university student, you may attend a study abroad program, or work as an intern in another country. If you are a business person, your company may expand its business into the world market, and you may work as an expatriate. All of these opportunities are possible now, which highlights the necessity for intercultural communication. In short, since you live or work in this diverse society, you have to deal with cultural differences or cultural conflicts. This new way of life presents challenges if you are not prepared. Intercultural training is critical for you to become a successful communicator in a diverse environment at home and abroad, and for you to achieve intercultural competence to fulfill your specific career goals and tasks. In short, intercultural competence is a required competence for all professionals in the 21st century, and intercultural training is the most effective method to achieve intercultural competence.

Intercultural Case Study

Why They Did Not Understand Each Other

A Chinese manager was in charge of the budget for a building construction project. According to the meeting schedule, he was supposed to present his budget to the American general manager for approval. At the meeting he presented his team's work on their survey and worked out the total budget for the construction of the company's workshop and office building. After his presentation the general manager asked how the total budget came out.

He replied with a detailed account and was proud of his carefully-thought-out budget assessment for this large project. He explained several times to the general manager that he had had oversight of many large and small projects in the past and the budget assessment for this project was fully supported by his experience. However, his proposal was not convincing to the American general manager and then he was asked to explain again how the budget was constructed. Though the Chinese manager tried hard to convince the general manager that his budget was realistic, the general manager kept asking how the budget was determined. The result was a tense and uncomfortable situation in which the Chinese manager lost face. The budget meeting lasted the whole day, but they had not reached any conclusion. What's worse, their discussion resulted in interpersonal conflicts.

Analyzing the Issues in the Case

1. What is the cultural point for their conflict? How do the American and Chinese managers perceive each other's argument?
2. What the Chinese manager did reflects Chinese vague way of presenting arguments, while the American general manager would only be convinced by the specific way to work out this budget proposal. What suggestions do you have for the Chinese manager?

Learning Culture Through Proverbs

Work in pairs and exchange views on the meanings of the following proverbs, then try to find out their Chinese equivalents if there is any, and discuss the values transmitted.

Proverb 1: *A stitch in time saves nine.*
Proverb 2: *Once bitten, twice shy.*

Online Research—Using Key Words

For more information and resources, search the Internet with the following key words:

intercultural services, intercultural training, intercultural coaching, intercultural consulting, relocation services

Unit 11
Intercultural Business Communication

You might assume that if you know the appropriate ways to communicate in a business setting, whether face-to-face or by electronic methods, you will succeed wherever you work. Actually, intercultural business communication (IBC) is very different from business communication or intercultural communication. You need to learn about the intercultural model to develop a synergistic or hybrid culture that can bridge two cultural patterns of doing business. Several cases of international mergers or acquisitions will be analyzed to deepen your understanding of the cultural elements central to effective intercultural partnerships.

What You Can Learn from This Unit

1. Understand the role of culture in business communication;
2. Know what intercultural business communication is and what it can do in today's global business world.
3. Tell the difference between intercultural communication and intercultural business communication;
4. Be aware that cultural differences may present obstacles in business communication;

Questions for Intercultural Awareness

1. In today's increasingly global business world, more and more foreign countries have set up joint ventures or multinational corporations in China. What challenges might these companies encounter and why do you think so?
2. How are you prepared for those challenges if you intend to work in those companies?
3. Some people say a mastery of foreign languages can resolve all the problems that may occur in intercultural working environment. What's your opinion?

What's Wrong?

Geely-Volvo Acquisition

Zhejiang Geely Holdings Group Co., Ltd. and Ford Motor Co. signed an acquisition deal on March 28, 2010 and on August, 2010 Geely took 100% ownership of Volvo, after paying Ford $1.3 billion. Li Shufu, Geely's chairman, has described the deal as the "poor boy from the countryside" (Geely) marrying the "rich girl from the city" (Volvo). When interviewed by *21st Century Business Herald* about the Geely acquisition of Volvo, author Zhuang described the deal as a cross-cultural marriage, with Li, Geely's chairman, and Stefan Jacoby, Volvo's CEO, sharing the same bed, but having different dreams for the future of Volvo. They also have different cultural views: Li is Chinese from Zhejiang province and founder of Geely Automobile; Jacoby is a German with a long career as a Volkswagen executive including a stint in Asia and the U.S. Two years after the acquisition, the newlyweds' life was fraught with intercultural problems which are now surfacing in their daily life.

On November 10, 2010, Li Shufu met visiting Swedish King Carl XVI Gustaf and Swedish scientists and businessmen in Zhejiang's capital Hangzhou, where Geely is based. Li answered questions concerning Volvo's future and whether it would cause job losses in Sweden. When asked by King Carl XVI Gustaf how Geely would guarantee that Volvo's standards would not be undermined after Geely's acquisition, Li said, "We are not just keeping Volvo's standards, but helping Volvo regain its past glory and surpass Mercedes-Benz and BMW." Li also presented a different concept of Volvo's future cars. He envisioned Volvo building big cars rather than small cars which would be tailored to the Chinese consumers in part because many of Volvo's concepts are too advanced and not entirely suitable for the Chinese market.

King Carl XVI Gustaf also asked whether three new manufacturing bases to be set up in China would push Swedish suppliers out of business. Li replied that the Swedish people had nothing to worry about since Geely follows a localized strategy, which means that all Volvo cars sold in Europe will be researched, developed and manufactured in Europe, so European supplies would not be affected. In addition, Volvo plans to set up plants in three Chinese cities: southwest China's Chengdu, east China's metropolis Shanghai and northeast China's Daqing.

On November 13, 2010, author Zhuang made a presentation to the Geely-Volvo delegation in Shanghai on the cultural integration after the Geely-Volvo acquisition. He discussed what Geely and Volvo should do next. In the following pages, we'll share what the author has discovered since the acquisition deal closed and what his perspective is into its solution.

Onion Model

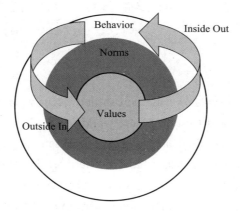

Outside-In Model We can see the inner layer only after peeling off one layer after another, eventually arriving at the core influence on individuals' thinking—their values. The implication is that by observing people's behavior and analyzing why they act the way they do, we can perceive societal norms and values.

Inside-Out Model The Onion Model is bi-directional. When we understand the values and norms of a culture, we can gain insight into and predict people's behavior, including cognitive styles and communication patterns. Knowledge of these can help us to make appropriate interpretations of the behavior of a cultural-different person and avoid some misunderstandings. If misunderstandings have occurred, knowledge of values and norms can assist us in resolving them—they

225

serve as the keys to understanding.

Intercultural Model

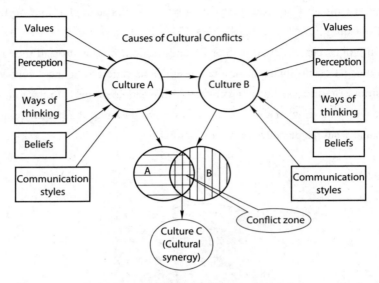

This diagram shows how cultural conflicts occur when people from two cultures (Culture A and Culture B) are working together, for example, in a Sino-U.S. company. Conflicts are inevitable because each culture has its own patterns that influence business relations. The intersection of Culture A and Culture B can be defined as a conflict zone whereby co-workers disagree on tactics, strategies and management styles. However, the Intercultural Model suggests that a third hybrid culture, Culture C, be developed as a synergistic solution. A road map can be created by the two cultural partners in which mutually-agreed upon goals and behavior develop common ground and result in diminished conflict.

Application of the Onion Model and the Intercultural Model to the Geely-Volvo Acquisition

Let's apply both the Onion Model and the Intercultural Model to the Geely-Volvo acquisition. What have Li Shufu, chairman of Geely and Stefan Jacoby, CEO of Volvo said that may form the basis of misunderstanding and conflict?

Our analysis reveals four categories of intercultural problems:

Decision Making Li made the decision right after the acquisition that Volvo would build three manufacturing plants in China. His announcement was made public without consulting the management team. When asked by the media for his comments, Jacoby openly and directly disagreed with Li and stated that any decision should get approval from the management team.

Strategic Vision Li claimed that Volvo should expand its production to grow its market share quickly, believing that he knows the Chinese market best. Jacoby replied that they need to be cautious in its expansion, believing that he has more experience with the product.

Product Vision Li envisioned the design and manufacture of large-sized cars, because Chinese consumers like big cars. Jacoby believed small-sized cars would be better because a smaller car would have low carbon emission and less energy consumption, a long-time goal of Volvo.

Communication Misunderstandings When asked by King Carl XVI Gustaf how Geely would guarantee that Volvo's standards would not be undermined following the Geely acquisition, Li said, "We are not just keeping Volvo's standards, but helping Volvo regain its past glory and surpass Mercedes-Benz and BMW." However, the King did not understand what Li meant, thinking why Li was not giving a reply as he expected Li to tell him how he was doing now rather than his determination.

If we analyze these four categories of problems from a managerial perspective, it is difficult to resolve their disputes as each of them believes he is right in thought and action and each would find it hard to persuade the other to change his mind. Thus, conflicts occur. However, when these problems are analyzed from intercultural perspectives, that is, to discern the norms and values that underlie their ideas and positions in vision and in daily management, we can perceive cultural factors behind those business problems. The following are proposed solutions for the four categories of intercultural problems mentioned above:

Solution for Decision Making Li is using a common Chinese method of management. He has adopted a hierarchical posture whereby as chairman of the board his authority is unquestioned and therefore, consultation with other members of the management team is unnecessary. He has been in the senior position as founder and president of Geely for many years. Jacoby, however, expects to be consulted both because he is CEO and because he is accustomed to a more inclusive management style. The solution to this issue lies in mutual and frequent communication between the chairman and the CEO. This may involve Li presenting his rationale as to why it is so important for Volvo to set up three manufacturing bases in China.

Solution for Strategic Vision Li desires to make a profit quickly as he has made an enormous financial commitment to acquire Volvo. He sees the path to profitability as expansion of production. Otherwise the expenses of running Volvo would overtake the revenues. But Jacoby thinks otherwise. He believes that by working closely with the Volvo senior management team to slowly promote brand image followed by increased production, revenues and expenses will be balanced. To solve this problem, Li and Jacoby need to spend time trying to understand the rationale behind each other's views and the role of management in shaping strategic planning. The key is to communicate with each other about their basic management philosophies and business models.

Solution for Product Vision Both Li and Jacoby are correct in their views regarding the Chinese customers' preference for big cars and the environmental impact of small-sized cars with low carbon emission and less energy consumption. The point for them is to find the balance between two views, therefore effective communication is the only way out so that each will find that the view held by the other is also right. Perhaps the synergetic path is to produce large cars initially to please the consumers while embarking on an advertising campaign to persuade the consumers that smart people care about the environment and they should also purchase "green" cars.

Solution for Communication Misunderstandings Li's reply to King Carl XVI Gustaf's concerns reflects the Chinese indirect way of communication. The King expected Li to be direct and specific by commenting on how and what he would do to maintain Volvo's high standards. Upon hearing Li's reply, the King was shocked, and didn't ask anything further, thinking Li was unwilling to give an answer or he was trying to hide something. Thus the King and his delegation members had a negative image about Li, but Li and all his Chinese staff thought his answer reflected Chinese people's confidence and pride. On the following day when the author met with the Volvo management team, he made a presentation to them. He analyzed the recent conversation between the King and Li from an intercultural perspective, which clarified their doubts over Li's reply and helped them understand typical Chinese communication patterns and styles. Potential conflict was reduced and intercultural awareness was heightened.

All in all, what has surfaced in these early days of the Geely-Volvo acquisition are normal business-related issues common to any acquisition but complicated by the cultural rationale behind each party's behavior and way of thinking. The solution to their disputes is linked to their understanding of each other's cultural rationale. This includes the role of the leader, the relationship between superiors and subordinates, profitability timetables, the appropriate way to respond to questions, and understanding of local consumers. Any effort to resolve the business conflicts cannot be limited to standard managerial solutions but intercultural perspectives which highlight cultural factors behind business problems and the development of synergistic, hybrid solutions.

This is what intercultural business communication aims to do in its study and application.

Discussion

1. What went wrong in the early days of the acquisition? Can you identify the seeds of intercultural conflicts?
2. Are these problems management related or interculturally related? Why do you think so?
3. Discuss the proposed solutions to their problems.

Reading 1

The Theoretical Foundation for Intercultural Business Communication: A Conceptual Model (Part 1)

A theoretical framework of intercultural business communication must include business as an essential variable where business is not just used to illustrate a point, but where business as an organization or activity becomes an integral part of the theory. As the term implies, "intercultural business communication" deals with intercultural issues, communication, and business.[1] It is the communication among individuals or groups from different cultural backgrounds in a business environment. As such it has its own identity separate from business communication, intercultural communication, and international business. Some authors use the term "international business communication," some use "intercultural communication." In this article I will use the term "intercultural business communication" for intercultural business communication within and between countries.

We can build on the research in intercultural business and intercultural communication to model the intercultural business communication process.

How Can We Model the IBC Process?

The proposed model in Figure 1 combines intercultural strategy, communication strategy, and business strategy. The number of variables that influence each one of the strategies is huge. This model does not claim to provide an exhaustive list of all the variables but only a sample of some of the most important ones.

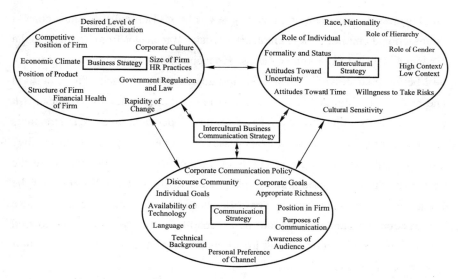

Figure 1 Intercultural Business Communication: A Conceptual Model

How Does Business Strategy Contribute to IBC?

Some may ask, what difference does it make whether we discuss intercultural communication or intercultural business communication? Why does business need to be a variable of similar weight to culture and communication? The answer is that intercultural business communication does not take place in a vacuum but in a business context. Suchan makes the point that business communication must take into account the specific business context; the same is true for intercultural business communication.

I argue that intercultural business communication is more than the sum of its parts,[2] that the process actually results in a new synergy and presents a new construct. When the business or corporation is on the sidelines of the intercultural communication process, it is difficult to reach the synergy resulting out of the interaction of the three variables. As Perkins maintains, most research on intercultural business communication concentrates on language and cultural differences and typically provides only a superficial view of a "mechanized and depersonalized Modern Corporation."

When two businesspeople from two different cultures interact, they bring their own backgrounds with them, but they also step outside their own cultural and business environment and create a new context. Bell calls this new context "transactional culture." For example, if a financial manager from Thailand and a financial manager from France discuss financing options of a joint venture, they will be more successful if they have an understanding of each other's cultural and business background. They need to find out the tolerance for financial risk that each side is willing to take. They also must understand investment structures in each country. For example, are businesses practicing equity or debt financing? Do individual investors prefer bonds or stocks? However, understanding the other side does not automatically bring success. Even the willingness of the French manager to conform to Thai rules does not solve the problem because the practices of Thailand may not be acceptable in France. They need to find a new way—a transactional culture—that is acceptable to both parties, their governments, cultures, and corporations.

In this effort, businesspeople must understand the impact of key organizational concepts such as hiring practices, promotion policies, decision making, competitive environment, financial regulations, business laws, and governmental requirements on the intercultural business communication process. They must also understand the relationship of business and culture in a particular environment. What is the social status of business? What influence does culture have on organizational structures? In addition, in the intercultural business communication process, the participants also bring with them their own corporate cultures. Out of all of these parts, the new transactional culture emerges. The result is a complex system of layers of culture, communication, and business. It would be impossible to tear out the business and simply substitute another context such as medicine or religion.

The difference between intercultural communication and intercultural business communication is not just that the latter takes place in a business.[3] In intercultural business communication the business strategies, goals, objectives, and practices become an integral part of the communication process and help create a new environment out of the synergy of culture, communication, and business.

As the following example illustrates, knowledge in intercultural communication is a precondition for successful intercultural business communication, but by itself it is not enough. A Peace Corps volunteer who has spent two years in Colombia has gained valuable insights into parts of Colombian culture. She is able to adapt to a more high-context communication approach, is able to accept different time orientations, and has learned to focus on the group rather than the individual.

While all of this insight is helpful in conducting business, it is not enough. In addition to the general culture, she now needs to also be aware of the business culture and business environment in Colombia. She needs to be able to relate the business objectives of a firm to cultural behavior, and she needs to be able to compare and reconcile different business approaches in Colombia, her native culture, and the rest of the world. She needs to know how the organizational structure of a firm will influence the development of business strategies, the flow of information, and the decision-making process. In short, she needs to understand the business context in which she will practice intercultural business communication. Her understanding of the business environment in her own background and in Colombia will help her develop an approach to intercultural business communication that draws on her background in culture, communication and business. The business knowledge is not merely added to intercultural communication; it is instrumental in developing a transactional culture of intercultural business communication.

How Does Intercultural Strategy Contribute to IBC?

Businesspeople need to take into account the national culture, the general business culture, and the specific corporate culture. In addition, they must be aware of individual communication styles. After all, cultures do not communicate with each other; individuals do.[4] Chinese culture cannot talk to Japanese culture except through the discourse of individual Chinese and individual Japanese people. The focus on individuals also helps avoid the traditional tendency to talk about the categorical Chinese, Japanese, or Arab audience. While a simplistic view of culture easily leads to stereotyping, research supports the assumption that a majority from a particular culture share certain cultural characteristics. For example, as a general rule, Japanese culture is more group-oriented than is U.S. culture. Without any generalizations, meaningful intercultural business communication would become even more difficult than it is already. To concentrate only on the individual and approach every intercultural communication situation from ground zero would be exhausting and not very productive.

We need to be aware that businesspeople are members of several cultures. They are tied to their corporate culture, the industry culture, the general business culture, and their national culture. A multinational company may have a very strong corporate culture that may negate some of the traditional cultural characteristics of a subsidiary country. For example, a Mexican employee of Procter & Gamble may have completely accepted a corporate culture of timeliness and punctuality that, at least in the work setting, is replacing the traditional polychronic time orientation of Mexican culture. In the international business culture, managers have many interests and reference points in common, and thus they converse easily among themselves.

Based on Hall, Hofstede, Victor, Beamer, and Trompenaars, the values that will influence the cultural strategy are the individual, the role of hierarchy, attitudes toward formality, high context versus low context orientation, time orientation, attitudes toward risk and uncertainty, the relationship of individuals to the universe, and feelings of a culture's own importance as expressed in the self-reference criterion. But this strategy will always take place in the business context. Just as people from different cultures create a transactional culture for their business strategy, they create a transactional culture for the intercultural strategy.

Vocabulary

as such　就其本身而论
depersonalized *adj.*　去个性化的
equity *n.*　股票
from ground zero　从零开始
self-reference *n.*　自我参考
variable *n.*　可变因素

Notes

1. As the term implies, "intercultural business communication" deals with

intercultural issues, communication, and business.

本句大意为：顾名思义，跨文化商务沟通主要解决跨文化问题、沟通问题，以及商务问题。它不同于跨文化沟通、商务沟通，以及跨文化商务。它是来自不同文化背景的个体或团体在商务环境中的沟通与交流。

2. ...intercultural business communication is more than the sum of its parts...

跨文化商务沟通不仅仅是跨文化、商务与沟通这三个部分的简单概括，而是这三个元素相融合产生的新的概念。它是指在商务环境中发生的跨文化沟通，所以应该融合到跨文化沟通的过程中去，如果把商务从跨文化沟通过程中区别出来，很难达到三者的协调及平衡。

3. The difference between intercultural communication and intercultural business communication is not just that the latter takes place in a business.

本句大意为：跨文化沟通与跨文化商务沟通的区别不仅仅在于后者发生在商务场合。在跨文化商务沟通中，需将商业目标、策略以及实践融入到沟通中，在文化、沟通及商务三者的共同作用下产生一个新的环境。

4. After all, cultures do not communicate with each other; individuals do.

商务人士需要考虑民族文化、一般商业文化，以及具体的企业文化。除此之外，他们还必须意识到个人的沟通方式。文化不会互相交流，但是个人会。个人是文化的载体。比如，只有在中国人与日本人对话沟通的时候，才可体现出中国文化与日本文化的交流。注重分析个人差异可以避免将各国人范畴化。

Discussion from Intercultural Perspectives

1. What does the field of intercultural business communication deal with?
2. What is the difference between intercultural communication and intercultural business communication?
3. When you study intercultural business communication, what is the objective of your study? To know the theories, the content, the methods, or something else?

Reading 2

The Theoretical Foundation for Intercultural Business Communication: A Conceptual Model (Part 2)

How Does Communication Strategy Contribute to IBC?

In their comprehensive review of intercultural business communication research Limaye and Victor make the point that most communication models are linear process models depicting a sender who sends a message to a receiver who then provides feedback to the sender. Furthermore, most of these models are developed by Westerners and rely on Western cognitive frames. Yet, many cultures have their own different cognitive frames which determine what is considered logical and rational in their cultures.

As a result, people think differently, approach business problems differently, and communicate differently. In order to integrate these differences into intercultural business communication, the model needs to break away from the Western approach and incorporate different mind-sets and cultural orientations.[1]

Over the last few years, several researchers in intercultural business communication have worked on a system approach to communication that is more culture neutral. For example, Beamer developed an approach to intercultural business communication competence that is applicable to most intercultural communication situations, but it is not focused on business.[2]

Yan also criticizes the traditional Western-based models and maintains that they distort the communication process by placing one of the participants, most likely the sender, in a dominant role. She prefers a model where sender and receiver work together, and she offers a consensus approach as an alternative to the process models. While her criticism brings out some of the shortcomings of the process models, I believe that the working together and the cooperation of sender and receiver and the process models are not mutually exclusive.

In Yan's view, the process approach is unethical because it is by definition manipulative. However, one can argue that if the goal is the building of consensus, then listening, cooperation, and discussion of common goals are as important in the process approach as in consensus approach.

Leiniger ties together four components in her model: global mission, global management strategies, international communication approaches, and individual rhetorical strategies. The model also shows the relationship among the four variables. It emphasizes the business context. All communication is clearly tied to global company strategies. By getting away from the traditional process approach and concentrating on a more systemic approach to communication, Leiniger's model seems to overcome some of the problems that Limaye and Victor and Yan criticize as inherent in all process models.

At the top of her model is the global mission which determines global strategies, which determine international communication approaches, which then determine individual rhetorical strategies. The model illustrates how a given company determines its intercultural business communication strategy, but it does not show us what happens when people from different cultures and different businesses communicate. When we apply her model to two businesspeople or two groups from different cultures, her model helps us determine what each side does, but it does not establish the link or interaction.

Communication strategy is influenced by corporate communication policies and personal preferences. For example, a policy that limits all memos to one page influences all written communication in the firm regardless of whether that communication is domestic or international. A communication strategy is also influenced by the availability of technology and the functional expertise of the communicator. Furthermore, people have personal preferences for the use of communication channels; some may prefer the telephone to memos.

Language also influences communication strategies. People who do business in a foreign language bring many of their own cognitive frames to the communication; therefore, the view that non-native speakers writing in English ought to master its logic ignores the cultural complexity of the language. If the business partners do not speak a common language, the entire intercultural business communication approach will be influenced by the dynamics of interpreters.

Just as the study of culture is not an end in itself, so communication is not an end in itself. In intercultural business communication the communication has a business purpose. The channels, levels of formality, use of technology, content and style of delivery are influenced by cultural and business considerations. The objectives of the business, the level of internationalization, the structure of the organization will help determine the intercultural business communication strategy. A communication strategy that does not take the specific business context into consideration will not be effective.

The proposed model pictures a dynamic interaction among the three variables that shape intercultural business communication. Changes in one area will affect not just the strategy in that area but also the strategies in the other two; ultimately any change will also have an impact on intercultural business communication.

How Does the Proposed Model Help Us Focus IBC Research

Studies in this category are relatively new, but they show that intercultural business communication is developing its own identity. The three studies I will discuss are rather different, but all three address the intercultural strategy, business strategy, and communication strategy. The extent of the synthesis into intercultural business communication varies, but it is addressed.

Forman presents a case study of Euro Disney. In exploring some of the major intercutural communication problems that Disney faced when establishing its park in France, she addresses the intercultural, the communication, and the business strategies and the resulting intercultural business communication fiasco.

Alkhazraji, Gardner, Martin, and Paolillo explore the acculturation of Muslim immigrants into U.S. organizations. The acculturation involves cultural adjustments, changes in communication patterns, and integration into the workplace. The findings are based on a survey of immigrants. As a result, we see the acculturation through the eyes of the immigrants, their perceptions, their opinions, and their concerns. This approach limits the discussion of intercultural communication somewhat.

The last study I will discuss provides a theoretical overview of professional intercultural communication and then illustrates the theoretical concepts with the help of a case study. Perkins emphasizes the need for business context. She argues that without this context intercultural communication is ill-focused and not effective. Furthermore, the focus cannot just be on business in general; it must be on the specific workplace context. As corporations change, their business strategies change; therefore, the business context is fluid. The same is true for the cultural context. We have to become more aware of variations within cultures. By seeing cultures as a set of shared meanings, we will have difficulties studying "zones of differences within and between cultures." The cultural changes will require changes in business strategies. For example, Perkins foresees an ever-changing growing number of niche markets. In order to be able to communicate effectively in this environment, we need to develop dynamic communication systems that can respond to these changes.

Summary

This article has shown that the cultural strategy, the business strategy, and the communication strategy are interrelated. Together they formulate an intercultural business communication strategy that presents a new construct which is greater than the sum of its parts.

In order to advance the field of intercultural business communication, we need to:

- Place our studies clearly into a business context. As we have seen, business is not just a vehicle for the discussion of intercultural communication. The business context shapes the cultural and communication strategies which in turn shape the business strategy.

- Conduct further research on the relationship between culture, business, and communication and the implications for the development of a new transactional culture. We need to ask: What role do the communication, culture, and business background of people play in developing adaptation strategies for effective intercultural business communication? What are the implications for specific workplace communication situations such as evaluations, training, and job assignments? What effect do changes in one area have on the other two areas and on the whole? For example, how will political changes in China affect business and culture, and how will these changes influence how Chinese workers and managers communicate with managers from other countries? How will foreign managers in China react to these changes? What are the business, culture, and communication constraints on adapting their intercultural business communication strategy?

- Identify additional variables that influence each strategy as presented in the model (see Figure 1 in Reading 1). The model does not provide a definitive list of all salient variables. As our environment changes, some variables may diminish in importance while others will grow. Traditional letters play a lesser role now than even ten years ago, while fax and e-mail play an even bigger role. We should examine how the changes in technology have affected the cultural, business, and communication strategies and what the implications are for the intercultural business communication strategy.

- Examine the impact of the theoretical foundation of intercultural business communication for curriculum development and teaching methodology.

Vocabulary

acculturation *n.* 文化适应
constraint *n.* 限制，束缚，约束
distort *v.* 歪曲，扭曲
dynamics *n.* 动态
fiasco *n.* 惨败
incorporate *v.* 合并，吸收
manipulative *adj.* 控制的
salient *adj.* 显著的

Notes

1. As a result, people think differently, approach business problems differently, and communicate differently. In order to integrate these differences into intercultural business communication, the model needs to break away from the Western approach and incorporate different mind-sets and cultural orientations.

众所周知，不同文化背景的人思维方式、处理问题方式不同，沟通方式也不同，当这些差异都反映在跨文化商务沟通中时，就会产生跨文化冲突。这个模型就是将不同的思维方式与文化导向整合在一起，形成一种双方都理解的沟通方式，进而促成共识。在跨文化商务沟通中，不能单以西方思维方式看问题，也不能单以东方思维方式看问题，这种单一思维方式是文化冲突的根源。

2. ...Beamer developed an approach to intercultural business communication competence that is applicable to most intercultural communication situations, but it is not focused on business.

不同文化的人具有不同的认知方式，进而导致他们的思维方式不同，所以他们在面对不同的商务问题时会产生不同的解决方式及交流方式。若要将这些差异都整合在跨文化商务沟通中，就需要整合不同的价值观取向及文化取向。本句大意为：比默研究出一种适用于大多数跨文化沟通情境的跨文化商务沟通能力，但它并非侧重商务。

Discussion from Intercultural Perspectives

1. "Beamer developed an approach to intercultural business communication competence that is applicable to most intercultural communication situations, but it is not focused on business." What is the implication for people who will work in an international setting?

2. "Perkins emphasizes the need for business context. She argues that without this context intercultural communication is ill-focused and not effective. Furthermore, the focus cannot just be on business in general; it must be on the specific workplace context." What does Perkins mean by "the focus...must be on the specific workplace context"? In what other workplaces can the intercultural business communication model be applied?

3. What is the objective of the study of intercultural business communication?

Intercultural Lens

Challenges and Opportunities in Global Mergers and Acquisitions

In the 21st century, the wave of mergers and acquisitions (M&A) will reach a record level in cross-border mergers and acquisitions for a variety of reasons, such as overseas expansion, additional emerging markets, and the desire to be more competitive. However, many of these mergers and acquisitions will fail to achieve their expected objectives. In spite of this, mergers continue to be a popular business strategy worldwide.

What Goes Wrong with M&A

Studies indicate that approximately 65% to 85% of mergers fail. A recent article in the *Harvard Business Review* estimates the number at 70%. Though there are many reasons for their failures, often one particular factor can be pinpointed: a failure to develop and execute an appropriate post-merger integration (PMI) strategy.

For all those failed mergers, there are different factors. However, there is only one primary factor that can determine their success: the development of cultural synergy. Pekala discovered that cultural integration is ignored in the majority of business combinations. In some studies of international M&As, there is a vague concept of cultural integration, which refers to the integration of different corporate cultures rather than the integration of different national cultures. Or cultural issues in their studies may represent different corporate cultures as well.

All executives are either competent in management or technology. These are the areas in which they feel comfortable. Thus, they tend to concentrate more on "hard" issues of the merger like the integration of the markets, products, brands, human resources, leadership organization, etc. than on "soft" issues like understanding cultural differences, resolving misunderstandings, building up core values, and making cultural synergy. More often than not, though, once the integration of "hard" issues is completed, executives would commence the operation of their new corporations ignoring the issue of cultural integration.

Culture is intangible, abstract and seemingly invisible. Yet it is reflected in management practices and people's behavior. If cultural differences are not managed well, they will become the leading cause for the merger failure. If dealt with properly or even capitalized on, cultural differences can become an asset for merged corporations and a source of innovative thinking and planning.

In summary, the THREE leading causes for cross-border merger failure have been pinpointed as follows:

- Executives are too focused on post-merger intergration of "hard" issues, paying little attention to or ignoring culture and human factors.

- Executives are ignorant of cultural factors that can make a difference in mergers. This may happen to domestic mergers between two corporate cultures in the East like the Shanghai Auto merger of SsangYong Motor or in the West like Daimler Chrysler (Daimler-Benz and Chrysler). In both situations, executives were unprepared to manage the cultural issues that were bound to surface at different managerial levels once the merger deal was closed. In these cases as in many others, the problems were mainly human or cultural related issues. Therefore, any approach to resolve them solely from managerial perspectives will not be effective.

- Executives are weak in intercultural competence. They cannot analyze a culture-related problem in their management when they are confronted with the wide range of problems at the post-merger phase. Or, if they identify a cultural source of the problem, they don't know how to develop culturally synergistic solutions and quell the tensions and conflicts that developed. Though more studies have offered some solutions to cross-border merger failures such as cultural due diligence, cultural integration, or cultural synergy, they will not be implemented if executives are not aware of its necessity. Therefore, a critical solution to successful global mergers is to enhance the executives' intercultural competence. With their awareness and skills, they will "walk the walk" of cultural synergy rather than being limited to "talking the talk" of the importance of cultural integration in cross-border mergers.

How to Diagnose Merger Failure

Mergers have two phases in cross-border M&A: pre-merger and post-merger. The pre-merger phase focuses on each merger party's interest or benefit, including the bid price for the merger or market, products, technology, human resources, marketing, organization structure, and leadership committees. The post-merger phase mainly focuses on the integration of corporate cultures and national cultures in the new company. So post-merger issues are related to the cooperation and communication between people from different cultural backgrounds, and cultural integration.

Occasionally the media focuses on a pre-merger deal failure and mistakenly describes the collapse as a merger failure. An example is the pre-merger fiasco of Sichuan Tengzhong Heavy Industrial Machinery and the Hummer division of America's General Motors. To be precise, this was a failure of a merger deal negotiation rather than a failure of a merged corporation, because at that time a new organization had not been formed. At the pre-merger negotiation phase no compromises should be made, but instead each party should prioritize its own interests and benefits in whatever decision it makes. Therefore each should maintain its principles and interests in discussing all the issues on the merger agenda. If these issues are not resolved, or are not well thought out, and the merger deal is closed, these issues will inevitably contribute to disappointment or catastrophe in the future. These business matters are more difficult to resolve once the merger is implemented, and therefore can become an insurmountable barrier to effective communication and smooth cooperation in the future. Despite thoughtful pre-merger discussions, certain managerial issues do not surface because they are masked by positive financial or market situations. In other words, when all is well, growth smoothes away problems, conflicts and differences. But when finances decline or market shares plunge, an inevitable negative spiral sets itself into motion.

At the post-merger phase almost all the organizations focus on the integration of finance and business-related work, but pay little attention to the two different national cultures' integration. These mergers that ignore cultural synergy are at their peril as disregard of cultural factors is the leading cause for merger failure even if pre-merger issues have been resolved successfully.

How to Make Cross-Border Mergers Succeed
With the typical merger failures diagnosed to cultural causes, cultural

synergy can be created by developing a third or hybrid culture—Culture C. The development of a hybridized culture becomes a core value or a cooperative principle in the new corporation. Culture C is not an ideal concept but it can be constructed with specific values and norms that can guide employees from different cultures as to how they should interact, write, speak and behave in the work setting. The rules and patterns of Culture C will enable co-workers to effectively and harmoniously communicate in their work environment. Within this hybrid environment, cultural conflict can be minimized. If it occurs, employees possess the intercultural competence skills to manage and solve conflict. Without creating Culture C and its synergetic results, all globally merged corporations will pay a steep price eventually.

Cultural synergy is the practical solution, and it can be achieved through intensive intercultural training focused on developing skill-oriented intercultural competence. Author Zhuang has designed an intercultural communication corporate training program with cultural synergy construction for the client company as the primary goal and intercultural competence of each employee as the path to the goal. These training objectives supplant customary intercultural communication goals focusing on the cultural differences between the merger or acquisition partners.

Our conclusion is that global mergers and acquisitions may fail due to the lack of cultural synergy, and creating a synergistic environment will contribute to the success of mergers and acquisitions.

Intercultural Case Study

Why Best Buy Failed in China

The famous United States-based consumer electronics retailer Best Buy announced on February 22, 2011 that it had decided to stop running its nine stores in China. This surprise announcement effectively signaled the end of Best Buy's eight-year China story in which it spent three years preparing for its market entry and five years expanding to nine stores located in Shanghai, Beijing, Suzhou and Hangzhou.

Best Buy disclosed its decision to close three of its stores in Shanghai at an upper management meeting on the afternoon of February 21. Just one day later it officially announced its plan to shut down all of its nine stores in China. Although the withdrawal seemed a little hasty, there were earlier signs that Best Buy's business was not running well in China. According to related reports, in Shanghai alone last year, there were already three contracted Best Buy projects that failed to finally settle themselves. Last November, Best Buy released the first-to-third quarter financial report that showed a meager 4% sales increase in the Chinese market compared to its total $38.5 billion global sales during the same period resulting in more than a 100% increase from a year earlier. The other part of Best Buy's business, the Chinese electronics brand Five Star acquired in 2006, also opened around 30 new stores between 2006 and 2010, a very small number compared to other Chinese electronics retailers that are seeing rapid expansion.

Opinions speculating on why Best Buy's failed in the Chinese market do not differ much. Most analysts believe it expanded too slowly to survive in the face of strong competition from other Chinese electronics giants such as Gome and Suning, both of whom currently boast over 1,000 stores nationwide.

Experts say that Best Buy's decision to stick to its American business model brought about its failure in the Chinese market, although the model has been working very successfully in Western markets. The model is composed of three parts. First, Best Buy purchases all of its products directly from suppliers and prices them independently. This is in contrast to its major Chinese competitors, who lease separate parts of a store to retailers of distinct brands and take a portion of every retailer's sales profit. Second, Best Buy hires a whole staff as its own sales team while the majority of sales people in most Chinese stores come from the supplier side. Finally, the American company utilizes a non-commission policy for its sales staff in order to avoid biased promotions that will disturb customer decisions.

Although the Best Buy model aims to please both suppliers and consumers by reducing the price competition between suppliers, creating a friendlier shopping environment, and providing better services such as the opportunity to try products before purchase, it does not seem to suit the Chinese market very well.

Chen Can, senior consultant at Analysis International, says the Best Buy model requiring self-purchased property and commodities as well as a bigger team of sales staff leads to a significant cost rise which results in a price disadvantage.

One employee of a local electronics supplier described the Best Buy model as a "wall" instead of a "bridge" between suppliers and customers.

Both Chen and home appliance expert Chen Qingqi pointed out that Best Buy failed to please its suppliers because they do not really receive very many orders from the company due to its small market presence. In addition, the frequent requests for customized products from Best Buy also increased supplier costs.

Chen added that most importantly, Best Buy did not please its customers. The price advantage seriously outshines any advantages in management.

Many consumers even commented that the Chinese name of Best Buy—*Baisimai*—as a bad one for marketing. *Baisimai* literally means "to buy after thinking 100 times."

Ironically, its business model, just as its Chinese name, tries too hard to educate consumers about high-end service value when lower price is typically the only value that motivates them to make quick decisions. The electronic giant's overconfidence in transforming the Chinese consumer philosophy finally hurt its overall performance in the Chinese market.

Analyzing the Issues in the Case

1. What is the difference in the retailer's management between Best Buy and local Chinese retailer stores like Gome and Suning?
2. What are the main factors leading to Best Buy's failure in China and why?
3. Why did Best Buy stick to its American business model to run Best Buy in China?

Learning Culture Through Proverbs

Work in pairs and exchange views on the meanings of the following proverbs, then try to find out their Chinese equivalents if there is any, and discuss the values transmitted.

Proverb 1: *We never miss the water till the well runs dry.*
Proverb 2: *All things are difficult before they are easy.*

Online Research—Using Key Words

For more information and resources, search the Internet with the following key words:

global mergers and acquisitions, pre-merger phase and post-merger phase, cultural synergy, cultural integration

Unit 12
Public Diplomacy and Intercultural Communication

Communication not only takes place between two people but also between two corporations, two governments, and between large institutions and the public. So far in this textbook, we have discussed the importance of considering intercultural dimensions in interactions with a culturally-different person. The same is true for the messages of public diplomacy. There are many possibilities for communication mistakes, misunderstandings, and misinterpretations. How do government officials and leaders know whether the communication has been successful or not? Why does the global public sometimes have negative perceptions of the government that is sending forth the messages? Like other countries, China has been struggling to improve its public diplomacy and this unit explores this topic.

What You Can Learn from This Unit

1. Understand what public diplomacy is;
2. Understand the difference between public diplomacy and governmental diplomacy;
3. Understand why our government is promoting public diplomacy;
4. Understand what intercultural communication can do for public diplomacy.

Questions for Intercultural Awareness

1. What is public diplomacy? Can you list some examples?
2. Why does the foreign public or media sometimes misinterpret China's messages?
3. What is the main barrier in conducting public diplomacy?

What's Wrong?

Why China Is Promoting Public Diplomacy

Since the 1980s with the implementation of the policy of reform and opening-up, China has experienced tremendous development in its national economy and in the daily lives of the Chinese people. However, China's fast growth has also bewildered many countries in the world. They wonder why China's economy keeps growing while dozens of countries have suffered huge economic losses. Citizens of many countries have become suspicious of and anxious about China's growth. They worry about losing the competitive edge of their industries which will diminish their influence in the world. The result is that the "China threat" debate periodically flares up in Western Europe, North America and even South America.

The Chinese government is concerned about the world's perceptions of it. Obviously, the global media's perceptions of China are inaccurate and biased. Here are some examples of the issues China is grappling with:

- Why is Western media's coverage of China unfair or biased?
- Why is the image about China in the world distorted?
- Why are China's good intentions to help other countries and regions (e.g., Africa) incorrectly interpreted?
- How can the Chinese people help the world to see the real China or present a more balanced and accurate image to the world?

One obvious reason for the possible distortions is the limited knowledge about China held by the foreign public and media. However, the underlying reason may well be cultural differences in how governments communicate with the press to shape their images, that is, culturally-derived public relations may lead to global misinterpretations of the messages China intends to transmit.

To transmit a clearer message about China, Zhao Qizheng, spokesman for the 11th Chinese People's Political Consultative Conference (CPPCC) makes the following suggestions:

- To help the world genuinely understand China, we cannot simply count on Western media coverage being fair and unbiased.
- The communication skills of every Chinese person are important tools in helping the world understand our nation.
- All related materials should also be written in readily readable foreign languages.
- We also need well-trained spokespeople to provide timely answers and explanations.

The suggestions flow from experience and practice. Zhao developed a career in conducting public diplomacy about China. The following are anecdotes from Zhao's book *Public Diplomacy and Cross-Cultural Communication* to showcase how he confronts the issues presented to him:

- Zhao compares China's social reality to an apple: It is much better to give the whole fruit to a foreigner when presenting China rather than just apple jam, juice or even vitamin C. Foreigners can bite and taste the apple by themselves, and it gives them room to digest and ponder it.

  Comment: It is a good practice to present the whole picture of China to the world so that people can form judgments by themselves. Otherwise the foreign public would assume the story they hear is not the true or full story and that important aspects of the story are intentionally being hidden. Further, foreign media and the public might create different stories based on their own interpretations and understandings of the situation. By then, opinions would already be formed and it would be too late for the Chinese government to clarify the situation. It is much easier to shape an opinion than to change one.

- Zhao aims to explain and write about China in an easy and understandable way so that even foreign high school students can understand the issues. He suggests using the "ABC" method rather than the "XYZ" method.

  Comment: By this analogy, Zhao suggests employing a direct (Western "ABC") approach to telling a story in contrast to an indirect (Chinese "XYZ") way of relating information. Direct and detailed information would remove ambiguity and therefore result in more uniform and accurate interpretations.

- Zhao suggests that in many cases, the Chinese government should be engaging in cross-cultural communication that is more balanced and factual, instead of shaping the message to convey a positive image of an event.

Comment: Actually, cross-cultural communication is a two-way communication model in which the sender and the receiver exchange information and share their views with each other. The goal is to understand each other's intended messages so as to achieve effective communication. Public diplomacy can achieve full effectiveness only by carrying out cross-cultural communication.

Discussion

1. Why is Western media coverage of China unfair or biased? Give some examples.
2. What are the barriers in conducting public diplomacy in order for the world to see real China?

Reading 1

China Needs More Public Diplomacy, Zhao Says

China needs a bigger public diplomacy campaign to better present the country to the world, said Zhao Qizheng, spokesman for the Chinese People's Political Consultative Conference (CPPCC), on Monday.

In an exclusive interview with the *China Daily* in the Great Hall of the People, the chairman of the foreign affairs committee of the National Committee of CPPCC said governmental diplomacy and public diplomacy[1] are mutually complementary.

"Governmental diplomacy represents a country's sovereignty. (But) in many other international exchanges, many different people also participate, including leaders from public and sub-governmental organizations, influential people such as scholars, opinion leaders, and social activists, and ordinary people. This is public diplomacy," Zhao said.

President Hu Jintao's speech to Yale University students in 2006 is a typical example of China's public diplomacy, which has existed for many years, Zhao said.

In 2001, the Boao Forum for Asia (BFA), a non-governmental international organization, was inaugurated, committed to promoting regional economic integration and bringing Asian countries even closer to development goals.

Last year, the BFA, based in Hainan province, attracted a record 1,700 participants, most of whom were leaders in government, business and academia in Asia.

Compared to governmental diplomacy, public diplomacy can better "explain" China's national condition and policies, and "present" the country to the world, Zhao said.

"In such communications, participants from both sides don't need to restrict their talks to diplomatic rhetoric, as neither is there to sign some treaty or make some announcement for their countries," he said. Participants in public diplomacy can discuss a wider range of issues with more active and straightforward expressions, he said.

Internationally, public diplomacy was first used in 1965 by Edmund Gullion, a career American diplomat, according to the United States Information Agency Alumni Association. It refers to the spreading of knowledge about a country's foreign policy via communication with foreign public audiences.

Though public diplomacy has existed in China for a long time, "the campaign is not big enough," Zhao said, when asked what the main difficulty is.

Most Chinese who currently do public diplomacy are those with rich work experience in international trade and communication, heads of China's multinational corporations, and research fellows of international affairs in Chinese universities, he said.

But during this year's two sessions of the CPPCC and the National People's Congress, Zhao has seen momentum to facilitate the country's public diplomacy.

The foreign affairs committee of the CPPCC on March 1, just two days before the annual session opened, published a new journal, *Public Diplomacy Quarterly*. As its editor-in-chief, Zhao wrote in the inaugural statement: "The aim and mission of this journal is to facilitate China's public diplomacy."

Foreign Minister Yang Jiechi, at his annual news conference on Monday, said Chinese diplomats are encouraged to go to the public, especially universities and media, this year.

Chen Haosu, a CPPCC member and president of the Chinese People's Association for Friendship with Foreign Countries, said the upcoming Shanghai Expo would be a "very good arena" for China's public diplomacy.

The Expo is expected to draw a record 70 million visitors from home and abroad from May 1 to October 31. According to the organizing committee, 192 countries and 52 international organizations have confirmed their participation.

In the same interview, Zhao stressed Beijing doesn't mean to export any "Chinese model[2]," despite the term becoming an international hot issue.

He said it's better to use China "case" than "model" when terming the country's growth path over the past decades.

"Case means a fact. But when you say model, it's more or less like a sample or example. Then others may think China is propagating[3], or competing with other country's models," he said. "How can other countries emulate the Chinese model directly without adapting it to its own national condition?"

Following the country's continuous economic boom, there has been an upsurge in the international community to discuss a "Chinese model," or similar terms, over the past several years.

David Shambaugh, a China studies expert at George Washington University, pointed out "some individual elements of China's development experience are unique..."

China's model is unique in that it flexibly adapts to elements imported from abroad and grafts those elements onto domestic roots in all fields, producing a unique hybrid and eclectic system, Shambaugh said. This is China's real "model," he said.

Zhao has his own definition of the "China model": "It is a summary of China's social development ideas, policies, practices, achievements and fallacies since 60 years ago, when PRC was founded, and especially in last 30 years since the reform and opening-up started."

But China "case" is better, he stressed, as it is still an evolving concept that may be clearer by the mid-21st century.

Vocabulary

editor-in-chief *n.* 总编辑
fallacy *n.* 谬误
graft *v.* 使成为一部分
inaugurate *v.* 为……举行创建仪式
momentum *n.* 势头
sovereignty *n.* 主权
upsurge *n.* 热潮

Notes

1. governmental diplomacy and public diplomacy
   政府外交是横向的，它代表国家主权，通过交涉、谈判，最后达成共识。政府外交之外的一切外交活动都是公共外交，比如在一些国际交流活动中，参与其中的非政府组织领导者、学者及社会活动家等比较具有影响力的人物，及普通大众等，都属于公共外交的参与者。

2. Chinese model
   外国人用"中国模式"特指中国过去几十年的发展道路。与"中国模式"一样，"中国崛起"，"中国已成为世界第二经济大国"等表述也会让人产生误解。

3. propagating
   propagating意为"对外宣传、传播"，带有政府主导的贬义色彩，也容易让人产生误解，所以，"宣传"不能译为propaganda，而应译为publicity。

Reading 2

Public Diplomacy Gains Ground

Though having only several decades of history, New China (PRC)'s public diplomacy has yielded many results. "We have made much progress in negotiating with foreign governments, congressmen, and military officers, but lack experience in dealing with the public and media agencies," Vice Foreign Minister Fu Ying said at a forum on public diplomacy held Saturday by Beijing Foreign Studies University (BFSU).

The international view of China often swings between overestimation and underestimation, either warning of the "China threat" in the face of Chinese achievements, or "China collapse" when any problems arise.[1] One major reason is that the number of cultural experts is limited, and another is that China's public diplomacy has yet to be improved, Fu noted.

The current leadership attaches even more importance to public diplomacy. President Hu Jintao said in July last year that public diplomacy would be a focus of all foreign affairs in the future, raising it to national strategic level for the first time.

The Ministry of Foreign Affairs upgraded the administrative level of the department in charge of public diplomacy last year and began to set up news centers at international summits. The 2008 Beijing Olympic Games and 2010 Shanghai Expo also created opportunities for foreigners to learn more about China. The moves were mainly led by the government representing a sovereign nation.

Zhao Qizheng, head of the foreign affairs committee in the Chinese People's Political Consultative Conference, believes that public diplomacy covers all activities except for government-to-government diplomacy, and that non-governmental agencies and the public should play a bigger role in the future. Zhao hailed the establishment of a public diplomacy center at BFSU on August 26, the first non-government think tank that addresses the field in China, suggesting the university train more professionals in translation, and especially political wording.[2] "The primary task is to improve translation, as adverse effects would trigger more misunderstandings," Zhao, also the honorary director of the center, said.

Fu said Chinese officials and enterprises are sometimes either awkward or slow when dealing with the media. Unlike their foreign counterparts who respond to misconceptions in a timely manner,[3] she said some Chinese enterprises sometimes take a long time to clear up allegations by foreign media of being spies or having Chinese military backgrounds. She suggested that special and systemic training in this field is vital. "Just being able to grasp foreign languages and knowing their policies is not enough."[4]

Some foreign critics said China has failed to realize that what foreigners really want to know about the country "is not *kung fu* or Chinese medicine, though these are good." "We want to know about the tremendous changes happening in China, such as why it only takes China decades to complete a job that other countries have spent centuries doing, and why Chinese policies change every five or seven years," Johan Galtung, a Norwegian scholar of conflict and peace, said at the forum.

"Rome was not built in a day, and public diplomacy should be a long-term endeavor, which is one of the keys to its success," Li Yonghui, professor of international relations at BFSU, told the *Global Times* yesterday. "The integration of non-governmental resources and establishment of a tracking system to assess the impact of public diplomacy input is also important," Li said.

Vocabulary

allegation *n.*   指控
swing *v.*   摇摆
trigger *v.*   引发

Notes

1. The international view of China often swings between overestimation and underestimation, either warning of the "China threat" in the face of Chinese achievements, or "China collapse" when any problems arise.

   本句大意为：国际上对于中国的发展往往偏向两个极端：一个是过于高估，比如当看到中国发展取得的成就时，就会宣扬"中国威胁论"；另外一种是过于低估，比如当看到中国发展中存在的一些问题时，就会宣扬"中国崩溃论"。

2. …suggesting the university train more professionals in translation, and especially political wording.

   北京外国语大学公共外交研究中心成立于2010年8月，旨在推动公共外交领域研究，向政府公共外交实践提供智力支持。赵启正认为由于负面影响会引起更多误解，所以提高翻译水平是当务之急，他建议大学培训一些翻译工作者，尤其是政治方面的专业人才。这说明我们对这些词语的翻译容易让人产生误解，因为国外读者不能理解这些词语所表达的真正含义，所以就会产生不同的版本的理解。

3. …Chinese officials and enterprises are sometimes either awkward or slow when dealing with the media. Unlike their foreign counterparts who respond to misconceptions in a timely manner…

   本句大意为：中国官员及企业在处理媒体问题时有时反应比较迟缓，而外国官员及媒体会及时澄清或处理报道中的误解。这些差异正说明东西方文化处理问题方式的不同，在面临媒体提出的问题时由于我们不善于直面问题，害怕正面冲突，往往会采取回避方式。正是这种回避方式使西方媒体确信，他们的疑问或质疑确实是我们的问题所在。

4. Just being able to grasp foreign languages and knowing their policies is not enough.

   仅仅学好一门语言并且了解他们的政治是不够的，还要知道如何才能使对方真正了解我们，这才是最关键的。

Discussion from Intercultural Perspectives

1. Why Chinese officials and enterprises are sometimes either awkward or slow when dealing with the media? Are there any cultural factors behind their behavior?
2. What might be the consequences of Chinese officials and enterprises responding slowly or ambiguously to the questions posed to them?
3. The Chinese sometimes avoid dealing with some sensitive issues face to face. How would the Westerners interpret such behavior?
4. What competence is needed to conduct public diplomacy? Why do you think so?

Intercultural Lens

Origins of the Term "Public Diplomacy"

According to a Library of Congress study of U.S. international and cultural programs and activities prepared for the Committee on Foreign Relations of the U.S. Senate, the term "public diplomacy" was first used in 1965 by Dean Edmund Gullion of the Fletcher School of Law and Diplomacy at Tufts University. It was created with the establishment at Fletcher of the Edward R. Murrow Center for Public Diplomacy.

The Murrow Center, in one of its earlier brochures, described public diplomacy as follows:

"Public diplomacy...deals with the influence of public attitudes on the formation and execution of foreign policies. It encompasses dimensions of international relations beyond traditional diplomacy, the cultivation by governments of public opinion in other countries, the interaction of private groups and interests in one country with those of another, the reporting of foreign affairs and its impact on policy, communication between those whose job is communication, as between diplomats and foreign correspondents, and the processes of intercultural communications.

"Central to public diplomacy is the transnational flow of information and ideas."

Public Diplomacy and Traditional Diplomacy

Public diplomacy differs from traditional diplomacy in that public diplomacy deals not only with governments but primarily with non-governmental individuals and organizations. Furthermore, public diplomacy activities often present many differing views as represented by private individuals and organizations in addition to official views.

Traditional diplomacy actively engages one government with another government. For example, in traditional diplomacy, U.S. Embassy officials represent the U.S. Government in a host country primarily by maintaining relations and conducting official USG business with the officials of the host government whereas public diplomacy primarily engages many diverse non-government elements of a society.

Zhao's Statements About Public Diplomacy

- Public diplomacy deals with many international exchanges where many different people participate, including leaders from public and sub-governmental organizations, influential people such as scholars, opinion leaders, and social activists, and ordinary people.
- Compared to governmental diplomacy, public diplomacy can better "explain" China's national condition and policies, and "present" the country to the world.

Evident Causes for Public Diplomacy Mishaps

- Chinese media covers stories and information in a Chinese way so that international publics could not understand the intended messages.
- Faced with questions or issues at a press conference, spokespersons would try to answer them in abstract terms or diplomatic rhetoric. While this

indirect style of speaking is to avoid confrontation, the foreign press may perceive the responses as evasive and covering up the truth.

• When Chinese officials use words or expressions referring to Chinese literature, poetry, or history, the international media or public might incorrectly interpret the speakers' intended messages and therefore a different understanding of the messages might be reported throughout the world. The result would be unintended opinions formed among the global public.

Intercultural Perspectives into Public Diplomacy Mishaps

Common Causes for Conflict First, conflict occurs when people misinterpret each other's behavior. Second, conflict arises from perceptions of incompatibility, such as perceiving certain personality or group characteristics as incompatible. Third, conflict happens when people look at the same situation but from different perspectives.

Different Communication Styles In low-context culture and high-context culture, differences in communication styles can be clearly seen.

A low-context culture is one in which the meanings of a communication message are stated clearly and explicitly, without depending on the context of the communication. A low-context culture requires direct, detailed and unambiguous speech or writing that is focused on the precise transmission of information. High-context culture is one in which the meanings of a communication message are found in the situation and in the relationships of the communicators or are internalized in the communicators' beliefs, values, and norms. This type of communication happens primarily among people in homogeneous cultures. The communication context plays an important role in the interpretation of a communication message. A high-context culture requires indirect communication because the goal is more focused on interpersonal harmony than the transmission of information.

Different Roles of Conversation Partners In a conversation, the roles the partners play vary according to different styles of conversation.

Listener-oriented style claims that the listener has the responsibility to understand the speaker, which means if the listener could not understand the speaker, it is the listener's fault. Speaker-oriented style assumes it is the speaker's responsibility to make the listener understand his or her point so that the speaker would explain his or her statement as clearly or explicitly as possible.

Different Ways of Thinking The distinction here regards the structure of organizing thoughts: general to specific vs. specific to general.

Eastern people tend to deal with issues or make statements starting with general views or statements, sometimes without giving any specific or personal reply in the end. Western people think from specific to general, that is to say, when asked to make comments or reply, they would cover this issue in a sequential order or confront the issue face to face, expressing their personal opinions, and finally make a conclusion. These differences in thinking can be observed in writing, speaking, discussion, problem solving, evaluation, etc.

Albert Einstein shed light on this issue by saying we cannot solve problems by using the same kind of thinking we used when we created them. What we can learn from his statement is that we should shift our thinking or perspective when dealing with communication in a cross-cultural context. We can then discover the real cause for communication obstacles and find paths around them.

Intercultural Case Study

National Image Lights Up Times Square

As advertising spaces go, you cannot get much more high profile than New York's iconic Times Square.

An estimated 1.7 million people pass through the landmark every day, making it a prime location to promote major brands—or, in China's case, a national image.

On Monday, there was a new addition to the usual billboards for Coca-Cola and Samsung: a 50-meter display called "China

Experience," a looped 1-minute promotional video featuring some of the nation's most famous faces.

The display, which opened a day before President Hu Jintao's arrival for a four-day state visit to the United States, is part of a major campaign to promote China's image among Americans.

Also included in the project is a 30-second commercial to be aired on U.S. television and a 30-minute documentary, according to the State Council Information Office.

Experts welcomed the move on Tuesday, including one professor who told *China Daily* he hopes the project will undo some of the damage caused by anti-Chinese advertisements used by several candidates during last November's mid-term elections in the U.S.

The promo in Times Square, which will run until February 14, features a range of successful people, such as NBA basketball star Yao Ming, pianist Lang Lang, film director John Woo, hybrid rice scientist Yuan Longping and Alibaba founder Jack Ma. It also features ordinary Chinese from across the country.

The 30-minute documentary, which was also funded by the central government, is also a mix of celebrities and ordinary citizens, with each offering a glimpse of the country's politics, economy, or society.

According to a report by *Guangming Daily*, a Beijing-based newspaper, one scene shows ethnic youngsters using cell phones in a remote, mountainous area of the Xinjiang Uygur Autonomous Region, while another has a man catching fish with cormorants in the picturesque southern city of Guilin.

"These scenes illustrate social changes and sustainable development," director Gao Xiaolong told *Guangming Daily*.

Analysts in China have in the main responded positively to the Times Square billboard promo, as well as wider plans to promote a truer image of China abroad.

"Advertising is a crucial platform to let people know about (a brand)," said Huang Shengmin, dean of School of Advertising, Communication University of China. "This project is a milestone to signal that China is now open to embrace the world."

Launching the campaign to coincide with Hu's visit to the U.S. was "a very smart choice," he said, adding: "It is difficult to evaluate what extent these commercials and the documentary will promote China's new image, but one thing is for sure: It's a long-term project."

"It is important to promote China in the U.S., especially during a time when Chinese and Americans have a huge perception gap," said Niu Xinchun, a U.S. studies specialist at China Institute of Contemporary International Relations.

"Many Americans, for example, think China's rise is taking away U.S. jobs, and there were lots of negative views about China during the midterms. So it's important for both sides to facilitate communication through mass media and between Americans and the Chinese."

Last week, the Pew Research Center published a study that found 20 percent of Americans see China as a global threat, while 22 percent feel the country is an adversary. Yet, the same research also showed that 58 percent believe it is "very important" to build stronger ties between China and the U.S.

A survey of Chinese residents jointly conducted by *China Daily* and Horizon Research Consultancy Group, also published last week, revealed that the number of people who view Beijing's ties with Washington as "very important" has doubled in the past year, while most believe relations will remain stable or improve despite recent turbulence.

"These commercials are pretty good and are catered to Western viewers and ideas," added Niu. "I think it's a good idea. It's time to improve (China's) image in the West."

However, Yu Guoming, vice-dean of School of Journalism and Communication, Renmin University of China, said he feels the country would be better served by efforts to foster a culture of understanding, rather than simply relying on advertising campaigns.

Yu suggested the first thing should be to help people overseas to understand that the Chinese people "are not monsters" by promoting shared values.

Analyzing the Issues in the Case

1. According to this case, what kind of image was projected to American people? Positive or negative? Why?
2. What is the cause for the misinterpretations of China made by Americans?
3. What lesson can we draw from this case? What are the practical implications for the Chinese government?

Learning Culture Through Proverbs

Work in pairs and exchange views on the meanings of the following proverbs, then try to find out their Chinese equivalents if there is any, and discuss the values transmitted.

Proverb 1: *The true friendship seeks to give, not take; to help, not to be helped; to minister, not to be ministered unto.*

Proverb 2: *A hedge between keeps friendship green.*

Online Research—Using Key Words

For more information and resources, search the Internet with the following key words:

governmental diplomacy, public diplomacy, soft power, public relations

Acknowledgements

We are very grateful to the authors and publishers of all the articles, reports, and stories we have chosen as the text for this textbook. Every effort has been made to obtain permission to use previously published materials. Some materials have been adapted and any error is unintentional. We regret that we have been unable to trace the copyright owners of a number of the materials. We apologize for this. We intend to show every respect for intellectual property rights, and hope our pleading for the permission to use the related material for teaching purposes will receive kind and generous consideration.

Unit 1

Reading 1

Myron W. Lustig, and Jolene Koester. *Intercultural Competence: Interpersonal Communication Across Cultures*. Pearson/A and B, 2006.

Reading 2

Gary P. Ferraro. *The Cultural Dimension of International Business*. Prentice Hall, 1998.

Unit 2

Reading 1

Kathy J. Irving. *Communicating in Context: Intercultural Communication Skills for ESL Students*. Prentice Hall, 1986.

Reading 2

Jan Gaston. *Cultural Awareness Teaching Techniques*. Pro Lingua Associates, 1984.

Unit 3

Reading 1

Judith N. Martin, and Thomas K. Nakayama. *Experiencing Intercultural Communication: An Introduction.* Mayfield Publishing Company, 2001.

Reading 2

Myron W. Lustig, and Jolene Koester. *AmongUS: Essays on Identity, Belonging, and Intercultural Competence.* Pearson College Division, 2005.

Unit 4

Reading 1

Jonas Stier. "Internationalisation, Ethnic Diversity and the Acquisition of Intercultural Competencies," *Intercultural Education.* 14(1): 77–91, 2003.

Reading 2

http://www.intstudy.com/articles/ec184a13.htm

Unit 5

Reading 1

Carley H. Dodd. *Dynamics of Intercultural Communication.* McGraw-Hill Companies, Incorporated, 1997.

Reading 2

Gary Althen. *American Ways*: *A Guide for Foreigners in the United States.* Intercultural Press, 1988.

Unit 6

Reading 1

Elizabeth A. Tuleja, and James O'Rourke. *Intercultural Communication for Business.* Thomson South-Western, 2005.

Reading 2

Fons Trompenaars, and Charles Hampden-Turner. *Riding the Waves of Culture: Understanding Diversity in Global Business*. McGraw-Hill Companies, Incorporated, 1998.

Unit 7

Reading 1

Judith N. Martin, and Thomas K. Nakayama. *Experiencing Intercultural Communication: An Introduction*. McGraw-Hill Higher Education, 2005.

Reading 2

Vickie Marie. "Living in Paradise: An Inside Look at the Micronesian Culture" in *AmongUS: Essays on Identity, Belonging, and Intercultural Competence* by Myron W. Lustig and Jolene Koester. Pearson College Division, 2005.

Unit 8

Reading 1

Gary Althen. *American Ways: A Guide for Foreigners in the United States*. Intercultural Press, 1988.

Reading 2

Patrick R. Moran. *Teaching Culture: Perspectives in Practice*. Heinle & Heinle/ Thomson Learning, 2001.

Unit 9

Reading 1

John C. Condon. *With Respect to the Japanese: A Guide for Americans*. Intercultural Press, 1984.

Reading 2

William I. Brustein. *Journal of Studies in International Education*. 11: 382, 2007.

Unit 10

Reading 1

Hu Wenzhong, Cornelius N. Grove, and Zhuang Enping. *Encountering the Chinese: A Modern Country, an Ancient Culture.* Intercultural Press, 2010.

Reading 2

Nan M. Sussman. "Working abroad and Expatriate Adjustment: Three Disciplinary Lenses for Exploring the Psychological Transition Cycle of International Employees," *Social and Personality Psychology Compass.* 5(7): 393–409, 2011.

Unit 11

Reading 1

Iris I. Varner. "The Theoretical Foundation for Intercultural Business Communication: A Conceptual Model," *The Journal of Business Communication.* 37(1): 39–57, 2000.

Reading 2

Iris I. Varner. "The Theoretical Foundation for Intercultural Business Communication: A Conceptual Model," *The Journal of Business Communication.* 37(1): 39–57, 2000.

Unit 12

Reading 1

Zhang Haizhou. "China Needs More Public Diplomacy, Zhao Says," *China Daily.* March 11, 2010.

Reading 2

Ji Beibei. "Public Diplomacy Gains Grounds." *Global Times.* September 15, 2010.

外研社英语专业文化类教材

西方思想经典导读

编著：孙有中

　　本书旨在通过对西方文化史的纵向考察和对西方思想经典文献的深度阅读，帮助学习者拓宽知识面，提高人文素养，培养思辨能力。

◆ 详尽注释化解原著阅读障碍，精心导读引领学子登堂入室

◆ 在学术训练中延伸英语学习，在英语学习中深化学术训练

◆ 文学、史学、哲学融为一体，阅读、写作、讨论贯穿始终

英语国家社会与文化

主编：梅仁毅

　　本书介绍了英国、美国、加拿大、澳大利亚、新西兰和爱尔兰六个主要英语国家的社会与文化背景，每单元内容包括中文导读、课文、注释、练习、研究任务。

◆ 课文简明易懂，语言地道，图文并茂；注释详尽，对重要的文化知识点进行介绍

◆ 练习形式多样；研究项目别出心裁，侧重培养学生搜索信息、调查访谈等多方面的实际工作能力

◆ 多数练习附有答案，方便学生自主学习

欧洲文化概况

编著：Duncan Sidwell（英）

　　本书从历史的角度阐述了欧洲文化的产生、发展和现状，系统介绍了欧洲文化的源流发展。

◆ 以具体的历史史实介绍欧洲文化，增加了趣味性和可读性

◆ 注重文化的横向比较，把欧洲文化的发展放在世界文化发展的宏观背景中，引导学习者深入思考

◆ 内容丰富，随书附带的CD-ROM光盘提供更多教学内容

澳大利亚社会与文化

编著：夏玉和　李又文

　　本书内容涵盖澳大利亚自然环境、历史变迁、移民与移民政策、原住民的历史与现状、文学艺术和语言、政治与经济体制、外交政策等各个方面。

◆ 由长期从事澳大利亚研究的中外学者撰写，语言地道，通俗易懂，又不失其学术研究的深度与价值

◆ 每章均有内容简介及对文章难点的中文注释，方便读者自学

◆ 每章均设思考题，帮助读者深化所学内容

美国研究读本

编著：梅仁毅

　　本书分为两辑。第一辑从政治、经济、社会、文化与教育四个方面阐释美国社会的基本体制；第二辑从美国国内政治、外交政策、经济发展、社会文化四个方面介绍美国进入21世纪以来发生的重大变化。

◆ 内容丰富翔实，全面介绍美国社会的基本框架与长久原则

◆ 题材广泛新颖，深入解读20世纪80年代以来美国的发展

◆ 导读提纲挈领，提供相关背景知识，概括各选篇主要内容

◆ 练习启发思维，引导学生思考各选篇主旨，促进自主学习